A SACRED TRUST

Stories Of Jewish Heritage & History

Rabbi Eugene Labovitz
Annette Labovitz

Combined Volumes
Two and Three

Jewish Cultural Literacy Series

Isaac Nathan Publishing Co., Inc.
Los Angeles

Stories Copyright © 1995 & 1998 by Rabbi Eugene Labovitz and Annette Labovitz.

Maps and Time Lines Copyright © 1995 & 1998 by Isaac Nathan Publishing Co., Inc.

Second Printing, combining original Volumes Two & Three

All rights reserved. Printed in the United States of America. No part of this book may be used or reproduced in any manner whatsoever without written permission from the Isaac Nathan Publishing Co., Inc., except for brief quotations in reviews for inclusion in a magazine, newspaper or broadcast.

> **NOTICE: Publication of this work involved extensive research and costs, and the rights of the copyright holders will be strictly enforced.**

Library of Congress Cataloging-in-Publication Data

Rabbi Eugene Labovitz, Annette Labovitz
  A Sacred Trust: Stories of Jewish Heritage & History
Volume Two and Three combined
  1. Jewish History   2. Jewish Stories   Jewish Literature
  4. Polish Jewry   5. American Jewry   6. Israel, State of, history
ISBN 0-914615-02-5
Library of Congress Catalog Card Number: 94-68316

Manufactured in the United States of America by
Isaac Nathan Publishing Co., Inc.
22711 Cass Avenue, Woodland Hills, CA 91364
(818) 225-9631 FAX 225-8354   e-mail david@inpubco.com

DEDICATED TO
THE MEMORY OF
RABBI SHLOMO CARLEBACH Z"L

Our beloved friend and teacher Rabbi Shlomo Carlebach, passed away on Cheshvan 16, 5755/October 21, 1994. Through his inspirational music and holy stories, he, a *talmid chacham* and sweet singer of Israel, identified with Jews from all over the world.

Shlomo epitomized the essence of life, and brought 'life" to so many. Hundreds, if not thousands, credit their finding Judaism because of his unique form of outreach, which he began long before the *teshuva* movement.

He was not "just a storyteller," as he often said. Rather, he transmitted through holy stories the essence of what a Jew could aspire to become. His knowledge of the Chassidic *rebbes,* and the stories about them, was intimate. Ishbitz, Lublin, Belz, Ger, Bobov, Stolin, and Breslov, are just a few among many of the great dynasties that he restored to "life" after the Holocaust.

He was the *rebbe* of the six million who were murdered during the Holocaust, the Russian *refuseniks,* and Israel's soldiers who defend the holy land.

Shlomo taught us how to sing the praises of God. The words to his creative melodies were based upon passages from the prayerbook, the psalms, and biblical and prophetic writings. His genius in creating inspiring melody, his method of teaching, and his undying love for his people, no matter where they were on the religious spectrum, combined into a human being that was unlike any other.

His love of Torah, his explanations of the lines of the Talmud, and his interpretation of the prayerbook were the inspiration for those who called themselves his disciples.

"*A-ve, a-ve, reh-chev Yisrael u'fa-ra-shav:* Our father (rebbe), our father (rebbe), the chariot of Israel and its rider.' (*II Melachim*, II Kings 2:12) With his chariot (airplane) he showed us how to connect heaven and earth. He was the leader in the battle for Jewish souls, he showed us the way in a time when strong leadership is paramount. He is sorely missed.

Rabbi Eugene and Annette Labovitz

Dedication

in memory of our parents

Yitzchak Elchanan ben Eliezer v'Rochel
Isadore Kwalwasser
and
Bryna bat Yehoshua Yisrael v'Chava Bracha
Bertha F. Kwalwasser

Menachem Zev
Mendel Labovitz
and Chana
Hannah Gottesman Labovitz

Reuvan ben Moshe
Ralph Epstein
and
Rochel bat Yisrael
Rachel Wrubel Epstein

Avraham Yitchak Giller
and in honor of
Tanya Brocha Giller

✡

Contents

Volume Two

Part Four
The Silver Age of Polish Jewry

Introduction 313
Kaddish 317
The Repentant Tailor 325
Equal Citizenship 337
The Rabbi's Daughter 347
The Forgotten Story 359
The Righteous Proselyte 369
The House of Rothchild 377
An Unusual Torah Scholar 387
Just One Kopek 395
The Pintele Yid 401
Remember Who You Are 415
The Holy Shekel 421
Quick Thinking 429
A Woman Ahead of Her Time 433
Don't Let The Lights Go Out 443

Volume Three

Part Five
The American Jewish Experience

Introduction 451
The First Jews in New Amsterdam 455
The Light of a Small Candle Shines at Valley Forge 461
Rebbeca and Judah 467
Concerning the Jews 477

The New Colossus 483
Rochel Leah's *Parochet* 489
A Bintel Brief 503
Tuition 509
One Survivor's Story 513
In Memory of Shlomo 531

∽

Part Six
Our People Return to Our Land
Introduction 537
Be Careful How You Speak 541
When Will the *Messiach* Come? 551
Once He Cried 553
The Determination of a *Yerushalmi* 561
A Fragment of Torah 567
The Afikoman That Restored Life 577
Let Our Work be for Peace 591
Kfar Etzion 599
From Moscow to *Yerushalayim* 611
The Iranian Connection 625
Why Did You Come to Israel? 635
Don't You Think It's Time? 643
I Have a Dream 649

∽

Sources, Further Readings and Footnotes i
Three Volume Index ix

Preface - Volumes Two and Three

Volume I of *A Sacred Trust: Stories of Jewish Heritage and History*, described the period from the destruction of the second Holy Temple to the expulsion of Spain, approximately fifteen hundred years later.

Through the narratives of the most important stories that every man, woman, and child should know to be Jewishly culturally literate, we explored the transfer of the center of Jewish life from *Eretz Yisrael* to Babylonia. We examined the way Jewish life was lived during the period when the Talmud was written, when Jews lived side by side with their Moslem neighbors for hundreds of years.

We followed the shift of the center of Jewish life to western Europe. In this part of the world, the story changed drastically, for instead of a relatively secure contact, the floodgates of hate and consequent persecution followed. But parallel to the Medieval Europe experience, the Golden Age was flourishing in Spain; Jews were totally integrated into the population, There was no difference between Moslem and Jew, except for religion.

Volume II tells the story of the *Silver Age of Polish Jewry*, Readers who have previewed the stories which tell this part of our history have commented how different the chapter of Jewish life in eastern Europe was from medieval Europe. It is marked by autonomy; it is as if the Jewish community thrived as a state within the Polish/Lithuanian/Russian state for more than four hundred years.

True, problems with non-Jewish neighbors existed. But the Jews who arrived in Poland at the invitation of King Boleslav in the middle of the 1200's built a foundation for modern Jewish life. *Chassidim, mitnagdim,* and the development of *yeshivot* as we know them today, had their source in eastern Europe. These institutions are being rebuilt in America and in *Eretz Yisrael*, fifty years after the Holocaust. We are struggling as a people to make certain that we *"Do Not Let the Light's Go Out."*

As the stories come closer to modern times, for they are arranged chronologically, the values that have kept our people alive become more focused.

What are these Jewish values? Study and transmitting Torah from generation to generation, caring for those less fortunate than ourselves, maintaining our Jewish identity, recognizing that the spark of holiness, the *pintele yid,* always smolders within us and only needs to be ignited with the flame of knowing how precious it is to be a Jew.

We hope that the stories in Volume II will help our readers and users continue to explore our precious and unique heritage with the goal of understanding what proceeded our generation.

By understanding the experiences and values of our ancestors, we will be able to build meaningful Jewish bridges into the future.

Volume III is the conclusion of *A Sacred Trust: Stories of Jewish Heritage and History.* These three volumes were conceived as a Jewish cultural literacy series.

The Jewish community finds itself in the midst of a struggle over issues of identity and continuity. We offer for your consideration the thought that literacy must precede identity and continuity, for if we do not know what is expected of us, how can our actions identify us as Jews?

To make our lives rich and meaningful as Jews, we need to gain basic fundamental knowledge. Acquisition of knowledge is necessary in two areas: we need to know that our past is the bridge that leads us into the future; we need to learn about those specific behaviors which characterize us as Jews. Through the stories in these three volumes, a total comprehensive portrait of what a Jew can aspire to be
becomes apparent.

In addition, many of the stories in Volume III were constructed from personal interviews. The people who shared their stories, the people who were in the forefront of history as it happened, make the "present" relevant. They lived through specific events and chose to share their memories for posterity. They are truly our link from the past to the
future.

Stories have different genres, and many variations, often depending on the teller or writer. But the goal of the stories is to transmit from one generation to the next the message of our cultural roots. What was it like to have lived in a specific country, in a specific century? How have the heroes and heroines celebrated holy days, and observed rituals? We have met exemplary role models who have inspired us with their Jewish message; people who have taught us, through the words of the narrative, what it means to be a Jew.

This volume includes stories of the American Jewish community, from the first settlers who arrived on these blessed shores in search of a better life, to those who completed the acculturation process in the present. It also includes stories of the rebuilding of our Holy Land, of pioneers returning in droves to rebuild the land that lay fallow for almost two thousand years, that was a sacred memory, and now has once again become the site of a flourishing Jewish homeland.

The stories in these three volumes will help you discover our rich Jewish heritage. We vision rabbis, educators and students, parents and children, grandparents and grandchildren, *chavurot*, adult education groups, everyone who wants to know, pursuing this yearning for knowledge through the beautiful medium of holy stories.

Rabbi Eugene Labovitz
Annette Labovitz
March, 1995
Adar, 5755

Part Four
The Silver Age of Polish Jewry

Time Line

| 70 c.e. | 600 c.e. | 1000 c.e. | 1400 c.e. | 1600 c.e. | 1800 c.e. | 2000 c.e. |

Location: Eastern Europe (Poland, Lithuania, Russia.)

Introduction

Boleslav, King of Poland, beckoned to the Jewish people to migrate to his land. He wanted them to help its economic development. To show them how much he desired their presence, he extended to them a charter of privileges, guaranteeing safety. For their part, the Jews were searching for a haven of refuge, a sanctuary from the violence that had been part of their lives in the Franco/Germanic lands since the advent of the Crusades, one-hundred fifty years before. They arrived little by little, establishing themselves, informing their brothers of the good conditions, encouraging them to follow. Eventually a large Jewish population settled in Poland/Lithuania. The period is known as the Silver Age of Polish Jewry, beginning in 1264, the year the first charter of privileges was granted. This period of relative security lasted approximately four hundred years until the horrible Chmielnicki massacres in 1648-1649. In spite of the terrible tragedy, the Jews remained in Poland/Lithuania. When Hitler marched into Poland, on September 1, 1939, more Jews lived there than in almost any other place in the world.

During the thirteenth, fourteenth, and fifteenth centuries, some Jews settled in the cities, others were craftsmen or merchants, and some administered the estates of wealthy *pareetzim* (singular, *poretz*). Occasionally, a *poretz* found a pretext for faulting his tenant and took steps to imprison or expel him from his land (*Kaddish,* Chapter 32; *The Repentant Tailor,*

Chapter Thirty-three). The Jews were permitted to establish autonomous governing councils in the major cities that were responsible for the welfare of the inhabitants of the area.

Toward the middle of the sixteenth century, the charter of privileges was reconfirmed by Prince Radziwill. (*Equal Citizenship,* Chapter Thirty-four)

During these approximately three hundred years, a native generation of rabbinic leaders created a center of Torah learning in Poland/Lithuania that illuminated the darkness of exile existence and became the forerunner of today's *yeshivot*.

The fortunes of the Jewish people changed drastically in 1648, for Jews suffered from the political and social upheavals around them. The Ukranian Cossacks were Greek Orthodox; the Poles were Roman Catholic. The Ukranians resented being ruled by the Poles who forced them into serfdom; they loved the freedom to roam the open Russian territory which bordered Poland. The Jews, living in unprotected *shtetlach* which dotted the Polish countryside, were empowered by the Polish king to collect the taxes. Bogdan Chmielnicki, leader of the Ukranian Cossacks unleashed his fury at the Jews who were representatives of the detested king. It took the Polish king ten years to restore order. In the meantime, the Cossacks ravaged the Polish countryside, slaughtering both Jews and Poles (*The Rabbi's Daughter,* Chapter Thirty-five).

The Jewish people felt totally helpless. They wondered how much longer the exile would last. When Shabbetai Zvi, the false Messiah appeared on the scene in 1665-1666, many people believed that he had come to remove them from exile and lead them back to *Eretz Yisrael*. When he converted to Islam to save his life, the Jewish people realized that he was a hoax, and their sense of despair grew. Now they felt hopeless as well.

The Baal Shem Tov, *Rebbe* Yisrael ben Eliezer, lifted up their spirits. He was the founder of the *chassidic* movement. He imbued the Jewish people with a love of God and a deeper understanding of learning and observance; he emphasized prayer as a focal point of Jewish life; he taught them to serve God with joy, no matter their personal situation. He often said that his father made him promise that he would love every Jew (*The Forgotten Story,* Chapter Thirty-six; *The Pintele Yid,* Chapter Forty-one).

In neighboring Vilna, Lithuania, the opponents of *chassidism* rallied around Rabbi Elyahu ben Shlomo Zalman, the Gaon of Vilna. They were called *mitnagdim,* for they feared *chassidism* as another sect that would influence people away from mainstream Judaism. They emphasized intense scholarship and ethical sensitivity (*The Righteous Proselyte,* Chapter Thirty-seven). Today, two hundred and fifty years later, there is little difference in practice between *chassidim* and *mitnagdim.*

The House of Rothschild, the legendary European bankers, started with a blessing from the *chassidic* rebbe, Rebbe Tzve Hirsh Halayve Horovitz of Tzortikov (*The House of Rothschild,* Chapter Thirty-eight).

In Poland/Russia, Jews suffered under cruel Tzarist regimes. Jewish children were kidnapped to serve for twenty five years in the army. The government wanted to Russify the Jews, i.e., to force them to assimilate (*Remember Who You Are,* Chapter Forty-two). *Pareetzim* imprisoned Jews who were late in paying their rent, or kidnapped the children and forcibly tried to convert them (Just One Kopeck, Chapter Forty).

The majority of Jews living in eastern Europe were not influenced by the emancipation movement in western Europe where the ghetto walls crumbled around them. The Jews were permitted to participate in society, after almost a thousand years of discrimination. The lure of the secular world resulted in many western European Jews abandoning Judaism (*An Unusual Torah Scholar,* Chapter Thirty-nine).

Jewish leaders convened to decide which roles emancipated Jews could fill in emerging modern governments. They pondered over the issue: will emancipated Jews remain loyal to their heritage? (*The Holy Shekel,* Chapter Forty-three)

People who hated Jews tried to discredit them in the eyes of the government. Sometimes a quick thinking Jew could cancel all the intended harm (*Quick Thinking,* Chapter Forty-four).

The way Jewish women were educated radically changed towards the beginning of the twentieth century, for a charismatic woman happened on the scene. She realized that if women were to be the guarantors of the next generation, they needed to be educated in order to transmit their Jewish heritage (*A Woman Ahead of Her Time,* Chapter Forty-five).

Poland/Russia/Lithuania, with their borders constantly changing on the battlefield and by political maneuvering, was home to the majority of world Jewry until the eve of World War II. During the Holocaust, the Jewish people, who had lived in eastern Europe for hundreds of years were totally annihilated (Don't Let *The Lights Go Out,* Chapter Forty-six).

These are the stories of our eastern European ancestors.

A Sacred Trust
— Commentary —
Kaddish

There are questions asked frequently regarding the recitation of the *kaddish* prayer.

1. If the *kaddish* is designated as the prayer to honor the memory of the dead, why is there no mention of either the name or the death of the deceased?
2. Why is the prayer recited in the Aramaic language rather than in Hebrew?
3. What consolation is derived by the mourner in reciting a prayer that praises God in the time of his grief?
4. If the deceased had an opportunity to deliver a message to the mourners, what would he/she say?

The message would include the first words of the *kaddish: yitgadal, v'yitkadash sh'may raba,* may the name of God be praised. The deceased says, in spite of the pain that is felt over my loss, "May God's Name be praised."

The deceased wants the mourners to comprehend his message, so he speaks in Aramaic because that was the language of the people, and it was easily understood.

There is no mention of the deceased because he is uttering the message, and the words of the *kaddish* are the consolation repeated by the mourners.

By helping the miller's wife raise the money for the recitation of the *kaddish* for all those who passed away without having any one to say *kaddish* for them, the soul of the banker's father ensured that the message of the *kaddish* would bring consolation to those people, also. At the same time it would elevate their souls to their eternal resting place.

—*Authors*

The Silver Age of Polish Jewry: Chapter Thirty-two

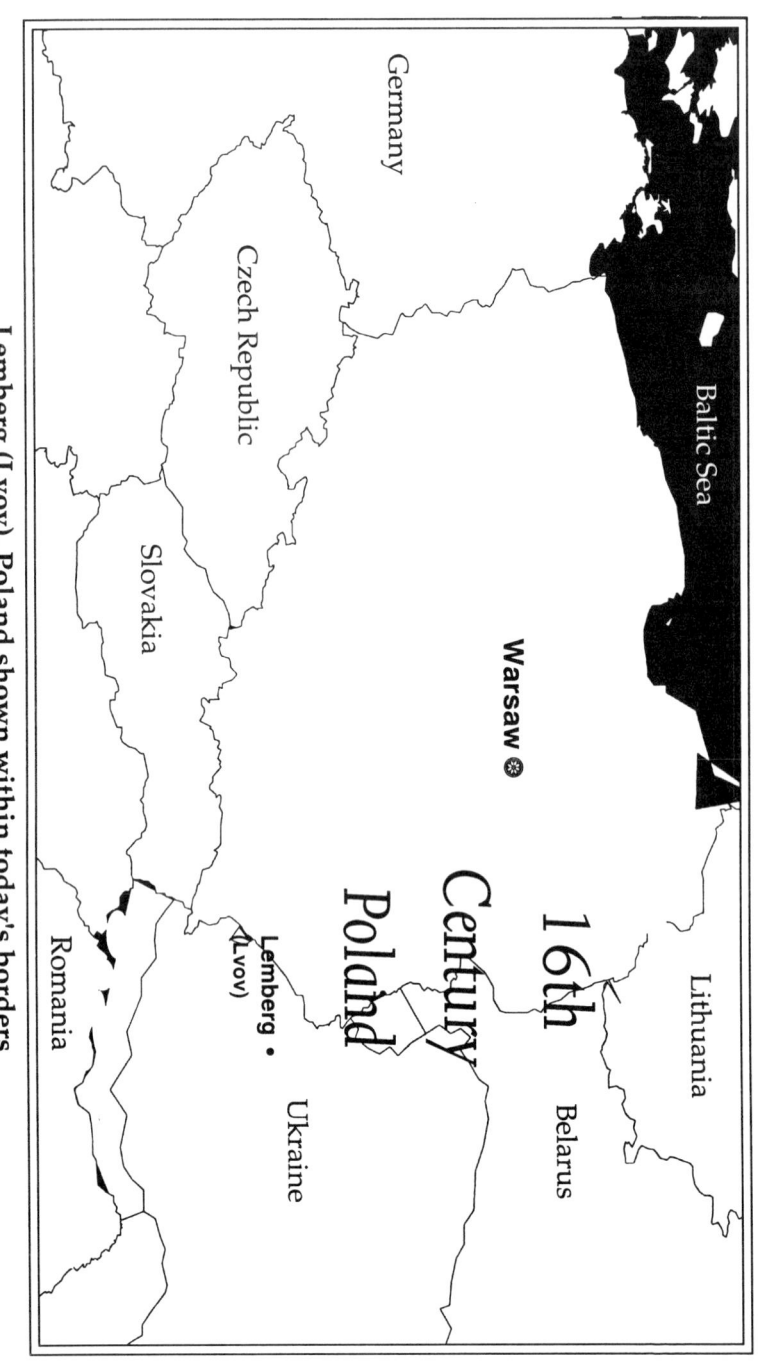

Lemberg (Lvov), Poland shown within today's borders

Chapter Thirty-Two
KADDISH

Time Line

| 70 c.e. | 600 c.e. | 1000 c.e. | 1400 c.e. | 1600 c.e. | 1800 c.e. | 2000 c.e. |

Location: Eastern Europe (Poland, Lithuania)

[**Ed.** *Kaddish* is a prayer praising God, recited with congregational responses at the close of individual sections of a prayer service. It is recited by a mourner following the study of *Torah*, *Tehillim* (Psalms), or *Talmud*, and after specified prayers during the service.]

[**Ed.** The first Jewish settlers immigrated to Poland from the Germanic lands, seeking refuge from the Crusades, the Blood Libels, and the accusation that they caused the spread of the Black Plague. Under the protection of a charter of privileges granted Jews by the Polish Kings Boleslav (1264) and Casimir (1344), they thrived economically and intellectually for a period of almost four hundred years. The immigrants were granted equal citizenship, and they lived a generally secure and content life. They established *kehilot*, (*kahal*, singular) autonomous governing councils and great *yeshivot* whose leaders illuminated Polish Jewish life. The leaders of the *kehilot* had to approve the representative appointed by the king. He had no right to interfere in any internal affairs regulated by the *kahal*.]

Lemberg (Lvov), located east of Cracow, was an important Polish city with a sizable Jewish population. The Jews of Lemberg thrived as merchants, trading in skins, cattle, wool, and clothing. Their economic success added abundantly to the king's treasury.

Pinchas, who lived on the estate of a *poretz* and leased the flour mill, ran into a head-on confrontation with him because he had not earned enough money that year to pay his rent.

At first, the *poretz* extended the due date for the rent, hoping that the miller's business would prosper. He realized that by taking away the mill or imprisoning the miller, he would never see his money. So he waited patiently, occasionally sending messages to the miller that his time was running out.

The miller always responded to the *poretz*: "Please, be patient. Just give me a little more time. I know things will get better. As soon as I have the money, I shall pay every *zloty* of the rent I owe!"

The *poretz* waited for a year. Finally, knowing that the miller would never pay, he ordered his servants to imprison Pinchas and his children. They broke into his house in the middle of the night, beat him and his sleeping children, overturned the furniture, broke windows, and shouted at the top of their voices: "The *poretz* has commanded us to imprison you and your children until someone pays what you owe. The *poretz* wants his money now. No more delays!"

Panic stricken, the miller's wife, slipped out of a back window, ran under the cover of darkness to the forest on the edge of the *poretz's* estate, and hid for the night under the shelter of a big oak tree.

When dawn broke, she stealthily made her way to Lemberg, to the house of Rabbi Asher ben Rabbi Yitzchak HaKohen.[1] She wanted him to help her raise the money to rescue her husband and children from the *poretz's* prison.

The Rabbi of Lemberg received her very kindly. He listened to her tell of her family's misfortune. When she finished, he responded: "I will give you a letter describing the plight of your family, requesting that the Jewish community respond generously. Stand on the main street in the marketplace, show my letter to the passers-by, plead your cause. Since Jews are compassionate, it should not take you too long to raise the money you need."

The Rabbi of Lemberg sat down at his desk to write the letter. Handing it to the woman, he also placed ten *zlotys* in her hand.

Gratefully, she left the Rabbi's house, and went out to the marketplace. She remained there for a few days.

She had almost collected enough to pay the ransom. Looking forward joyfully to being reunited with her family, the frightening thought suddenly occurred to her: "What if they are no longer alive? What if the *poretz* starved or beat them to death, God forbid?"

"Here I am collecting money to redeem them and they might already be dead, God forbid. Dead? Who will say *kaddish* for them?"

With heavy heart, she trudged home.

The next morning, while standing in the marketplace again, she noticed a gentle looking man, carrying a velvet sack, ostensibly containing his *talit* and *tefilin*, walking in the direction of the *shul*. She ran towards him, crying: "My husband and children have been imprisoned by the *poretz*. I don't know if they are still alive. If they are dead, who will say *kaddish* for them? Please, I beg you ... take this money. Say *kaddish* for them." She placed half the money she had collected in his hand. She stopped crying for a moment, and, as if in an afterthought, she moaned: "Before you go, tell me your name."

"My name is Tuvia," he answered. He continued in the direction of the *shul*.

She did not know whether to collect more money to redeem her imprisoned husband and children. "If they were dead," she thought, "at least *kaddish* was being said for them."

She could not rest. Suddenly, it occurred to her: "Tuvia is going to say *kaddish* for my family. If they are dead, I have no use for the money I have left. I will ask him to say *kaddish* for all the people who have passed on without children, without anyone who could say *kaddish* for them!"

She ran after him. He was just about to enter the *shul*. "Wait, she yelled, at the top of her voice. "Wait, I have another favor to ask of you."

Tuvia turned around.

Breathlessly, she said: "When you recite *kaddish* for my

family, I would like you to say *kaddish* for all the people who have passed on without children, without anyone who could say *kaddish* for them. Will you do it?"

When he nodded, she placed the rest of the money she had collected into his hand. Then she returned to the marketplace, wondering what to do next.

All at once, the thought occurred to her: "What if I gave Tuvia the money for nothing? What if he forgets to say *kaddish*?"

She ran to the *shul*, climbed up the stairs to the women's gallery, sat down, and waited until the end of the service, till the time for the recital of the *kaddish*. Tuvia stood up and began: "*Yis-ga-dal v'yis-ka-dash sh'may ra-bah...*"

She returned to the marketplace. Confused, fleeting thoughts gave her no peace.

"Are my husband and children dead or alive?" she pondered. "Maybe I should continue to collect money to ransom them."

She decided to remain, showing the rabbi's letter to the passers-by. Around mid-morning, she noticed an elegant carriage approaching in the distance. Sleek white horses, harnessed to the carriage, trotted along at a brisk pace. She realized that the passenger in the approaching carriage must be a very wealthy man, so she raised her hands, waved frantically, trying to stop the carriage. A fashionably dressed man stepped down from the carriage.

"What's wrong? Why did you stop my carriage?" he queried.

Not hesitating, she handed the rabbi's letter to the man.

He finished reading it, and said: "I am going to give you a note addressed to the local money lender. I have all my money deposited with him. Take this note to his home, and he will give you the money you need to pay the ransom for your family."

The woman thanked him profusely, and ran all the way to the

money lender's house. She knocked loudly on the door. A servant admitted her.

She showed him the note. Examining it carefully, he said: "Please, sit down. I will be back in a few minutes."

The servant showed the note to his master. He emerged from the drawing room and asked: "Where did you get this note?"

She described the man who had stopped his carriage in the marketplace.

"Please, come into the drawing room," he urged. He pointed to a comfortable looking chair and told her to be seated.

He spoke softly. "Please, look at the portraits hanging behind me. Can you pick out the portrait of the man who gave you the note?"

She scanned the faces on the portraits, one by one, then pointed to the last portrait in the row.

"That is the man who helped me," she said.

The money lender lowered his eyes, blinking back tears. He sighed, then spoke in broken sentences: "I want you to know that the portrait you pointed to is a portrait of my father. He passed away twenty years ago. What did you do today that merited my father to come from his eternal resting place to give you this large sum of money?"

She started from the beginning, omitting no detail. When she reached the part of the story where she ran after Tuvia to give him additional money to recite *kaddish* for those people who passed away without children, or for those people whose children did not recite *kaddish* for them, he sobbed uncontrollably.

"I want you to know, that I now understand why my father came from his eternal resting place to give you this large sum of money. My father was a very committed Jew, but I did not follow in his footsteps. Rather, I became very involved in business. It didn't seem important to me to make the time to recite *kaddish* for him, for the elevation of his soul into its eternal resting place. Apparently, the *kaddish* of the gentle man that you hired to say *kaddish* for all those people who passed away without their children reciting *kaddish* for them elevated my father's soul to its final eternal resting place. He must have returned to this world to thank you for what you did."

He rose, walked over to the safe, opened it, withdrew the amount of money that was written on the face of the note, and gave it to the woman.

Running breathlessly to the *poretz*, she handed him the money. Silently, she thanked God as her husband and children were released.

[**Ed.** This story was written for posterity by Rabbi Asher ben Rabbi Yitzchak Hakohen in the records of the Jewish community of Lemberg.]

A Sacred Trust
— Commentary —
The Repentant Tailor

Tailors are frequently found in Jewish folk tales, perhaps because they had so little status in real life. Tailors were people who worked with their hands, and in a culture in which men of the mind or men of the heart were honored, they were not considered very important. But in this story and in the many others like it that abound, tailors win redemption.

This is a story about sin, about a man who wanders away from his family and his people and becomes part of the entourage of the *Poretz*, the Polish noblemen. There he lives in limbo—ostracized by the Jews, treated lightly by the *Poretz*.

And then, something happens. Someone arrives, who has the power to change his life. A *Rebbe* arrives who speaks to the whole group that shares Shabbat with him—and yet the tailor, (and probably everyone else who is present) feels that he is speaking just to him, just to his own innermost soul. The tailor hears the message and begins his long journey back from sin to repentance. In the end he climbs to a level higher than anyone could have ever imagined.

Cynics will say that such a story could never have happened for people can't change that much. Evil can't be undone this way. Tailors can't become saints. Let them believe that if they want to...but if you are not so cynical, read this tale and wonder. Could it have really happened? And if it happened then, could it perhaps happen again—to you? to me?

Who knows? Perhaps it could?

Rabbi Jack Riemer

Editor of **Torah Fax** *and Director of the National Rabbinic Network. Author of* **Wrestling with the Angeles,** *and editor of* **The World of the High Holy Days** *and* **So That Your Values Live On.**

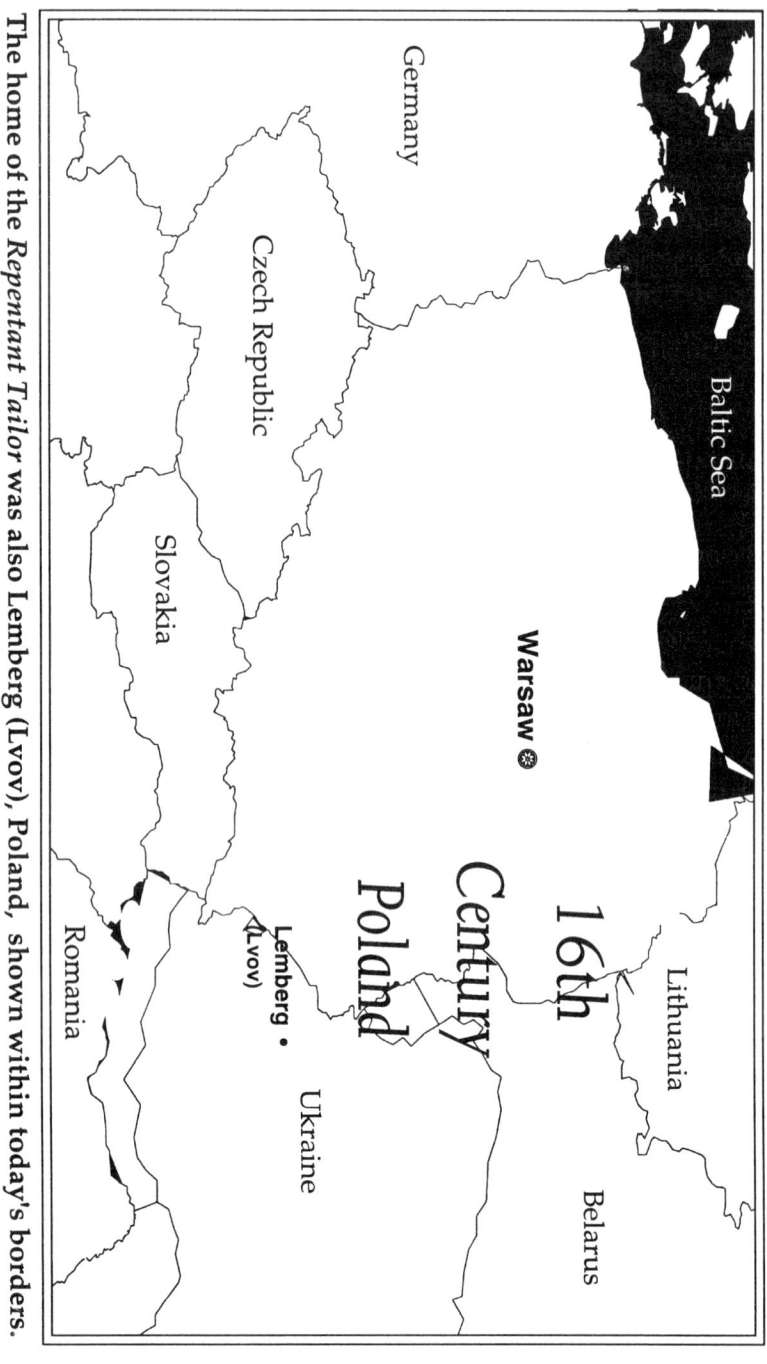

The home of the *Repentant Tailor* was also Lemberg (Lvov), Poland, shown within today's borders.

Chapter Thirty-Three
THE REPENTANT TAILOR

Time Line

| 70 c.e. | 600 c.e. | 1000 c.e. | 1400 c.e. | 1600 c.e. | 1800 c.e. | 2000 c.e. |

Location: Eastern Europe (Poland, Lithuania)

[**Ed.** The *kahal*, the autonomous governing council, controlled much of Jewish life in Polish cities during the fifteenth and sixteenth centuries. It supervised education, religious institutions, and was generally responsible for the care of the poor, the widowed, the orphans, and the sick. It ostracized people who refused to conform to the standards of the Jewish community.]

The tailor of Lemberg was poor because he was a sloppy craftsman. The first time a person wore a garment he had sewn, the seams opened, the hem dropped, and the fabric split. The people grew tired of inferior workmanship and took their business elsewhere. The tailor did not try to improve his skills; rather he rationalized his unfortunate situation.

"They don't patronize me because they don't want me to earn a living," he thought bitterly. "They are to blame for the miserable condition in which my wife and I are forced to live."

The tailor was blessed with natural wit. Since he was blind to his own faults, he decided to seek the means of earning a livelihood outside the Jewish community.

One day he heard that the *poretz* was looking for someone to entertain him and his courtiers each evening after dinner.

"A lot of people laugh at my jokes," the tailor decided. "Why should I struggle at tailoring when I can make a lot of money entertaining the *poretz* and his friends. I think I will apply for the job."

The *poretz*, who lived in a luxurious mansion at the top of the hill, agreed to hire the tailor on a temporary basis.

"If you make us laugh, I will retain you permanently," he said.

Each night after dinner, he told funny stories to the *poretz*, his family, and their guests. Afterward, he returned to his modest house in the *shtetl*.

At the beginning of the second week, the *poretz* commented: "Why don't you stay here? I have a nice room for you on the second floor, with a window overlooking the valley. It's a comfortable, airy room. As long as I am pleased with your work, you may call this room your home."

"Why should I live in squalor when I can live in luxury," thought the tailor. "There's no need for me to go home every night."

He accepted the *poretz's* offer. It did not take long for him to become accustomed to the ways of the non-Jewish world. The tailor ate the *poretz's* food, and slowly became addicted to his wine. Intoxicated, he found it much easier to tell the type of jokes that pleased the *poretz*. On occasion, he returned home to visit his wife. Always drunk, he beat her before returning to the mansion. The *kahal* ostracized him. The tailor of Lemberg became a social outcast.

He had grown accustomed to sleeping half the day in the *poretz's* mansion. One Friday afternoon, after many months in the employ of the *poretz*, the tailor opened his eyes, blinked two or three times in the gleaming, sunlit room, and stretched. He swung his feet over the side of the bed and hobbled over to the window. Peering down into the valley, he beheld an unusual sight. The innkeeper directed furniture carriers and food vendors into the inn amidst much excitement. It seemed that the innkeeper was making special preparations for important guests for *Shabbat*.

He stood at the window a long time, turning in one direction, then another, wondering from where the guests would come. About an hour later, he saw a carriage approaching from the west. As the carriage drew closer to the inn, the tailor was able to detect that a dignified looking rabbi sat in the front with the wagon driver, and the carriage was filled with what appeared to be about ten young men. He remained standing at the window until he saw the innkeeper run out to greet the rabbi and his students.

Excitedly, the tailor fled through the mansion searching for the *poretz*. When he found him, he screeched excitedly: "I have to go to spend *Shabbat* in the inn!"

The *poretz* was furious that the tailor didn't want to entertain on the most important night of the week.

"I don't understand you. Haven't I treated you well? Isn't my house, my food, my wine good enough for you? Why do you want to go to the inn?" thundered the *poretz*.

"You really don't understand," muttered the tailor. "I was looking out my bedroom window at the valley. I noticed a lot of commotion at the inn. Workers moved around furniture. Food vendors brought in lots of extra food. Then some important guests arrived. Something exciting must be happening down there. If you let me go, I will be able to create new material from my observing at first hand all the goings on. I will be able to entertain you even better."

The *poretz* thought for a moment. "I'm a little tired of his stories. Maybe I should let him go. He is such a natural wit. Chances are he will come back with great material."

Turning to the tailor, he said: "All right, I'll let you go, but remember, you must return here early Sunday morning."

"Of course I will," said the tailor sheepishly. "But remember, I am a social outcast in the Jewish community. Unless you order the innkeeper to take me in, he will refuse, and then our whole plan will be for naught. Write a note to the innkeeper ordering him to let me stay in the inn for *Shabbat*."

Armed with the note, the tailor descended the hill and headed for the inn. The innkeeper was in a quandary when he entered and handed him the note. He did not want the social outcast to be with him, especially on this *Shabbat* when he was hosting a distinguished rabbi and his students.

Nevertheless, pretending to welcome the tailor, for he did not want to anger the *poretz* in any way, he said: "You can have the first room on the right side of the stairs on the third floor. Why don't you go up there and make yourself comfortable. I'll send someone to call you when dinner is ready."

As the tailor climbed the steps, the innkeeper realized that he was faced with a new dilemma: how to seat the social outcast at the table without offending his distinguished guests.

"I know what to do. I will instruct my servant to set the tables for *Shabbat* in the shape of a rectangle. I'll seat the rabbi at the head of the table, his students on each of the long sides, divided equally, and the tailor at the far end. That way he will not be close to the rabbi."

The rabbi and his students prepared themselves for *Shabbat* and went off to the synagogue to pray *Kabbolat Shabbat*.

[**Ed.** The Friday night service is called *Kabbolat Shabbat*, welcoming the *Shabbat* Queen.]

The tailor remained in his room. When the guests returned from the synagogue and were seated in the dining room of the inn, the innkeeper sent a messenger to call the tailor as he had promised. He seated the tailor opposite the rabbi at the far end of the table.

During the course of the meal, the rabbi usually discussed the Torah portion for that particular week. However, this time he deviated from his usual custom and used as his theme a subject totally unrelated to the weekly Torah reading. He spoke on the theme of repentance. His students wondered why he had deviated from his usual custom, but they listened respectfully and did not comment. The outcast tailor did not move from his seat.

During the *Shabbat* luncheon, the rabbi again spoke on the subject of repentance. This time, he delineated explicit wrongs that people commit, and urged them to repent. The tailor's eyes did not move from the rabbi's face the entire time. As he spoke, the rabbi stared at the tailor, as if his eyes penetrated the tailor's soul.

When the meal ended, the rabbi announced that he wanted to be alone for the remainder of the *Shabbat*. Some of the students went to their rooms to rest, others went for a leisurely walk, and others sat down in the garden to study the Torah reading for that week. Only the tailor remained glued to his seat. He sat there until nightfall, until three stars appeared in the sky.

Then he bounded up the stairs and banged on the door of the rabbi's room.

The rabbi opened the door and said in a soft voice: "Please, come in. I have been expecting you!"

The tailor started to cry uncontrollably. He muttered: "I am the one that you spoke about last night and this afternoon. I am the one that has committed all those wrongs.

But I want you to know that I am ready to repent. Please, teach me how to mend my evil ways. Please teach me the path of repentance."

"To begin on the path of repentance, you have to fast for three days," whispered the rabbi.

The tailor continued crying: "Is that all there is to repentance? After all the sins I have committed? I know there must be more to repentance than that. Please, tell me what I have to do to be completely forgiven. I am ready to do anything to return to my people."

The rabbi said: "You're right! There is more. You must fast from one *Shabbat* to the next. During the weekdays, you must immerse yourself in the study of Torah. You must use every opportunity to do good deeds. Eventually, you will receive a sign that your repentance has been accepted."

The next morning, the tailor went to the synagogue. He joined the worshippers who had come to pray. After the service ended, he walked over to the bookshelves, withdrew a volume of the Talmud, sat down on a bench in the corner, opened the book, and began poring over the text.

The *shammish* was a bit disturbed, for he was responsible for opening and closing the synagogue. He wanted to close the doors for the day and leave to attend to other business.

"I can't wait around for you all day," he said gruffly. "Hurry, finish the passage that you are studying and come back for the evening prayers. I have other things to do."

The tailor did not know what to do. He needed to remain in the synagogue so he could follow the rabbi's instructions. Having no other alternative, he revealed his plight to the *shammish*.

The *shammish* was very understanding. "I'll tell you what I can do. I will lock the doors and you can remain in the synagogue. You will be able to study here all day. Tonight, I will return for the evening prayers and open the doors, as usual. No one need know our secret. After the evening service, I will make you comfortable on a long bench in the basement. You can sleep there."

The tailor nodded his head, and the *shammish* left. He accepted his hunger and loneliness as part of his repentance.

The week dragged by slowly. He looked forward to the first Friday night, hoping that he would receive a sign that his repentance had been accepted. But the worshippers arrived, prayed and departed, and the tailor remained in the synagogue all by himself with only a small *challah* and a piece of chicken that the *shammish* had brought him. There was no sign that his repentance had been accepted.

The second week dragged by even slower than the first. That Friday night, the worshippers arrived, prayed and departed. The *shammish* also departed, forgetting entirely that the tailor depended upon him for *Shabbat* food. The tailor groped for his bench in the basement, sat down forlornly, and began to weep. Anguished words of prayer gushed forth from the depth of his soul, for he desperately wanted to know if his repentance would ever be accepted.

He prayed for a long time, then fell into a fitful sleep. The tailor dreamed that *Elyahu Hanave* hovered over him, whispering: "Your repentance has been accepted. The sign that you will know that this is so is that within one hour's time the *shammish* will return to the synagogue, open the door and let you out. Return to your wife and your home. After *Shabbat*, sell your house and buy a new one near the *mikveh* (ritual bath). When you have done this, I will appear to you each night to teach you Torah."

The tailor awoke, startled. He was not certain whether to believe his dream or not. He sat on the bench patiently and waited for the arrival of the *shammish*. When he was about to give up in despair, he heard footsteps approaching through the open basement window on the cobblestoned walk above. He ran to the window and was able to make out the figure of the *shammish* approaching in the dark.

The *shammish* opened the door of the synagogue, ran down the basement stairs and said breathlessly: "Please forgive me for forgetting you. I went home and ate my *Shabbat* meal and then retired for the night. I was about to doze off when I remembered that you were still locked in the synagogue. I quickly put on my clothes and ran here as fast as I could."

The two men walked up the stairs and out the door of the synagogue. The *shammish* turned in the direction that he had come and set off for his home. The tailor also set off in the direction of his home. He walked quickly.

When he reached the house, he rapped on the door. "Open up," he pleaded. "Please open the door."

He had awakened his wife from a deep sleep. She recognized his voice but feared to open the door, thinking that he might be drunk again, that he had come to beat her.

"Please, open the door. Tonight is *Shabbat*. I swear that I will not hurt you."

She opened the door slowly. He walked into their house timidly and wished her a *Good Shabbos*. The penitent tailor walked over to the cupboard, took down the bottle of wine and a *kiddush* cup, recited the *kiddush*, ritually washed his hands and recited a blessing on a leftover piece of *challah*, helped himself to some food, then recited the grace after meals, removed a blanket from the cupboard, spread it on the floor, lay down and fell asleep.

His wife could not fall sleep. She could not believe that the man laying on the blanket on the floor was the husband who beat her periodically. She did not understand how his behavior had changed so radically in so short a time.

In the morning, she tried to satisfy her curiosity by asking him all kinds of questions. He responded: "Today is *Shabbat*. I don't want to discuss weekly matters on our holy day. Tonight, I will tell you everything that happened to me."

After *havdalah* (ceremony separating *Shabbat* from the weekday), he told her every detail of his life of the past few months, how he had tired of repeating the same jokes over and over to the *poretz*, how he tried to find new material, how he had met a rabbi who had set him upon the path of repentance.

"And," he whispered, "we cannot tell anybody anything. *Elyahu Hanave* will come to study Torah with me after we move into our new house near the *mikveh*."

It was the custom of the Rabbi of Lemberg to sleep during the first few hours of the night, rise at midnight, walk to the *mikveh*, immerse himself, and return to his study hall to study Torah until the breaking dawn. Some nights his *shammish* accompanied him. One particular night, as the rabbi and his *shammish* approached the *mikveh*, the rabbi noticed a light from the tailor's window.

"I'm so glad that the tailor is working on improving his craft," thought the rabbi. "If he becomes a better tailor, he can earn a fine living in this city."

The next night, the rabbi saw a light in the tailor's house again. This time he sent his *shammish* to find out why the tailor was working so hard, so late into the night.

The *shammish* reported back to the rabbi: "The tailor told me that he has many garments to sew. He told me to explain to you that this was the reason why he kept such late hours."

The following week, the rabbi noticed that the lantern was still lit in the tailor's house even though it was past midnight. The rabbi doubted that the tailor had so many garments to sew. He decided to find out for himself why the tailor stayed up so late each night.

The tailor responded to the knock. The rabbi stood on the porch and asked: "Why do you keep such late hours? Weeks have gone by since you moved to this house and since then I have noticed your candles burning every night on my way to the *mikveh*."

"I told your *shammish* that I have a lot of garments to sew. I have so much work that I cannot possibly finish it all during the day, so I work late into the night," responded the tailor diffidently.

The rabbi was not satisfied. He persisted in knowing why the tailor stayed up past midnight each night. Realizing that the rabbi would not leave until he knew the truth, the tailor decided to tell him: "*Elyahu Hanave* comes to study Torah with me each night."

The rabbi was astonished. "Ask *Elyahu Hanave* if I can sit next to you when he studies with you," he pleaded.

The tailor turned from the rabbi and entered the house. He was gone but a few moments before he returned.

"*Elyahu Hanave* said that it was not feasible for you to learn together with us.

[**Ed.** Why was the repentant tailor more deserving to study with *Elyahu Hanave* than the Rabbi of Lemberg? The answer is based upon the

Talmudic dictum: "In the place where penitents stand, even the wholly righteous cannot stand." Talmud Bavli, Berachot 34b]

"However, he told me to tell you that I may teach you the following morning what we studied the previous night. In order that you may believe me, he told me to give you a sign. He said that the sign would be that no one would die within the city limits of Lemberg all the while I live."

The rabbi agreed to accept the sign. Each morning he returned to the tailor's house to study with him the Torah that *Elyahu Hanave* had taught him the night before. The rabbi and the tailor studied together for many months. Each time the rabbi heard of a death, he quickly investigated. He always found that the deceased had lived in the vicinity surrounding Lemberg, not within the city limits.

About six months later, the *shammish* rushed into the study hall. I want you to know," he shouted, "that there has been a death within the city limits."

Instantly, the rabbi tore his clothes, for he knew that it was time to mourn for the man who had become like a brother to him, the tailor who had been his partner in Torah study.

Immediately, he made arrangements for the tailor's funeral. When he eulogized the tailor, he revealed what the tailor had achieved through repentance, that he had achieved the level of holiness of one of the *"lamed vav tzaddikim,"* one of the thirty-six holy righteous, who by their merit, the world exists.

After the funeral, the Rabbi of Lemberg wrote the story of the holy tailor in his diary for posterity.

A Sacred Trust
— Commentary —
Equal Citizenship

The basic theme of Rosh Hashanah, as reflected in the liturgy is *Malchut*, the establishment of God's kingship.

On the second day of Rosh Hashanah, we read of the birth of Samuel. We conclude, with the prayer of Hannah, in which she prays for a human king who will raise up the lowly and protect the oppressed. Hannah prays for a king who will reflect Divine kingship,

Ultimately, the prayer of Hannah is fulfilled through King David, who establishes the monarchy. And it is the ability of David to repent that secures his eternal kingship. It is therefore most appropriate that Rosh Hashanah, the day of kingship, also inaugurates the ten days of repentance.

Rabbi David S. Silber
Director
Drisha Institute for Jewish Education
New York

338
The Silver Age of Polish Jewry: Chapter Thirty-Thirty-Four

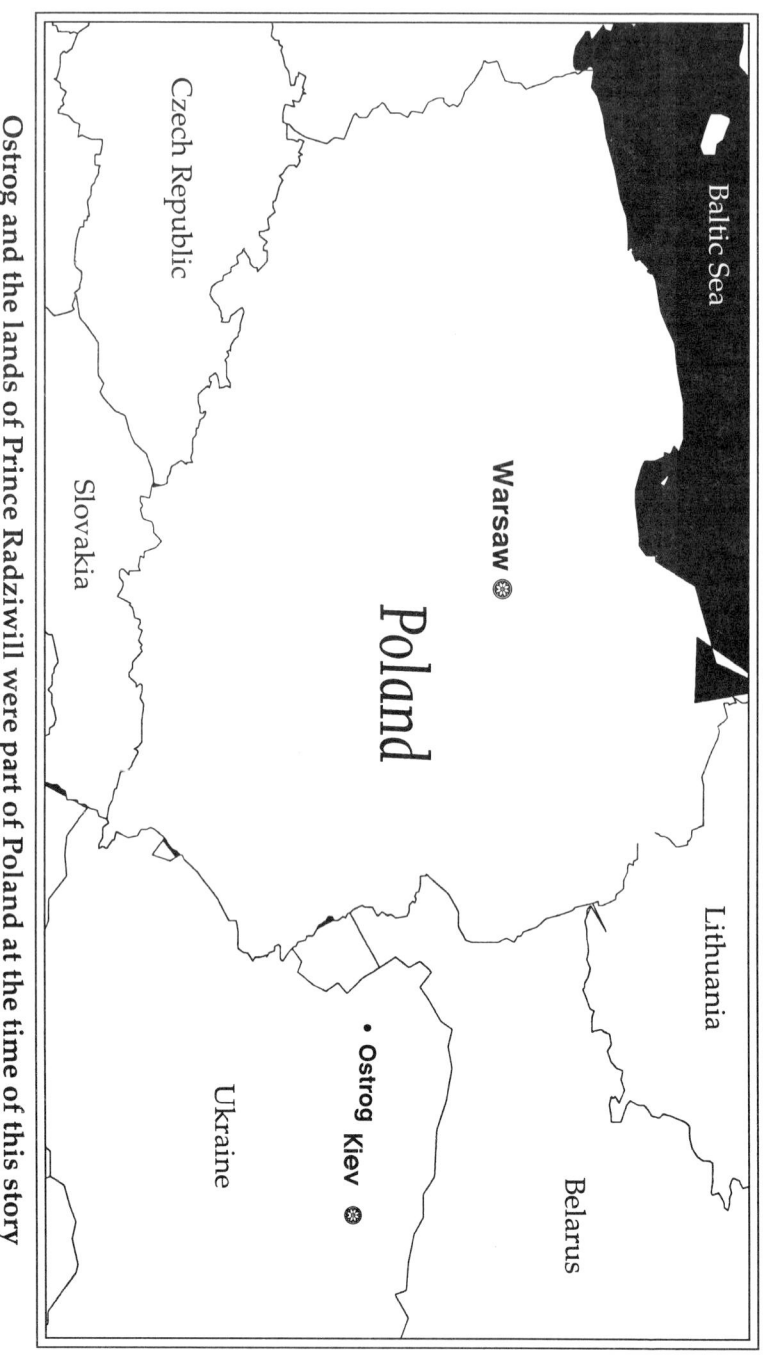

Ostrog and the lands of Prince Radziwill were part of Poland at the time of this story

Chapter Thirty-Four
EQUAL CITIZENSHIP

Time Line

| 70 c.e. | 600 c.e. | 1000 c.e. | 1400 c.e. | 1600 c.e. | 1800 c.e. | 2000 c.e. |

Location: Eastern Europe (Poland, Luthuania)

Young Prince Janus Radziwill of Volhynia[1] mused: "I have inherited vast lands from my father. He taught me how to be tolerant of Jews, to respect their commercial ability. Their prosperity makes me prosperous. I lease them land, and they act as administrators, hiring peasants to work it. Many of them live in fine estates, scattered throughout the region. Some of them own inns; some oversee the flour mills and the fisheries; some travel to the twice yearly trade fairs, Jaraslow in the fall and Lublin in the spring, returning with incredible merchandise; others are superior craftsmen. Their presence seems to keep the peasants under control. I can count my blessings at the hands of the Jews. But all these blessings are for naught, if I do not marry and produce an heir."

One of his advisors suggested that he marry a German princess named Elizabeth. "She will bring to this union a vast dowry," he said. "Her father is a powerful prince, and she is his only child. Eventually, you will be able to consolidate your lands and create a mighty empire!"

Prince Janus married Princess Elizabeth. She brought her dowry to the marriage; she also brought with her a malicious hatred of the Jewish people, which had been instilled in her by her parish priest from the time she was a little girl.[2]

Normally, Prince Janus paid no attention if a Jewish administrator was a day or two late in delivering the rent. Princess Elizabeth, however, ranted and raved: "Those Jews are cheating us of our money. They will destroy our holdings. We must expel them, for they will cause us great harm!"

"You are wrong, Elizabeth. My father taught me that if I respect the Jews that live on my land, they will prosper, and I will prosper with them. So far, my actions have proved correct."

They fought every time a payment of rent was delayed just one day.

"Why don't you try it my way, just one time. If you really love me, you will do what I ask."

Against his better judgment, Prince Janus signed a decree of expulsion against all the Jewish administrators that lived in the estates on his land. The expulsion was to become effective in three months.

The Jews were horrified when they heard the decree. They had been living comfortably in Poland/Lithuania for more than two hundred years. They had contributed to the economic development of the region; they had become relatively secure in this land whose kings had extended to them privileges of citizenship; they had raised a generation of native scholars who guided Jewish life.

The *parnas*[3] immediately sought the advice of the *Maharsha*,[4] who was living in Ostrog.

"Prince Janus Radziwill has decreed that the administrators of the estates must leave their homes in three months time. Where will they go? How will they protect themselves? Their families? They will be forced to wander aimlessly in the surrounding forests."

The Maharsha was equally anguished by their pain, but he had no answer. "We can only pray that something will happen to change the decree," he whispered.

The cool waters of the Dneipr River beckoned relief from the intense summer heat. Prince Radziwill led his horse to a tree near the river's edge, tied it, removed his clothing, folded it neatly on the marshland, and gingerly stepped into the water. The water lapped around his feet. He drifted slowly, enjoying the refreshing water, until it covered his shoulders; then he dove under, swam for a while, straightened up, treading water. He looked around; the sight was so wondrous.

The Carpathian Mountains rose in front of him. He lulled in reverie. The sudden neighing of his horse returned him to reality. He couldn't believe his eyes. A man, exactly his size, was wearing his clothes and riding off on his horse.

"Robber! Thief! Bandit! Swindler! Stop! Stop!" He shouted until no more words came from his hoarse throat. "That scoundrel is imitating me for some reason. No one will know that he is an impostor. How will I be able to extricate myself from this situation? Where will I find refuge? How will I protect myself? I will be forced to wander aimlessly in this forest!"

The sun began its descent. His shadow lengthened. His feet stuck in the underbrush as he wandered aimlessly, searching for a solution to his dilemma. Stickers pricked, brambles scratched, hunger tormented his stomach, and his body shivered.

Many dark hours later, he crossed a clearing and noticed a small cottage. "I must be near the outskirts of a village," he thought.

He continued in the direction of the cottage. As he approached it, dogs growled, waking the sleeping peasant. Prince Radziwill pounded on the door.

"Please let me in! I beg you, have mercy. I am Prince Radziwill."

The peasant lit a lantern, opened the door a crack, and peered at the nude man with the bloody feet standing in front of him. Frightened, he screamed: "The devil, the devil!"

He grabbed a *besom* (an early form of a broom) that stood near the door, raised it overhead, and struck the man facing him, pelting his head and shoulders with blow after blow.

"Go back to the four winds, where you came from, and leave decent people sleep in peace," he screeched, slamming the door.

The prince knocked on all the doors in the village and all the peasants reacted as if he were the devil.

Weary, unable to continue, he tumbled down against a large tree trunk and fell asleep.

He awoke to the smells of bubbling buckwheat cooking in a big iron pot over an open flame. A Jewish family huddled around the bonfire, their household goods stacked and tied on a wagon in back of them, a makeshift tent supported by rope tied to two parallel trees.

"Please, help me," he pleaded. "I am Prince Radziwill. I was swimming ... my clothes were laying on the marsh next to my horse. Someone, an impostor, took everything and left me like this. I have been wandering since yesterday afternoon."

Menachem laughed. "Just a few hours ago, Prince Radziwill passed through this way, making sure that my people obeyed his decree of expulsion. We are one of the families that were expelled, that will be forced to wander aimlessly in search of a new place to live. I don't believe that you are the prince, but nevertheless, my friend, I will not leave you in this condition. You are welcome to stay with us."

He walked over to the wagon, took a pair of pants, a shirt, a pair of shoes, and handed them to the prince.

They wandered together. Each time they approached a village, the prince tried to convince the priest and the community council of his true identity. The same reaction ensued each time: "Look at the Jewish Prince Radziwill! Ha! Ha!"

Sometimes, they spit at him, at times they chased him to the outskirts of the village, at times they threw stones. He remained with the Jewish family.

They headed toward Ostrog, to spend *Rosh Hashana*, *Yom Kippur*, and *Sukkot* in the city where the *Maharsha* lived. Menachem knew that the *kahal*[5] would find them appropriate home hospitality for the duration of the holiday season, and hoped they would help them resettle.

The *Maharsha* noticed the new family in the synagogue. "Who are you? Where do you come from? Are you comfortable in the community hospitality house?"

"My name is Menachem. We are one of the families that were expelled by Prince Radziwill's decree. We have lived in the forest since the expulsion order became effective. Now that winter is approaching, we desperately need to settle down, but we have no way to earn a living. And, in addition," he continued wearily, "we are caring for a deranged man who thinks he is Prince Radziwill. We found him wandering while we were camped in the forest, and have cared for him since.... We hope that the *kahal* in this city will act kindly toward us and help us resettle."

"I have to deal with first things first," said the *Maharsha*. "I want you to bring this man to me, the one who thinks he is Prince Radziwill."

He was dressed in the garments of a Jew, but he insisted he was Prince Radziwill as he stood before the *Maharsha*, pleading for mercy.

"I really believe you, but let me explain why I think you are in this terrible plight. My people have lived peacefully in this region for almost two hundred years. Your evil decree, the expulsion order, caused a tremendous upheaval in their lives. The expelled families are homeless. Their method of earning a living depended on their administering the estates upon which they lived. God, the judge of the whole world, wanted you to experience the pain that you caused."

"I am truly sorry ... I realize that I have committed a terrible wrong. I listened to my wife ... she told me that I would prove how much I loved her by decreeing the expulsion of the Jews from all my lands ... at first I resisted, for the Jewish people and my family have lived together peacefully for a long time ... my father instilled in me religious tolerance, but my wife was taught from early childhood to hate Jews, to make their lives miserable. I am solely responsible for my actions, for I should have resisted. I could have shown her how much I care for her in other ways. Please, tell me how I can make up for the terrible wrong that I have committed."

"Tomorrow is the first day of *Rosh Hashana*, the beginning of our new year. We believe that on this day, the entire world, both Jews and non-Jews, are judged for their actions. I see how contrite you are. During these two holy days, sit in the back of the synagogue, look into your soul, promise that you will not repeat this terrible mistake again. Search for a way to make amends, and hopefully, a way will become apparent to restore you to your position."

The night after the holiday, the *Maharsha* called the *parnas* and Prince Radziwill to his study. Turning to the *parnas*, he said: "You do not recognize that man, but his name is Prince Radziwill. He is truly contrite over the decree of expulsion. He has promised to rescind the decree and the administrators will be able to return to their estates. I need to help him return to his position. This is my plan."

The following Sunday morning, the *parnas* sat on the ledge of his wagon. The man sat next to him. The horses raced forward but were reined in a short distance from the gate of the Radziwill mansion. The *parnas* handed him a new set of royal garments.

"The Jewish community has purchased these for you. Put them on. Your wife is waiting in your carriage at the gate to accompany you to church."

That afternoon, a new decree was written. It reaffirmed the original charter granted by Kings Boleslav and Casimir and added some new privileges.[6]

"For the next five years, the Jewish people are exempt from any increases in their taxes.

"No Jew will ever be expelled from this region as long as Radziwills live.

"Any administrator that has already left his estate is welcome to return to his home.

"The synagogue of the *Maharsha* in Ostrog will be refurbished. It will be the most beautiful in the entire world.

"In gratitude for his having cared for me in the forest, I am appointing Menachem as my treasurer. He will be directly responsible to me."

Prince Radziwill served in the Sejm.[7] Throughout his political career, he always was mindful of the promise he made to the Jewish people.

A Sacred Trust
— Commentary —
The Rabbi's Daughter

This story is likely to inspire contradictory responses, even within the same reader. On the one hand, it is easy to admire the many fine traits of the Rabbi's daughter—her loyalty, her intelligence, her courage, and her love of her people. On the other hand, her double powerlessness, both as a Jew in a hostile Christian society and as a woman in a male-controlled culture, is one that most readers will find deeply troubling.

Judged by the standards of today's women heroes—leaders of governments, senators, Supreme Court Justices, doctors, professors, and business women, little Esther is not so impressive. But to use the accomplishments of today's women to belittle this medieval woman would be unfair. In fact, her accomplishments are all the more impressive because she was able to help out her people and find her father, despite her own limited resources. Using only her brains and her pluck, she made a difference for her community and for her family.

The lesson, then, of this remarkable woman is that smarts and heart are a pretty good start.

Rabbi Bradley Shavit Artson
Congregation Eilat,
*   Mission Viejo, California,*
Author of **It's A Mitzvah!**
   Jewish Living Step-By-Step

The Silver Age of Polish Jewry: Chapter Thirty-Five

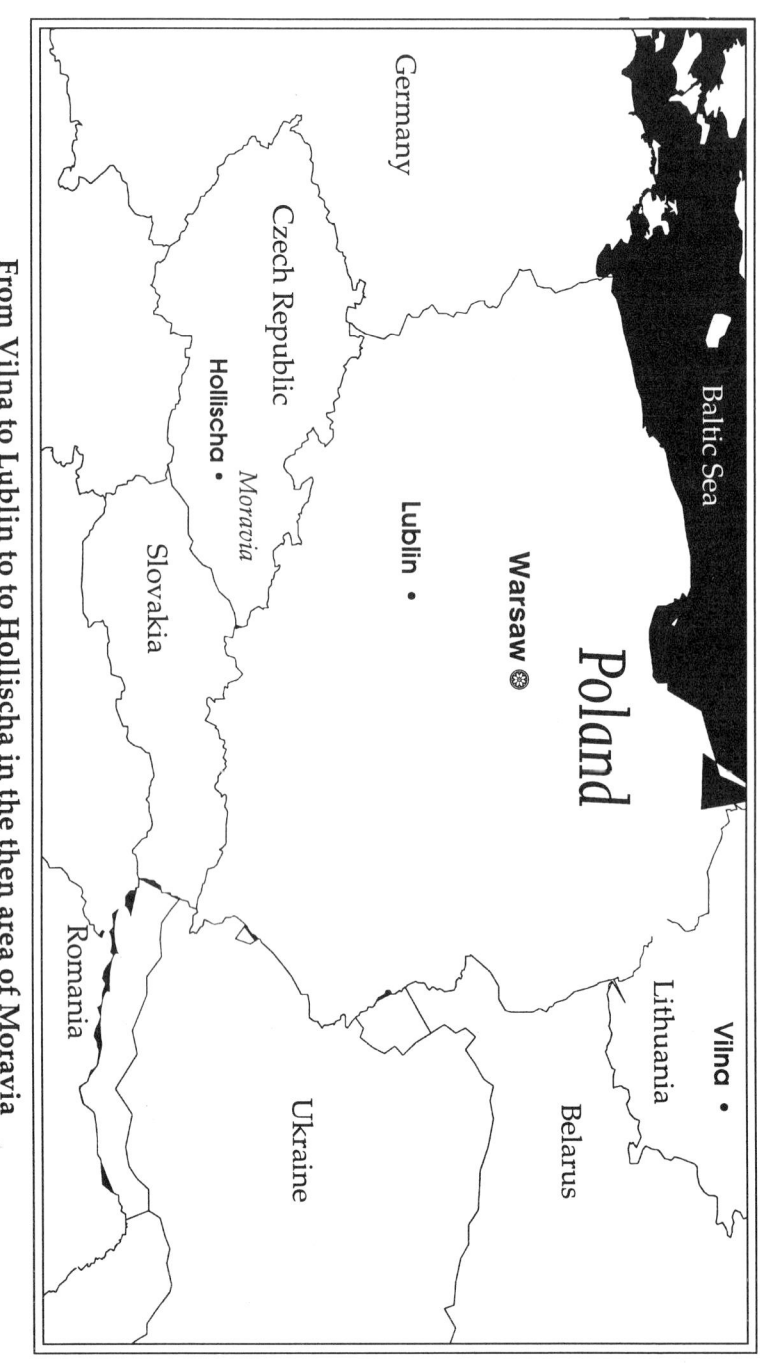

From Vilna to Lublin to Hollischa in the then area of Moravia

Chapter Thirty-Five
THE RABBI'S DAUGHTER

Time Line

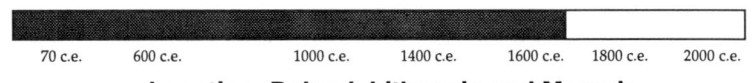

| 70 c.e. | 600 c.e. | 1000 c.e. | 1400 c.e. | 1600 c.e. | 1800 c.e. | 2000 c.e. |

Location: Poland, Lithuania and Moravia

Rabbi Shabse HaKohen[1] was considered a youthful prodigy. By the time he was twenty-four years old he had completed a brilliant commentary on the code of Jewish law, and had been appointed as the *dayyan* (chief judge) of the Jewish court in Vilna.

He married Miriam, the daughter of a wealthy merchant named Benjamin Zev, and granddaughter of Rabbi Moses Isserles,[2] the formost codifier of Ashkenazic Jewish law. Her father pledged to support the young couple, alleviating him of the responsibilities of providing a livelihood so that he might devote all his energy toward the study of Torah.

Assuming that they would live in relative security, as Jews had lived in Poland\Lithuania for hundreds of years, they were horrified as the Ukrainian Cossacks, under the leadership of Bogdan Chmielnicki, unleashed their fury upon both Poles and Jews living throughout eastern Europe.[3] The Cossacks ravaged once flourishing cities, decimating countrysides, murdering innocent men, women and children. The survivors fled, most just a few steps ahead of the perpetrators.

Rabbi Shabse, his wife and young daughter were among those familes who abandoned all their possessions to the marauding foe, and escaped to Lublin, searching desperately for sanctuary in a more hospitable place. Less than three months later, the Cossacks caught up with the survivors and attacked that city. The Jews were forced to flee again. This time, instead of remaining on Polish/Lithuania soil, Rabbi Shabse and his family headed westward and crossed the border into Moravia, settling in Dreznin.

The Moravian Jewish community helped absorb the unfortunate refugees, aided them in acquiring homes, and assisted them in reestablishing their businesses and trades. Because they knew of Rabbi Shabse's reputation, they appointed him as *Landesribbiner,* the chief rabbinical authority and decisor of Jewish law.

He reconstructed his *yeshiva* and settled down to teach and to write. However, this sanctuary proved to be short lived. The French Bourbons, determined to block the power of the Austrian Hapsburgs as the Thirty Year's War[4] concluded with the Peace of Westphalia, decided to return to the battlefield and their army threatened the safety of the inhabitants of Dreznin.

The French soldiers who attacked their house terrified Miriam, and she died from fright. Escaping with Esther, his five year old daughter, through a back window, he dashed toward the forest, only a few steps ahead of the invaders. Not noticing a fallen branch, he tripped and fell into the thick underbrush. Before he knew it, a husky French soldier, who had been stalking through the forest, snatched Esther from his arms and carried her off, a prisoner of war. He collapsed, grief-stricken from the death of his wife and the loss of his daughter.

"What can I do?" he sobbed. Resigning himself to the fact that he was powerless, he stood up, turned to find the way out of the forest, and trudged with a heavy plodding gait toward, what he hoped, would be safety.

The soldier returned to camp, carrying the screaming child in his arms. He had no idea what he was going to do with her. Esther's persistent screams aroused General Jablonska, who came running to investigate.

The Rabbi's Daughter

"She is a beautiful little girl," he said to the soldier. "Where did you find her?"

The soldier hesitated. "I snatched her from her father who was fleeing from our army."

General Jablonska was a compassionate man. He gently lifted the little girl from the soldiers arms, and raised her to his shoulder. He rocked her for a long while, until she stopped crying. He personally washed her scraped knees and elbows. He ordered a servant to bring her some food, but the child refused to eat.

"You must be very hungry," the general whispered to her gently. "Why aren't you eating?"

"Yes, I am hungry," whimpered the little girl, "but I am Jewish, and I am not permitted to eat food that is not kosher."

General Jablonska told the servant to remove the food he had brought and instructed him to bring some fresh fruit and vegetables in its place.

He was overtaken with the little girl. "I have decided," he announced that evening, "that I will take this child back with me to my home. She seems to be about the same age as my daughter, Marie. She will be a good companion for her. I will raise them together, as if they were sisters."

The girls shared the same room, received the same gifts, were educated by the same tutor. They only differed in their diet. Marie ate any food while Esther nibbled nuts, fruits, and vegetables, and ate one cooked meal a day that was brought to her from the town, by an old Jewish woman named Hannah.

The girls were inseparable.

One hot humid night, a few years later, Esther could not sleep. She lay quietly in her bed, not wanting to disturb Marie. Suddenly, she heard a hissing sound. Turning toward the sound, she saw a slithering snake, its fangs ready to strike, at the foot of Marie's bed. Panic stricken, she yelled at the top of her voice: "Help, help!" Her screams echoed through the mansion. The general appeared within seconds, followed by his wife and two bodyguards.

Pale, stuttering, Esther pointed to the snake coiled around the foot of Maria's bed.

The general grabbed his bodyguard's sword. With one swift stroke, the snake lay dead.

The general whispered to his wife: "I will never forget that Esther saved Marie's life."

As the girls grew older, it seemed as if they had one mind in two different bodies.

"No matter what happens in the future," Marie swore to Esther, "I will never forget our childhood. I hope we will never be separated, but in the event that we are, I want you to know that I will always remain loyal to our friendship."

Two years later, a fire broke out in the kitchen of the general's mansion. The flames rose rapidly through the girl's sleeping quarters, shrouding their bedroom in thick smoke. The odor of the singed tapestries awakened them. Screaming, panic stricken, Marie ran out the door of the bedroom toward safety. Esther jumped out the second floor window, landing in the flowerbeds below.

Badly bruised and shaken, Esther limped through the flower garden toward the fields that separated the general's mansion from the town. She did not know why she was running; but something compelled her to do so.

Suddenly, she was startled by the gruff voice of a tall, burly man who had emerged from nowhere, a knife drawn in his hand.

"*Gott en himmel*—God in Heaven," she moaned. "I have escaped from the fire only to die by the hand of this bandit. "

Then, as if a voice from within her formulated the words, she heard herself addressing him: "If it is money that you want, tell me the price for my life." Her words were amazingly assertive and controlled, but her body quivered.

"Take me with you to the town. Tell the *parnas* that you have a young girl to ransom. You know that a Jew is not allowed to close his eyes to the suffering of his captured brethren, because Jews are responsible for one another."[5]

> [**Ed.** The *parnas* of the community was responsible for collecting taxes, the execution of civil laws as they related to both the Jewish and the non-Jewish community, and social welfare.]

> [**Ed.** Ransoming hostages is a *mitzva* of such great importance that even money set aside for the upkeep of a synagogue may be used. *Talmud Bavli, Bava Basra 8b.*]

Tell him that if he doesn't pay your ransom demands, you will kill her. I know you will receive the money, and my life will be spared. We will both have what we want."

The tall burly bandit was enchanted by the girl's audacity. "You know," he admitted grumpily, "You are right. I do not want to kill you. I only want money. No one has ever bargained with me before. I will do as you request."

The bandit walked Esther toward the town.

Word spread rapidly that two strangers, a tall, burly man, and a young girl, demanded to see the parnas in the town square.

The *parnas* ran to meet them. "How can I help you," he asked?

The bandit growled: "I found this young girl in the fields. In order to ransom her, I want five hundred schillings. Pay me or she will die."

The *parnas*, a very wealthy merchant named Menachem, knowing the importance of ransoming hostages, said calmly: "I will not bargain with you, even though the price you ask is exorbitant. We Jews believe that human life is precious beyond the value of money. Wait here."

He returned in a very short time with the money. The bandit released his hostage.

"At last I can live again among my own people," sighed Esther gratefully to Menachem. "It has been so difficult remembering who I am ... it has been such a long time."

The *parnas* made arrangements for Esther to live with a well-to-do family. It did not take her long to learn to do what the other young girls did. Her face sparkled with joy as she ministered to the sick, cared for the widows and orphans, and prepared food for the aged.

The *parnas* watched Esther blossom. "She overflows with kindness," he mused one day, "she has the qualities of a true daughter of Israel; she will be a perfect mate for my son." After their wedding, the young couple settled down to married life.

Meantime, General Jablonska was replaced by a money hungry young captain. Knowing that no one would question his authority, he decreed the imposition of an exorbitant tax on the Jewish community, ten times more than they had paid the previous year.

Menachem pleaded with the captain: "Even if we sell everything we own, we will not be able to raise the money to fulfill your demands. Please reconsider!"

The captain was adamant. "You have no choice," he told the parnas. "Either you raise the required sum, or I will expel all of you from this town."

The rabbi decreed a day of fasting and prayer. Esther's physically exhausted and emotionally distressed husband returned home from the study hall.

"Let me try to do some thing to help," she insisted. "Since I know how to write in many languages, I will write to General Jablonska. He is a kindly man. He might be able to influence his successor to ease his demands."

"I don't think that will help," answered her husband, "but you can try. I think you should know that the captain is the general's son-in-law."

Esther's eyes lit up. "Then he must be Marie's husband," she whispered. "I have a plan. I will return to the house where I grew up. I will tell Marie of our plight. I know she will do everything in her power to help us."

The next morning, Esther gathered some sewing materials, placed them in a basket and headed for the mansion.

When she arrived, she knocked at the door. A servant responded: "How can I help you?" the servant asked.

"Please tell your mistress that her seamstress has arrived."

Esther was escorted through the mansion to the sewing room. The rooms seemed so familiar to her. She was standing face to face with Marie in a few short minutes. She was sure that Marie did not recognize her.

"I live in the nearby town," she began. "One of the merchants brought me some beautiful fabric from the fair in Lublin. I thought you might like me to sew you a new gown from this lovely fabric."

Marie picked up the fabric and rolled it absentmindedly through her fingers. She seemed deep in thought.

Suddenly, she said: "Tell me, who are you. Your voice, your face, your manner are so familiar. It seems to me that I know you from somewhere . . . that your voice is a voice out of my past."

"I am Esther. I grew up in this house with you. Remember the fire ... when I jumped from the second floor window that night.... I was bruised and battered, but my life was saved. Something compelled me to run away.... I ran through the fields ... a bandit found me and held me for ransom.... The Jewish community redeemed me.... I've recently married the son of the *parnas*."

"Esther, Esther, is it really you?" shrieked Marie joyfully. "I wondered if you were alive. We never found your body among the charred ruins of that section of the house. I've missed you so much." She extended her arms. The two women hugged and wept.

Finally, Marie spoke: "Why did you pose as a seamstress?"

"I had to find a way to see you. My people are faced with a

terrible crisis. I need your help. The new governor, your husband, demands exorbitant taxes ... if we are unable to pay, he threatens to expel us."

"I will go to talk to him right now," said Marie. "I will try to convince him that his demands are unreasonable."

The captain was surprised when his wife entered his office, accompanied by another pretty lady.

Marie introduced Esther to her husband. He listened attentively while the two women explained how they knew each other. Marie asked him to reconsider the imposition of increased taxes on the Jewish community, but he was adamant in his refusal.

Esther, knowing the general's reputation, interrupted the discussion between husband and wife.

"I have an idea," she said. "We can all benefit from it. Your father-in-law loved and cared for me as his daughter. If you let him know that you were the one who discovered that I was still alive, he will reward you handsomely. I'm certain that his gift to you will be far more valuable than the increased taxes you levied upon my people."

The captain smiled. "I like your plan. I will rescind my decree on the condition that my father-in-law acts as you think he will."

Ten days later, the *parnas* received word from the captain that the Jewish community would only have to pay the amount of taxes they had paid in previous years. There was great rejoicing in the town.

A few years later, one of the leading scholars of that generation visited the town. That *Shabbat* morning, every person gathered in the *shul* to hear him preach.

In the women's gallery, Esther sat on the edge of her seat, for the voice of the visitor was vaguely familiar. She couldn't remember where she had heard it. Then a flood of memories

The Rabbi's Daughter

washed over her, immersing her entire being with vignettes of her early childhood.

"That voice ... it sounds so much like my father's voice.... I can't be sure. I was so young."

When the services were over, Esther asked her husband to invite the distinguished guest to their home for the *Shabbat* meal.

They conversed about conditions of Jewish life in the town, about other Jewish communities, about the distinguished guest's travels. He reminisced: "I was forced to flee many times. I had a daughter. She probably would be about your age by now. First we fled from Chmielnicki and his hordes. Then we fled from the French. A French soldier kidnapped her." He lowered his head sadly.

Esther had no doubt in her mind that the distinguished guest was her father.

"Father, I am Esther, I am your daughter! I am the girl who was kidnapped in the forest." Their happiness was indescribable. After spending some time together, Rabbi Shabse returned to his home in Hollischau, where he spent the rest of his life.

A Sacred Trust
— Commentary —
The Forgotten Story

Words can either be holy or profane. When they are holy, they are uplifting. When they are profane, they are destructive.

Holy words, uplifting words should sometimes be whispered. Words of admonition can be destructive, and therefore, they should always be uttered privately. Words, when whispered with love, can renew within us our heritage. Harsh words of admonition can drive us away.

This story about an apostate teaches us much about words.

"Words that sincerely emanate from the heart, enter the heart."

—*Rabbi Moshe Ibn Ezra. Shirat Yisrael.*
Spanish Golden Age Poet.

Words that emanate from the heart can inspire true reprentance. Words that emanate from the heart of the truly repentant bring forgiverness.

—***Authors***

The Pale of Settlement

Approximate area at the end of the 19th century

✡

Area names are of the 19th century.
Specific boundries are today's boundries.

Chapter Thirty-Six
THE FORGOTTEN STORY

Time Line

70 c.e.　　600 c.e.　　1000 c.e.　　1400 c.e.　　1600 c.e.　　1800 c.e.　　2000 c.e.

Location: Eastern Europe (Poland, Russia)

Upon the instructions of the Baal Shem Tov,[1] his disciples settled in various distant *shtetlach* throughout the Pale of Settlement.

> [Ed. The Pale of Settlement was an area of eastern Europe located between the Baltic and the Black Seas from north to south, and by Russia, Prussia, and Austria from the east and west sides. The Jews were confined to small *shtetlach* in the Pale, to limit their settlement in other provinces of the Russian empire.]

They planted the kernels of the hundreds of *chassidic* dynasties that still flourish today, some of which are Belz, Bobov, Ger, Lubavitch, Moditz, Slonim, Stolin.

Shimon, one of the Baal Shem Tov's students, was not instructed to settle in a distant *shtetl*.

One day the Baal Shem Tov called Shimon into his private room: "Shimon," he said, "you no doubt heard that I have sent your friends to the far flung corners of this vast land. I hope that they will establish *chassidic* communities in these distant *shtetlach*. But since you are one of my best students, I have chosen you for a special mission.

I want you to travel from *shtetl* to *shtetl* to teach the Torah you learned, to tell over the stories you heard, to repeat whatever incidents occurred here in Medziboz. Although you do not understand the reason for this special mission right now,

I'm asking you to trust me and follow my instructions. Eventually, you will know why I did not request you to do the same job as I requested of your friends."

Shimon was very disappointed, for he had hoped he could settle down in one *shtetl* and there spread the teachings of the Baal Shem Tov. Instead, he was given a mission to wander. Nevertheless, knowing that he had to heed his rebbe's request, he packed a few of his belongings and set off to fulfill his wishes.

Wherever Shimon traveled, people urged him to share his rebbe's Torah thoughts, stories and deeds. He found that the Baal Shem Tov's reputation had spread through a wide area of eastern Europe, and therefore he always had an eager audience.

After many months of weary travel, Shimon arrived, late one Thursday afternoon, in a town much larger than the usual *shtetl*. He asked directions to the *shul*, and waited there until the people gathered for the evening prayers on their way home from work.

One man approached him. "We have heard that the Baal Shem Tov is sending emissaries to these far flung *shtetlach* to teach us. Since you are a stranger here, might you be one of those emissaries?"

Shimon nodded. "In that case," the man continued, "Asher, the wealthiest Jew in town asked that I tell you to hurry to his house as soon as you can. He is impatiently waiting for your arrival, as he loves to hear stories about the Baal Shem Tov. He lives in the large mansion at the end of the road."

Shimon ran towards the mansion at the conclusion of the prayers. It was very large, set far back from the main road, surrounded by tall trees, their crowns touching the heavens, and lush, verdant foliage alternated between blooming flowers in the thick hedges. He was warmly greeted by Asher.

"I've waited for your arrival for a long time," he said. "In order to welcome you properly, I would like to invite you and the entire Jewish community to share the three meals of *Shabbat* with my family. I want everyone to get acquainted with you. You will have a large audience to tell the stories, the incidents, the deeds, and the Torah learning of the holy Baal Shem Tov. In the meantime, I will show you to your room. You must be weary from your journey.

True to his word, Asher led all the men to his house from shul that Friday night after the *Kabbolat Shabbat* prayers. The women and children had already arrived. Families were seated together at long, white clothed banquet tables. The soft glistening candlelight blended well with the delectable fragrance of the *Shabbat* food. After *kiddush*, Asher's guests shared a sumptuous meal.

Relaxed, peaceful, they turned to face him as he rose and asked for their attention: "I have invited all of you here for a very special reason. You must know by now that Shimon, our special visitor, is a disciple of the Baal Shem Tov. He would like to share some of his rebbe's Torah thoughts and stories with us. Please give him your attention."

Shimon stood up next to Asher. Everyone's eyes focused on him. Mentally, he reviewed his opening sentence, but instead of speaking, his body started to tremble. He cleared his throat, coughed, tried to delay a few seconds until he could think of something to say, something that he wanted to share with this eager audience, but nothing entered his mind. He stood, speechless, then sat down, totally frustrated.

"You must be weary, or nervous," whispered Asher comfortingly. "After a good night's sleep, your mind will be more clear. Tomorrow, at the second meal of *Shabbat*, at lunch, I will introduce you again and you will be able to share with us whatever you like."

After the people finished their lunch, Asher arose to introduce Shimon. Again, Shimon went through the motions of preparing to speak, but no words came forth from his mouth. The people really had wanted to hear some of the Baal Shem

Tov's Torah thoughts.

Very disappointed, they did not return to the mansion for *shalosh seudot*, the third meal of *Shabbat*.

Asher sat across the table from Shimon. Silently, Shimon pecked at his food. He could not understand why, suddenly, he had become speechless. In all his travels, he had spoken at length to people hungry to hear the words of the Baal Shem Tov.

"Please, try not to be distressed," said Asher, as he breathed deeply, calmly. "It was my pleasure to invite everyone for the *Shabbat* meals. I have the feeling that eventually you will understand why you had difficulty speaking today. In the meantime, I am very happy that you were my Shabbat guest."

"As soon as *Shabbat* is over," said Shimon miserably, "I will have to continue wandering. I thank you for your hospitality and understanding." After *Shabbat*, Asher gave Shimon a large sum of money and provided him with a carriage.

"I would like you to use this carriage as you travel," he said. "It will certainly make your life easier."

Shimon thanked Asher profusely for his generosity, climbed into the carriage and set off for the next *shtetl*. Desperately, he tried to remember an incident, a story, a teaching of the Baal Shem Tov. He hadn't traveled more than ten minutes when part of a story flashed through his mind. Excitedly, he turned the horses around, and headed back for Asher's mansion.

He halted the horses, jumped down, ran towards the front door, and pounded impatiently on it.

Asher opened the door himself. Surprised at Shimon's return, he queried gently: "What can I do for you?"

"I was only ten minutes out of town," Shimon shouted excitedly, "when I remembered part of a story. It seems important that I tell it to you, so I returned."

Asher placed his hand around Shimon's shoulder and guided

him into a small private room. "Please, sit down," he beckoned. The room was furnished with a few small chairs. Books lined the walls. Candles glowed on the tables.

"Now, tell me what it is that you remembered."

"The tale that I will tell you has no ending, but I am certain that I must tell it to you.

I was very young when this incident occurred, but I remember it distinctly. Whenever the Baal Shem Tov traveled, he took me with him. Once, we traveled to a very distant town. Alexy, his coachman, sat next to him at the front of the wagon. It seemed that he always knew the shortest way. Sometimes it would take us only a very short time to reach a distant town.

Anyway, on that particular trip, I sat in back of the wagon by myself. Alexy guided the horses into the center of, what seemed, a deserted town. The streets were vacant; the houses were boarded up; every store was closed; every window was shuttered; and every door was chained and bolted.

The Baal Shem Tov signalled for Alexy to wait in front of a three story house. He motioned to me to walk up the path leading to the house and knock on the door. I did as he told me. I knocked then I pounded, but no one responded. I returned to the carriage. Then, he alighted and motioned to me to join him. Together we walked up the path. He knocked furiously, and within a few minutes, a frightened lady pulled the door open a crack.

"I must come in," he demanded.

"Please, be quiet," she quivered. "Don't you know that today is the day that a Jew will be executed in the town square. Any commotion will bring the authorities here. It would only cause more trouble for us."

The Baal Shem Tov ignored her pleas. He pushed the door aside and pulled me into the house after him. We climbed three flights of stairs and entered a room with a large window overlooking the town square. He still did not speak. He pushed me in front of him, pointing to the platform on which stood a shivering man, his hands tied behind his back, a hood over his face, a gallows nearby.

"Do you see that man?" he demanded. I nodded.

"Now, look to the right. What do you see?"

"I see a noble astride a stallion. He is dressed regally. He looks like a bishop of the church, and all the people in the mob that are crowding around the platform have their eyes on him."

"I want you to go over to that noble and tell him, that I, the Baal Shem Tov want to see him."

I did not question my *rebbe's* instructions. Trembling, I slipped down the stairs and ran as swiftly as I could, through the throng of spectators, to the place where the noble's horse stood. I pulled at the noble's leg to gain his attention.

He turned to see who was disturbing him. When his eye caught mine, I whispered: "My master, the holy Baal Shem Tov sent me to fetch you.

"He wants to see you immediately." I pointed to the window where I knew the Baal Shem Tov watched.

"Later. Tell him I will come later. Tell him that I am busy now, that I will come after the execution."

I ran back to the house, climbed up the stairs, and breathlessly told my rebbe what the noble said.

"Return to the noble," said the Baal Shem Tov. "Be very firm. Tell him that I want to see him immediately. Tell him that he is not to delay one second."

"I ran to do my master's bidding. The noble dismounted from his horse. He raised his hands, as if to stop the proceedings and then he followed me back to the house. I showed him to the room where the Baal Shem Tov waited. Strangely, I was not permitted to enter. I was told to wait downstairs. I don't know anymore of the story. I don't even know why I felt the urgent need to tell it to you."

The Forgotten Story

Shimon stopped speaking. He peered at the man sitting opposite him. Through the flickering shadow of the soft candlelight, he noticed that Asher was crying. He swayed back and forth in his chair, obviously in great pain.

"I can tell you how the story ends," he choked. "Then you will know why you were instructed to travel, why you had to repeat all the stories and teachings of the Baal Shem Tov. You will also understand why you were speechless over *Shabbat*. What you have told me tonight, had to be told in complete privacy.

"You see, I was that person who was dressed in the robes of a bishop of the church. I ran away from Judaism and converted to Christianity. I was promised great financial rewards and powerful positions. The more powerful I became, the more I persecuted my people. I ordered *shtetlach* to be plundered, people to be arrested on trumped up ritual murder charges."

[**Ed.** Ritual murder trials, although mostly associated with the Jewish experience in western Europe, were prevalent in eastern Europe also. Owing to the zeal of astute church champions, three important trials, ending in the conviction and execution of innocent Jews were tried by the highest court; the Tribunal of Lublin at Sandomir (1698-1710), Posen (1736), and Zaslav (1748). Jews who were tried were accused of murdering Christian children and using their blood to bake matzot for *Pesach*.]

"Every evil that I planned and brought to fruition had as its prize more power and more wealth. I had to prove that I was a good Christian. But as I grew older, my conscience began to bother me. I could not sleep. In my dreams, I witnessed Abraham, Isaac, and Jacob, the patriarchs of my people fighting for my soul. Their fighting tormented me.

"Then, I heard about the deeds of the Baal Shem Tov and I prayed night after night for him to come and rescue me. I arranged my church affairs, sold my property and exchanged the money for gold. In order not to arouse suspicion, I planned one more execution. You arrived to pull me away from the platform just as I was about to condemn one more Jew to death."

Asher's shoulders heaved, his head hung limp, the tears fell into his lap. He could not speak for a long time.

"When I followed you to that house," he continued, "when I stood face to face with the Baal Shem Tov, I realized that I could not go through with that final execution. I knew I would never return to that platform. The Baal Shem Tov told me what to do to begin the process of repentance. I was to study Torah and be hospitable to passers-by.

"He instructed me to move to this town and live off the money that I had accumulated while I was a bishop. I was to wait patiently for someone to tell me the first part of my story. When that happened, I would know that I had been forgiven in Heaven, that my repentance had been accepted. Now, I want to help you settle comfortably here by giving you half my fortune. Your days of wandering are over, for you have fulfilled the mission of the Baal Shem Tov."

> [**Ed.** The Supreme Secret Council of the Russian court was very opposed to Polish Jewish merchants who crossed the border in the vicinity of Smolensk to trade. Boruch Leibov, one of these merchants, audaciously built a synagogue in the nearby village of Zverovich for the Jews who lived there. The Greek Orthodox priest was convinced that the synagogue would influence his people to convert to Judaism. The Jews were arrested and deported beyond the Russian border.
>
> Boruch Leibov continued his business on both sides of the border in partnership with a Greek Orthodox retired navy captain who ultimately converted to Judaism. They were both arrested, brought to St. Petersburg, turned over to the "Chancellery for Secret Inquisitorial Affairs," tried, and condemned to torture on the rack until they confessed their crimes.
>
> The punishment for the crime of misleading a Christian was burning at the stake. The auto-da-fe was carried out in St. Petersburg, on a public square, in the presence of a large crowd of spectators, on July 15, 1738.]

∾

A Sacred Trust
— Commentary —
The Righteous Proselyte

The story of Count Potocki's conversion to Judaism is most inspiring, especially so since it took place in a time of growing hatred for Jews and Judaism. There were always a few remarkable individuals, like the Count, who brooked no resistance in seeking to ally themselves with the Jewish people for God's sake.

Once proselytes to Judaism were not so rare. Two thousand years ago, Judaism was a religion of outreach. Professor Salo W. Baron, Columbia's great scholar of Jewish history, has estimated that five to ten percent of the residents of the Roman Empire were Jews or Jewish sympathizers - people attracted by our emphasis on One, ethical God who brought the world a sense of moral and natural order.

In our open contemporary society, conversion has once again become a possibility. Thousands of people, dissatisfied with their religion of birth, have opted to become Jews. They have found Judaism's view of God, its emphasis on sanctifying life in this world, its stubborn persistence in the face of unbelievable calamities - to be qualities of great power and attractiveness.

These *gerei hatsedek* Jews by choice, are changing the contours of contemporary Judaism. They are drawn less by Judaism' s ethnic dimension than by its celebratory affirmation to life. These converts encourage born Jews to reexamine the Jewish jewels they all too often take for granted. Most of all, their election of Judaism a few decades after the Holocaust, highlights the eternal attraction of our faith. Despite the knowledge that six million people were killed just for being Jews, growing numbers of Gentiles have chosen to join an eternal faith and an eternal people and have become an overflowing reservoir of hope and inspiration.

Rabbi Stephen C. Lerner
Founder and Director
The Center for Conversion to Judaism
Teaneck, NJ and New York, NY

The Silver Age of Polish Jewry: Chapter Thirty-Seven

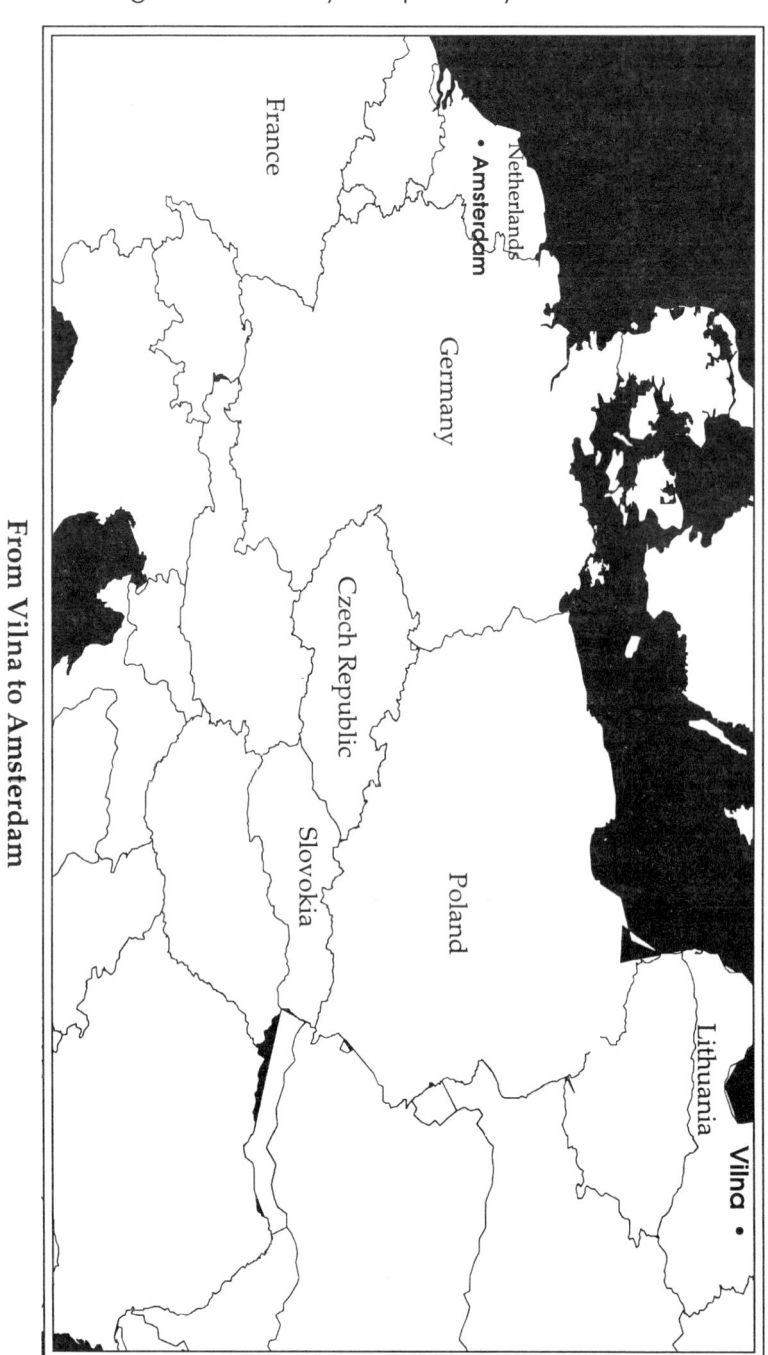

From Vilna to Amsterdam

Chapter Thirty-Seven
THE RIGHTEOUS PROSELYTE

Time Line

| 70 c.e. | 600 c.e. | 1000 c.e. | 1400 c.e. | 1600 c.e. | 1800 c.e. | 2000 c.e. |

Location: Lithuania

In Vilna, Lithuania, the *Yerushalayim* of Europe during the eighteenth century, the sing-song melody of Talmudic study reverberated through the open windows of the *bayt midrash* in harmony with the melodious chirping of the birds. Countess Potocki leisurely pushed a baby carriage along the path following the flow of the Zaretche River. She breathed deeply as she walked, enjoying the budding wild flowers and the delicious fragrance of the blooming trees.

"How wonderful it is to walk after being confined indoors so much of the winter," she thought. Her reverie was interrupted by the hysterical screams of her baby laying inside the carriage. She gently rocked it from side to side. The baby squirmed agitatedly, his hands trembling, his feet quivering. She lifted him and held him close to her, patting him lovingly. He continued to scream. She returned him to the carriage and continued to rock it. Nothing Countess Potocki did quieted the hysterical baby.

The Gaon of Vilna[1] and some of his students were crossing the Zaretche River bridge, heading for the small *shul* on Polotsk Street. The sharp wails of the hysterical baby pierced the whispering murmur of the gently rustling trees.

The Gaon turned to his students and said: "Wait here for me."

He crossed over to the path by the river, approached the perturbed mother, and asked if he could try to calm the hysterical baby. When she consented, he bent over, peered inside the carriage, smiled and stood upright. The baby stopped crying.

"What is your baby's name?" he asked gently.

"His name is Valentine, Valentine Potocki," she replied.

"Be patient with him. He has a great future!" he whispered.

The Gaon rejoined his students. Countess Potocki continued walking.

Many years passed. The baby grew into a young lad. His family indulged his every whim, but he was restless and dissatisfied with life. He was surrounded with luxuries that were bought with the profits of his family's lucrative liquor business, but his only companion was a horse that he rode through the wooded area outside the city. Sometimes he spent days at a time roaming the forests, sleeping under the trees. His family did not miss him, for his father drank himself into a stupor each evening, then spent the rest of the night cursing his mother. Valentine was very unhappy.

One Friday towards dusk, while riding his horse, he strayed into the Jewish section of town. He rode around aimlessly. He noticed, in one house after another, the reflection of the soft flicker of candlelight glowing through the windows. He dismounted, tied his horse to a tree and began walking toward the sound of an enchanting melody emanating from the farthest house at the edge of the forest. Stealthily, he peered inside the window. He saw a Jewish family celebrating *Shabbat*.

"This is so much different than my family," his thoughts rambled. "In my house, everyone eats separately; here the entire family is together. In my house, we eat the most expensive cuts of meat; here, it seems that dinner will consist of a twisted loaf of white bread and a herring. In my house, everyone is always shouting; here, the family is singing together." He stood by the window, entranced by what he saw, until the candles burned out and the Jewish family retired for the night.

He returned to the Jewish section of town the following Friday afternoon, and headed immediately for the house where he had heard the enchanting melody. "I want to join them so much," he reasoned, "but if I knock on the door, I might frighten them. Then they will stop singing!" So he returned for many weeks and merely watched silently from outside the window. Finally, he knew he had to reveal himself.

The following week, after he tied his horse to the tree, he walked up the path and knocked at the door. Inside, the Jewish family wondered who disturbed their *Shabbat* peace. When they opened the door and saw a young lad, dressed in the garb of wealthy nobility, they were visibly frightened.

"Please," he begged, "let me come in. My name is Valentine Potocki. I have been watching you from the window for weeks. There is something special about what you do each Friday night. I have to know what it is. I swear that I will not hurt you in any way. I just want to find out why your family is so different from mine."

The Jewish family invited him inside. They welcomed him warmly and shared their meager *Shabbat* meal with him. He remained until the candles burned out.

"May I return," he queried?

"You may return as often as you like," they responded.

Valentine Potocki returned to the Jewish family's home each Friday night for many months. Eventually, he asked if he could spend the entire *Shabbat* day with them. When they consented, his joy knew no bounds. He believed that he had found a purpose in life, a life-style that was spiritually gratifying.

He was eager to learn about Jewish law and thought; he wanted to know more than he was able to learn from the Jewish family. One Friday night, he confided to them: "I have been thinking about conversion to Judaism for a very long time, almost since the first *Shabbat* that I met you. I want to learn Torah, to find out what being Jewish really means, but I don't know how to proceed."

They were not shocked, for they had seen him change over the course of the many months he had spent with them.

"We must be very careful to formulate a plan that will not

endanger you or the Jewish community. You no doubt know that the church frowns upon Christians converting to Judaism, especially Christians from such a noble family as the Graf Potocki family. After all, your family has been part of the Polish aristocracy for a long time. We need to take our time; we need to make discreet inquiries on how to proceed. Give us two weeks."

After *Shabbat* dinner two weeks later, they told Valentine Potocki the plan.

"During the coming week, unobtrusively gather as many of your personal belongings and bring them here a little at a time. Arrange your financial affairs so that you can take enough money with you to support yourself. Make sure no one in your family knows what you are doing. Hire a coach to take you westward, making many different stops and changes along the way. Your destination is Amsterdam. We have found out that Jews are free to be Jews there. Leave next Sunday, so that you will have a week to travel.

"When you arrive in Amsterdam, seek out the Rabbi of the city and tell him that you have been spending *Shabbat* with us for many months. Tell him that you want to convert. We are sure that he will help you. Since your family is accustomed to you being away for many days at a time, they will not be suspicious when you do not return home for the first three or four days. We think the police will give up searching for you after a week or so. Everyone will assume that you met with a fatal accident. We hope that this plan will not endanger you or anyone in the Jewish community."

The plan seemed feasible. Valentine Potocki went to live in Amsterdam. He converted to Judaism and took the name of Avraham ben Avraham. He grew a beard and *payot*, donned the garb of an observant Jew, and studied Torah diligently for five years. He absorbed every nuance of Judaism much as a dry sponge absorbs water. The people of Amsterdam called him Avraham, the "learned Jew."

The Righteous Proselyte

The years passed quickly. Although he was happy in Amsterdam, he decided to return to Vilna. He wanted to marry one of the daughters of the Jewish family who had inspired him to change his life. After the wedding, the young couple settled in a house near her parents and became intensely involved in the Jewish community.

Avraham, the "learned Jew," loved to lead the worshippers in prayer. He noticed, however, that some people insisted on gossiping during the prayer service. He never tired of gently chiding them for their lack of respect in *shul*.

One *Shabbat* morning, as he was gently reminding one of the worshippers to refrain from speaking, the man reacted: "Who are you to tell me what to do?"

Standing in his place, gesticulating wildly, he yelled angrily: "How can any of you listen to him? Do you know who he really is? He is a convert. His real name is Graf Valentine Potocki. What does he know about Judaism? How dare he tell us what to do?"

A hushed silence spread over the *shul*. Many people were surprised that the "learned Jew" in their midst was a convert. Others were aghast at the nerve of the man who had spoken out of turn. Still others trembled when they realized the ramifications to the "learned Jew" and the Jewish community. They dreaded the day when the church representatives would find out that the heir to one of Poland's noble families had converted to Judaism.

It did not take long for word to spread through the Christian section of Vilna, that Graf Valentine Potocki was alive and well. His family was very surprised with this unexpected turn of events, for they had despaired of ever finding him. The police constable arrested him, took him to the army barracks, shaved his beard and *payot*, and summoned his mother to identify him. She pleaded with him to renounce Judaism, but he refused.

At the conclusion of the trial the court asked him if he wanted to speak. He answered calmly: "I know that I am accused of heresy, and that you will condemn me to death. I want you to know that I believe you will only be burning flesh and bone. As for the man who revealed my identity, please tell him that I forgive him because he gave me the opportunity to die for the sanctification of God's glorious and Holy Name."

While he was awaiting execution, a messenger from the Gaon of Vilna told him that it would be possible to save his life with kabbalistic secrets. He refused to consider it, preferring to die a martyr's death.

The execution of the "learned Jew" took place on the second day of *Shevuout*, 5509.[2] When his flesh could no longer withstand the pain of the scorching flames, he cried out: "Blessed be You, O Lord our God, who sanctifies His Name before the multitudes."

[**Ed.** During the time when the Crusades ravaged Jewish communities in the Franco/Germanic lands, the rabbis introduced a prayer which was recited following the martyr's recitation of *Sh'ma*. The blessing "Bless are You, O Lord our God, Master of the Universe, Who has sanctified us with His commandments and commanded us to sanctify His Name before the multitudes" has been repeated by martyrs throughout the ages.]

"*Sh'ma Yisrael*, Hear 0 Israel, the Lord our God, the Lord is One."[3]

A member of the Jewish community disguised himself as a Christian and bribed a local official for permission to gather the ashes and a finger from the corpse of the "learned Jew," which he buried in the Jewish cemetery in Vilna. The Jews of Vilna recited *Kaddish* at the grave of the "learned Jew," for many years to honor his memory.

[**Ed.** The Chafetz Chaim, Rabbi Yisrael Mayer HaKohen (1838-1933) explained that before the Revelation at Sinai, the Almighty asked each nation in turn if they would accept His Torah. All refused except the Jewish people who swore: 'we will do and we will listen.' (Sh'mot, Exodus 24:7). However, there were some holy souls among the nations who desired to accept the Torah. These were the righteous proselytes of all generations. Among them was Graf Valentine Potocki, Avraham ben Avraham, the "learned Jew."]

A Sacred Trust
— Commentary —
The House of Rothchild

Two profound lessons emerge from the story of the *House of Rothschild;* the justification of great success and the complex relationship of Jew and non-Jew in pre-modern Europe.

The prosperity of Mayer Anshel, his success in worldly terms, is grounded, so this story would have it, in his pious and humble beginnings. One is led to believe that Mayer Anshel was a reluctant entrepreneur, spurred on by necessity, not ambition or greed. He would have preferred study to business. Even while in business, his focus was the welfare of his clientele, not his profit. Wealth is a blessing, then, and the wealthy are to be honored, as long as wealth itself is not the goal. Mayer Anshel earned his right to success because of his early devotion to study, and his life-long qualities of kindness, caring and moral rectitude.

The relationship between Jew and non-Jew was most complex, as this story illustrates. Whether peasant or *poretz*, the non-Jew could determine the destiny of a Jew. So it is with political powerlessness, as we experienced before the founding of the State of Israel. Mostly, there was an uneasy truce. Peasants provided the daily livelihood of a Jewish innkeeper, a peasant woman assisted a Jewish household in the intimate tasks of housecleaning. But, stereotypically, the male peasants were also drunkards, and the female peasant an opportunistic thief.

The *poretz*, on the other hand, was now a kind, understanding ruler. But, this too was tenuous. "Could something have happened to change the decent relationship between him and my people?" the *rebbe* asked. As long as Jews are in exile, this story teaches, our safety, both in the world at large and in our very homes, is at risk.

Rabbi Nina Beth Cardin
Editor, Sh'ma
Visiting Lecturer, JTS

The Silver Age of Polish Jewry: Chapter Thirty-Eight

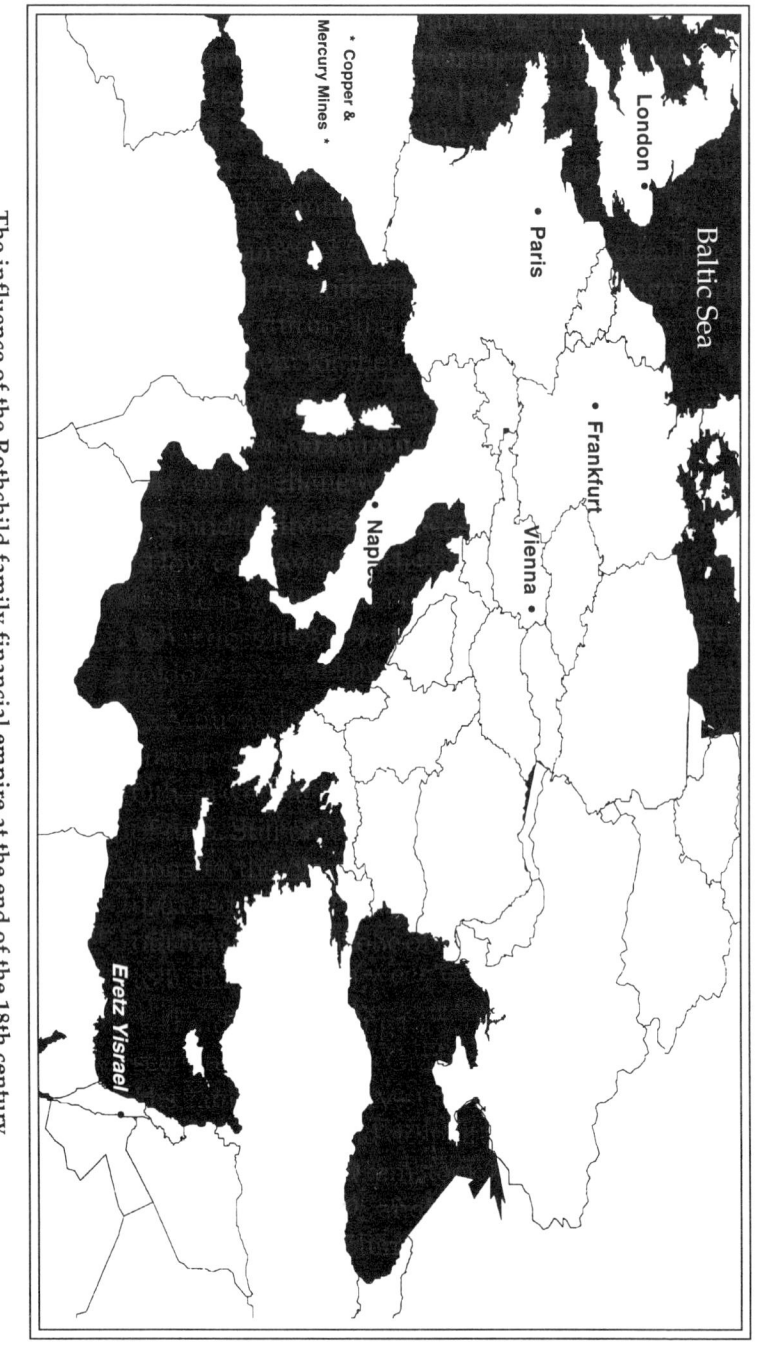

The influence of the Rothchild family financial empire at the end of the 18th century

Chapter Thirty-Eight
THE HOUSE OF ROTHSCHILD

Time Line

| 70 c.e. | 600 c.e. | 1000 c.e. | 1400 c.e. | 1600 c.e. | 1800 c.e. | 2000 c.e. |

Location: Pale of Settlement, Frankfurt

Rebbe Tzve Hirsh Halayve Horovitz of Tzortikov noticed that a modest, sincere young lad walked around the *bayt midrash* with sad downcast eyes. Inquiring, he found out that his name was Mayer Anshel,[1] that he had been recently orphaned, and that he had come from Frankfurt-au-Main to study. Attempting to make him comfortable in his new surroundings, Rebbe Tzve Hirsh appointed him to be his *shammish* and arranged for him to live with his family.

Mayer Anshel matured. His every action pleased Rebbe Tzve Hirsh, for he did more than was expected of him; the rebbe's appointments were arranged in an orderly fashion, the holy books that were left laying on the table in the *bayt midrash* were always returned neatly to their places on the book shelves, and the *tzedakah* money with which he was entrusted by the rebbe was always distributed fairly and compassionately.

When Mayer Anshel reached marriageable age, a match was arranged for him with a young woman who lived in Sneatin, a neighboring *shtetl*. Taking leave of Rebbe Tzve Hirsh, he went to live with his in-laws. Faced with the problem of earning a livelihood, he opened a little grocery business that flourished immediately, because his customers enjoyed the personal attention he gave each one of them.

In the meantime, the two sons of Rebbe Tzve Hirsh had married. Rebbe Shmelke went to live in Nikolsburg and Rebbe Pinchas went to live in Frankfurt-au-Main. Only one daughter, born during the latter years of his life, remained at home. At the appropriate time she would be matched with a proper young man. Rebbe Tzve Hirsh had saved a small amount of money towards her dowry and added it to the money he had inherited from his father. It totaled five hundred gold thalers, a sizeable amount for those days. He was the only one who knew where the money was hidden. The box was locked in a drawer of the bureau in his private room and opened once a year, on the night of the searching of the leaven, preceding *Pesach*.

Alone, customarily searching all the drawers, boxes, bookcases, under the bed and the furniture in his private room the year that Mayer Anshel was married, Rebbe Tzve Hirsh cautiously approached the bureau. The flickering little candle that he carried cast a soft glow as he lifted the key from its hiding place, unlocked the drawer, pulled it open, lifted the lid of the box. To his dismay, the box was empty. There was no sign that the drawer or the lock had been tampered with. He started to scream, and some people who had been in his house waiting for him to finish his search in his private room ran up the stairs. His face had turned ashen.

"The money for her dowry, the box ... it is entirely empty," he cried out to the first person who crossed the threshold. "The money has been stolen!"

The hushed silence was broken by the voice of a man standing in the rear.

"Only Mayer Anshel could have taken the money. He was the only one who had intimate knowledge of everything that happened in this house."

Another man demanded to know how he could accuse anyone without proof.

"Proof," he shouted "I'll supply you with proof! How do you think he has such a successful business? Most people struggle for a long time. What are the reports you hear about him? You hear that he is successful, that his shop is well stocked with merchandise. Where do you think he obtained the money to start his business?"

Rebbe Tzve Hirsh raised his hands to silence the commotion. "You have no right to accuse him without proper proof. He never gave me any reason to doubt his sincerity or his honesty the entire time he lived in this house. I don't know who stole the money, but I am certain that it was not Mayer Anshel!"

But the accuser did not give the *rebbe* a moment's peace. Finally, he decided to visit Mayer Anshel and hear the truth from his lips.

With a great deal of personal anguish pressing upon his heart, Rebbe Tzve Hirsh set off for Sneatin. He hadn't the faintest idea how to talk to a man that he believed innocent, but that others in his household were convinced was guilty.

He rode around the marketplace in his carriage for a time, struggling with different opening sentences. Finally, he asked directions to Mayer Anshel's house, and pointed the horses that way. When he arrived, he tied the horses to the hitching post and knocked on the door.

Mayer Anshel was so happy to see him. He moved away from the door courteously, extended his hand in warm greeting, and motioned for him to enter. He led him to the head of the table, gestured for him to sit down in the arm chair. Before he sat down to join his rebbe, Mayer Anshel personally served a cold drink and some cake.

"I am so happy to welcome you to my new home. Please tell me how your family is," began Mayer Anshel easily.

Rebbe Tzve Hirsh picked up the cue. He started to discuss all the members of his family. Then, while he was talking, he wove the incident of the missing money into the conversation. He was surprised at Mayer Anshel's reaction.

"Yes," he said, "I was among the few who knew that you had

hidden five hundred gold thalers for your daughter's dowry. I knew exactly where you had hidden the money, where you had hidden the key to the drawer. I am prepared to return the money to you. However, right now, I only have two hundred gold thalers on hand. I will give them to you, and I promise to send you fifty gold thalers a month for the next six months until the debt is paid."

Rebbe Tzve Hirsh could not believe the words he heard from Mayer Anshel. But when he handed him two hundred gold thalers, he accepted them quietly and promised himself that he would not reveal to a soul what had happened. He was happy that the accuser had not suspected someone without reason, that he had arranged for the lost money to be returned, that he had hopes of regaining the entire sum in the near future. He returned to Tzortikov that day.

Of course, this is not the end of the story; there are too many suspicious details still unresolved.

In a neighboring *shtetl*, a Jewish innkeeper decided to investigate a strange experience.

On their way home from the fields, the peasants used to stop in his inn to drink, to talk, to joke, to while away the time. One day, a peasant seemed in an unusually happy mood. Waving his broad arms around the inn, he announced in a rather raucous voice: "Friends, eat and drink to your heart's content; today I am paying!"

The innkeeper served more food and drink that evening than he had served for the past two weeks. The host peasant was a little tipsy when he rose to pay the bill. Walking a crooked line, he stumbled over to the innkeeper, withdrew a gold thaler from his pocket and gurgled: "This should take care of my debt."

"Wait a minute," mumbled the innkeeper. "This is not the money that is used here. I have never seen such a coin. How do I know its value?"

"Don't worry about it," replied the peasant. "You see, I was walking down the road, and I saw this shiny coin laying in the weeds at the side. Someone must have lost it. If you take it to the money lender in town tomorrow morning, he will tell you what it is worth. He will, no doubt, exchange it for zlotys and give you change. You can take what I owe you, and the next time I come in, you will give me the change."

Having no choice, the innkeeper took the gold thaler. The next morning he went to the money lender and found that indeed the gold thaler was very precious.

The following week, the same scene was repeated. When the scene was repeated the third week, the innkeeper became suspicious.

"How many gold thalers can one peasant find in the mud? People don't throw money around. He must have stolen them. I have to have some help to uncover the mystery."

That afternoon, when business had quieted down in the inn, the innkeeper went to see the *poretz*. The *poretz* owned vast holdings in the entire area and ruled it compassionately. He listened intently as the innkeeper unravelled his story.

"I have come to you for advice," concluded the innkeeper. "If the money was stolen, I would like to see it returned to its proper owner."

"Well, this is my advice," began the *poretz*, after a few moments of quiet thought. "It is a known fact that people who have too much to drink cannot hold their secrets. Therefore, the next time that peasant comes to your inn with his friends, increase the amount of liquor each time they ask for a refill. It won't take too long for the entire group to become completely inebriated. Then pretend that you want to join the crowd, and sit down with them. You should be able to get the peasant to confess how he obtained the gold thalers."

The innkeeper thanked the *poretz* and returned to the inn. He waited for the peasant and his friends the next week.

When they arrived, he followed the *poretz's* instructions.

When the entire group was intoxicated, he sat down next to them, pretending to be friendly, solicitous.

"Hey," he yelled at the top of his voice, pretending to be as drunk as them, "where did you find those gold thalers?"

"Hah, hah," screamed the peasant, almost choking on his laughter, "you didn't believe that I really found them. Listen," he motioned with his hand, lend me your ear, I'll tell you what really happened. You see, my wife sometimes works in Jewish houses, especially before their spring holiday. It seems that they are all crazy clean then. Last year, she noticed that their rebbe walked around the house with a little candle. It seemed to her that he was searching for something, so she followed him. He was so immersed in what he was doing, that he did not notice that she was right behind him. She saw him pick up a key, walk over to a bureau, open a drawer, remove a box, open it, count out the money that was hidden in it, return the box to the drawer, lock it, and replace the key. When he left the room, she stole the money. She brought it to me, and I figured that if there was no investigation for a year, it would be safe to use it. So I kept it hidden all this time. Now, the year has passed and I feel safe using the coins, one at a time! I'm a rich man! I'm a rich man! Hah, hah!" His sides shook with laughter.

The innkeeper was dumbfounded with the confession of the drunken peasant.

The next day he returned to the *poretz* with the information. The *poretz* sent one of his officers to the peasant's cottage, to search for and retrieve the money and to apprehend him until the investigation was concluded.

A few days later, that same officer appeared on the doorstep of Rebbe Tzve Hirsh's house.

"The *poretz* would like to invite you to visit him," the officer suggested gently. "Could you possibly come this afternoon?"

Rebbe Tzve Hirsh was a bit alarmed. "Could something have happened to change the decent relationship between him and my people?" he pondered.

Worrying would not solve his dilemma, so he asked one of his disciples to hitch his horse to the wagon and hurriedly started out for the *poretz's* mansion.

The *poretz* received him kindly. He was more puzzled when the *poretz* began asking him questions about the welfare of the Jews, about his personal family. Skillfully, the *poretz* directed the conversation to the amount of money needed as a dowry to marry off his young daughter.

"Surely, you cannot afford an adequate dowry from the money that you earn. Without money, how will you possibly arrange a proper marriage for your daughter?" persisted the *poretz*.

Rebbe Tzve Hirsh remained silent for a long time, then he whispered carefully: "I have five hundred gold thalers saved for my daughter's dowry from an inheritance I received from my father. It is locked in my private room."

"Could you please describe to me the type of box in which you keep the money?"

Rebbe Tzve Hirsh was stunned. He did not understand why the *poretz* asked him such a specific question. Unable to contain his curiosity, he replied: "The box is missing. It was taken when the money was stolen."

When the *poretz* heard Rebbe Tzve Hirsh's reply, he rose, excused himself for a moment, disappeared into another room, but returned shortly with a packet of gold thalers. He indicated to Rebbe Tzve Hirsh to count it.

"I believe this money belongs to you. When you count the money, you will see that four gold thalers are missing. They were spent by one of the peasants." .

Then the *poretz* preceded to tell the story of how he found out about the stolen money.

Rebbe Tzve Hirsh thanked the *poretz* for his consideration and returned home with mixed emotions: he was happy that the stolen money had been returned, but his heart was broken that he had permitted himself to suspect the innocent Mayer Anshel.

The remainder of the day, he walked around the *bayt midrash* a broken man.

"I have committed such a terrible wrong," he moaned. "I have besmirched an innocent person by listening to someone else's opinion without truly ascertaining the facts."

That night Rebbe Tzve Hirsh could not sleep. Early the next morning, he harnessed his horse to the wagon himself, and set off for Sneatin. Besides returning the money, he wanted to beg forgiveness from Mayer Anshel.

Mayer Anshel greeted him as warmly as he had the first time. When they finally sat down face to face, Rebbe Tzve Hirsh inquired: "I don't understand why you returned money that you had not stolen?"

Mayer Anshel stood up respectfully.

"You see," he said, "when I saw your anguish, I pretended to be the thief, in order to alleviate your pain."

"I beg you to forgive me," pleaded Rebbe Tzve Hirsh remorsefully. "I believed someone else's accusation without investigating the facts. I besmirched your reputation. I caused you pain, and you repaid me with good. I am returning your money," he continued, laying the money on the table. "I bless you that it will increase a hundred fold, that you, your children, and your grandchildren will enjoy its riches for all generations."

Rebbe Tzve Hirsh returned to Tzortikov. Mayer Anshel returned to his native Frankfurt-au-Main. The rest of the story of the House of Rothschild is history.

༄

A Sacred Trust
— Commentary —
An Unusual Torah Scholar

This touching tale has several relevant themes for the modern Jew: the assimilation from the Pale of Settlement to the blandishments of higher learning and science in western Europe; the alluring attraction of the world of wealth and social status in place of tradition and piety. This story of two centuries ago reflects the conflicts of today, and the pain that parents committed to tradition experience when their children abandon the values taught to them as children.

Fiction, of course, is a world of fantasy, and this lovely tale expresses the hopes and dreams hidden deep within our bosom. When Chaim David Bernard becomes Dr. David Bernard, we fear that another link in the chain of Judaism is broken. But through the dramatic web of occurrences that take place, the young doctor returns to his roots, and becomes Chaim again. In some respects we see here an example of the *Baal Teshuvah* movement in America and Israel. There are, of course, *baalay teshuvah* among all branches of Judaism, not just the Orthodox. Young people are returning to their roots in all groups of Jewish life in the nineties. The spiritual search for meaning through Judaism is influencing many young parents to reclaim what was lost in their earlier youth.

There are two interesting yet subtle messages at the end of the story. While returning to his roots, "Dr. Chaim" maintains his medical practice. He wants to grab both ends of the stick, to take *"yofyato shel Yefet be-oha lay Shem."* He returns, but not to the ghetto of yesterday. The other is the way his wife, Margaret, joins him in his pilgrimage. She says, with dramatic irony for the twentieth century reader, "I don't know what the sounds mean, but somehow, I think they are very important."

The returning Jews of our generation may not know what the sounds of traditional Jewish life mean, but they are drawn to them in a powerful way, and are willing to struggle to understand them. We must help them to do so.

Rabbi Dov Peretz Elkins
The Jewish Center, Princeton, New Jersey
Author of **Moments of Transcendence: Inspirational Readings for Rosh Hashanah and Yom Kippur; Prescription for a Long and Happy Life: Age-Old Wisdom for the New Ages,** *and many other books.*

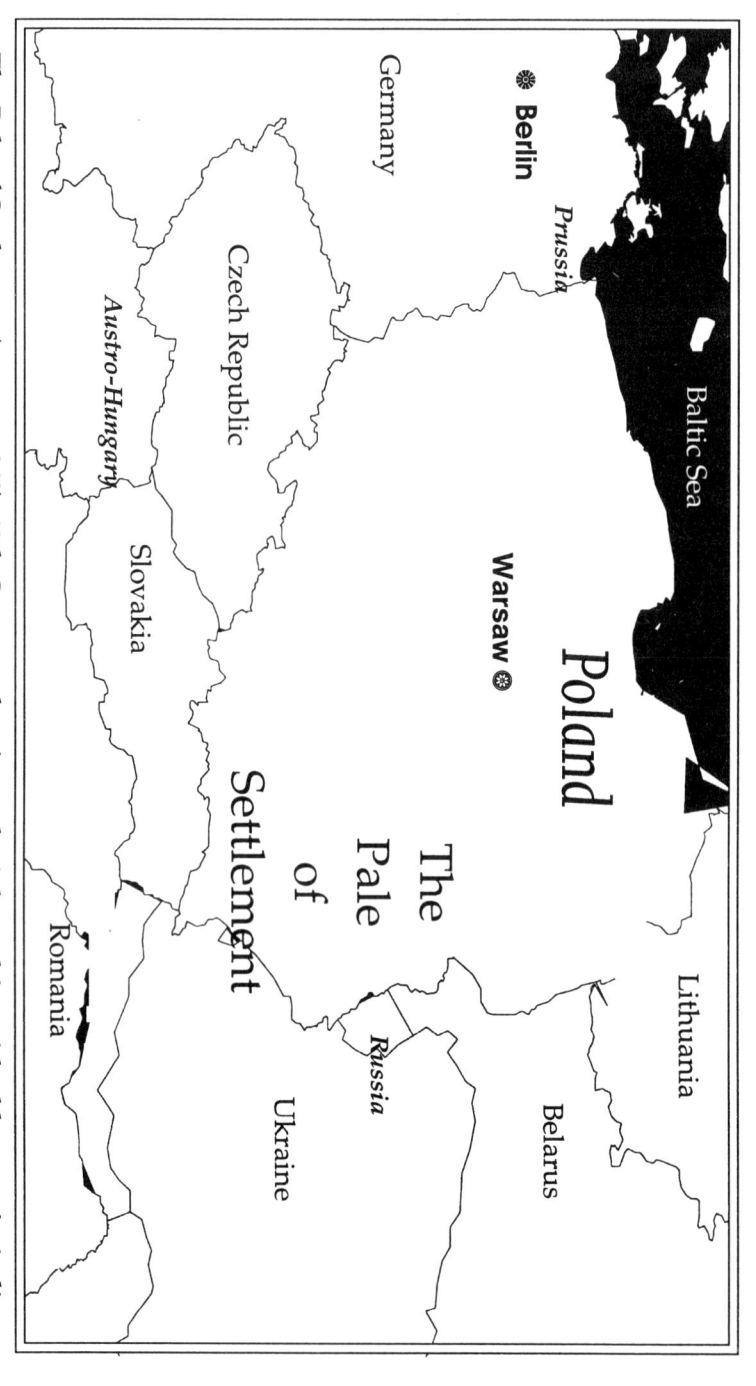

The Pale of Settlement (see page 360), 19th Century, showing today's boundries with old names in *italics*

Chapter Thirty-Nine
AN UNUSUAL TORAH SCHOLAR

Time Line

| 70 c.e. | 600 c.e. | 1000 c.e. | 1400 c.e. | 1600 c.e. | 1800 c.e. | 2000 c.e. |

Location: Pale of Settlement, Germany

Throughout the ages, cultures alien to Judaism influenced Jews away from the path of Torah. The struggle reached its peak during the Age of Enlightenment, occurring in western European countries during the seventeenth and eighteenth centuries. Jews had been released from confinement in the ghettos. They had been granted citizenship. Many opted to join the secular society and abandoned Judaism.

A child was born to an observant Jewish family living in the Pale of Settlement.

[**Ed.** The Pale of Settlement was that part of Poland that had been swallowed up by Russia during three consecutive partitions. Jews living in the Pale of Settlement were generally not affected by societal advances in western Europe.]

The parents, Chaya and Yissachar Dov Bernard named their son Chaim David. The boy proved to be exceedingly bright, and by the time he was ten years old, the *melamed*, the tutor who was supported by the townspeople to instruct their sons, informed Chaim David's parents that there was nothing more he could teach him.

"How shall we find a teacher for our son?" lamented Chaya that evening to her husband. "We both know that it will be a miracle for him to remain a committed Jew if he does not know what the Almighty expects of him!"

"What shall we do? We are so poor. We barely eke out a living. We can't afford to hire a more knowledgeable tutor from a bigger *shtetl*, nor can we afford to send our son to a *yeshiva*!" He bent his head over, staring aimlessly at the dirt floor.

Suddenly, he blurted out: "I have a plan. It might be a solution to our problem. My brother, the one who moved to Berlin, has become very wealthy. He has no children of his own. Perhaps he will help us pay for our son's *yeshiva* education. I will write him a letter this minute."

When Yissachar Dov's brother responded to the letter, he gladly offered to help educate Chaim David. However, he insisted that they send him to live with him in Berlin.

Although reluctant to part with their son, yet pleased with the opportunity to continue his religious education, they scraped together enough money to purchase a third class train ticket and sent him to his uncle.

Upon his arrival, Chaim David's uncle enrolled him in the finest secular, private school under the name of David, omitting his first name entirely. He showered upon him every conceivable luxury. At first David wondered why the food he was served tasted different than his mother's cooking. He attributed it to his uncle being able to afford meat, something he never ate at home, but when milk and butter were served on the same table, he was clearly puzzled. Day followed day, but there was no *Shabbat*. When the summer weather turned cooler, David expected his uncle to attend holy day services, but on the day that he calculated to be *Yom Kippur*, he was awakened like every morning and sent off to school.

David missed his parents and their way of life. He wrote to them regularly, but never mentioned the differences between the way they raised him and the way his uncle was raising him. Then the letters became more and more infrequent. Chaya and Yissachar Dov attributed this to the pre-occupation of their son with his studies. There was no way for them to know the truth. In reality, it did not take very long for him to forget the way he had been raised the first ten years of his life. His friends reinforced his new life style. Years passed.

One night, David's uncle spoke seriously to him. "What career would you like to follow?" he inquired.

"I was thinking," responded David, "that I would like to become a doctor and have the opportunity to save lives."

"That's a good choice. Because of my political influence, I will have no trouble arranging for your admittance to the medical school at the university," he answered.

David excelled in medical school. He graduated with honors, and with his uncle's help, he established a fine medical practice in a very short time. His reputation spread; he was consulted by kings, princes, and politicians. He never turned away a poor patient, and often, traveled long distances to attend to the seriously ill.

He married a lady named Margaret who had been born a Jew but had also been raised in an assimilated family.

One day, he received an urgent message that one of the high-ranking officers of the army, who happened to be a close personal friend of his uncle, was seriously ill. Packing some medical supplies, he set out immediately for the army camp, a two day's ride eastward by horse. He arrived too late. The officer had passed away that afternoon. Despondently, he rode around the army camp in the dark for a long time.

"I will take a different, longer route on my return tomorrow. I need to have time to think." He rode aimlessly, not realizing that he was travelling toward the Polish border. He found himself in the middle of a *shtetl*. He noticed throngs of people milling around a wooden building. Unbeknown to him, it was the *shul* of Rebbe Dovid Lelever.[1] Curious, he tied his horse to a tree, dismounted, walked around the edges of the crowds, then decided to enter the building. He sat down in the back row. He was surprised at the many people who were praying fervently, following the somber voice of the *baal tefilah*, the person who chanted the prayers. Memories of the time he had attended with his father flooded his entire being. He recognized that he had wandered into a *shul*. He reasoned that this day was *Yom Kippur*, the holiest day of the Jewish calendar year.

Although Dr. David Bernard did not understand the meaning of the prayers, he somehow felt at peace with himself.

Suddenly, as if by the signal of an invisible orchestra conductor, David Bernard heard the worshippers shout: "*Chay v'kayam nora u-marom v'kadosh*, Our God is living, awe inspiring, and most Holy."

> [**Ed.** This verse is the refrain of a *piyut* (prayer-poem) recited in the repetition of the "*Amida*" (the silent devotion) during *S'hacharit* (morning service) on *Rosh Hashana* and Yom Kippur. The *piyut* begins with "*Yimloch Hashem L'olam ... V'atah Kadosh Yoshayv Tehilot Yisrael ...* The Almighty shall reign forever ... You Holy One, listen to the prayers of Israel."]

The shouting was interrupted by the raised, waving hands of a frantic-looking man who stood at the front of the *shul*. "Please," he begged the worshippers, "does anyone know if there is a doctor in this *shul*? Our rebbe's daughter is in the throes of childbirth. She is having a very difficult time delivering her baby. Is there someone here who knows how to help?"

Dr. David Bernard stood up. Rushing to the front of the shul, he said: "Please take me immediately to the laboring mother. I will do everything in my power to help her."

Towards the middle of the afternoon, Dr. David Bernard delivered the laboring mother of her firstborn son, the rebbe's first grandchild.

Gratefully, the rebbe turned to the doctor and whispered: "You have saved my daughter's life. You have saved my grandson's life. Because of this, I will restore to you what you have lost. Please, remain with me the rest of this holy day."

David Bernard sat next to Rebbe Dovid Lelever the rest of that Yom Kippur day. He asked the rebbe why he should be a Jew; why he should study Torah; why he should observe the *mitzvot*. The rebbe responded as only a rebbe can. The sun began its descent in the heavens. The holy day was rapidly coming to an end. After the awesome blast of the *shofar*, Rebbe Dovid Lelever turned to Dr. David Bernard and said: "We have spent a few very holy hours together. Now, it is time for me to break my fast. Please, come home with me and join me."

The doctor was intrigued by the *rebbe's* manner; he could not say no to his request. The two men continued talking all night. The talking turned into learning; the learning aroused the doctor's curiosity. He wanted to devour all of the Judaism that he had missed.

They did not part until noon the next day. As his horse trotted along the road, Dr. David Bernard thought about his encounter with Rebbe Dovid Lelever. His heart ached at the thought of his having been cut off from his roots. He wondered if he could incorporate what he had learned into his present life-style.

"No matter how Margaret reacts," he decided, as he neared his house two days later, "I have to return to my roots, to my people."

From the distance, he noticed that Margaret was sitting on the front porch of their spacious house. "That's strange," he thought. "Margaret never sits outside during the day. I wonder how she will accept my decision to return to the Jewish community."

He was the first one to speak. "I have something very important to tell you," he began. "I had the most unbelievable experience yesterday. I think that it reshaped my life." He proceeded to describe to her everything that had happened from the moment his horse had wandered aimlessly into Lelev until he parted with the *rebbe*.

When he finished, she spoke: "Let me tell you what happened to me. I have been sitting here since, mulling over it, trying to understand it, searching for an explanation. You see, three days ago, about eleven in the morning, as I was very busy with the household chores, I suddenly heard a piercing sound which seemed to come from nowhere. At first, I didn't pay too much attention to it. But I kept hearing the sounds over and over, clearer and clearer. I rubbed my ears, I thought I was hearing things, but they wouldn't stop. Finally, mesmerized, I decided to memorize the sounds so that I could repeat them to you. This is what I heard."

She lowered her voice, and said haltingly: *"Chay v'kayam nora u-marom v'kadosh.* I don't know what the sounds mean, but somehow, I think they are very important."

"Those are the same words I heard in the *shul* in the *shtetl*," he said brokenly. "I know what they mean. Our God is living, awe-inspiring, and most Holy."

"I have decided, Margaret, that I must return to my roots, to my people. I was born a Jew. You were born a Jew. We don't really know what being Jewish means. It is obvious by the way we live. I have to study. I have to become part of the Jewish people. Will you explore our roots together with me?"

"Now I understand why I heard that piercing call too," she interrupted. "It is, as if, I also was being invited to return home. Yes, I will join you. Together, we shall find out what being Jewish means."

Margaret and Dr. David Bernard moved to Lublin. They became disciples of Rebbe Yaacov Yitzchak[2] who was known as HaChoze, the Seer of Lublin, and studied with him every day. He reclaimed the name he was given by his parents at birth, Chaim David ben Yissachar Ber. They lovingly performed the *mitzvot* that they learned. They consecrated a major part of their efforts to the *mitzva* of *hachnasat orchim,* hospitality to strangers. They were respected for their love and kindness to everyone.

They immersed themselves in learning. After the Seer of Lublin passed away, some of his disciples asked Chaim David Bernard if he would serve as his successor, but he refused because he did not want to give up the practice of medicine. Margaret was such an inspiration to Jewish women that many named their newborn daughters Margaret to honor her.

A Sacred Trust
— Commentary —
Just One Kopek

Ben Azai said:

> "A *mitzvah* draws forth another *mitzvah*."
>
> (Pirkei Avot 4:2)

In *"Just One Kopeck"* a group of rabbis must collect *tzedakah*, charity, from a miser. The story teaches us a variety of lessons:

1. Don't assume how another person will respond when asked to help.

2. Giving is an educational process, which is advanced by the patience and encouragement of a teacher.

3. The very act of giving, as Ben Azai taught us, reinforces our desire to give.

The lessons of this fine tale are applicable to the range of *mitzvot*, those acts which derive from our relationship with God. Each time we do a *mitzvah* we are rewarded with the motivation to do another *mitzvah*. Each time we do a *mitzvah* we discover a little more clearly who we are at our core.

Rabbi Elie Kaplan Spitz
Congregation B'nai Israel
Tustin, California

**Berditchev, now located in the Ukrainian nation.
(Borders are today's)**

Italics indicate 18th century regional names

Chapter Forty
JUST ONE KOPECK

Time Line

| 70 c.e. | 600 c.e. | 1000 c.e. | 1400 c.e. | 1600 c.e. | 1800 c.e. | 2000 c.e. |

Location: Pale of Settlement

This entry in the diary of a Volhynia country *poretz* illustrates the precarious conditions under which the Jews lived in Poland/Russia during the eighteenth century.

[Ed. *Arendar* is the term used for a lessee, originally of a farm, tavern, or inn on the estate of a *poretz* in Poland/Russia. The arendars, mostly Jews, provided a steady source of revenue for the *poretz*.]

"The *arendar* Hershko is ninety one rubles behind in payment of his rent. I will be forced to garnishee his possessions. According to the clause of my contract with him, I also have the right, in case of further non-payment, to imprison him, his wife and children as long as I like, until he pays his debt. I have already issued orders to have him chained and locked up in the pig-sty together with the swine. I have permitted his wife and three sons to remain in the inn. However, I took the fourth son, the youngest one, Layzer, to my manor where I will have him instructed in the Catholic catechism and prayers. I have already forced him to make the sign of the cross and eat pork. I was stopped from proceeding further with my plans to convert him when three Jews arrived from Berditchev. They remitted the debt of the arendar, thereby saving him from imprisonment and his son from forced conversion."

Rebbe Layve Yitzchak of Berditchev,[1] Rebbe Menachem Mendel of Vitebsk,[2] and Rebbe Shneor Zalman of Liadi[3] had heard that an innocent Jew had been incarcerated for being unable to pay the rent due the *poretz* on his leased inn. They learned that the *poretz* had kidnaped the youngest son for the purpose of converting him. In desperation, they decided to appeal to Motel, the wealthiest Jew in the area. They hoped he would give them the required sum to redeem the captives, even though he had never contributed anything to any cause before.

Motel, the miser, had built his mansion set well back from the road. Tall trees and thick hedges grew in front of an iron picket fence that surrounded the property, to discourage visitors. To further be certain that his privacy would not be disturbed, Motel permitted his vicious dogs to roam the grounds freely.

The three rebbes approached the gate. For a minute, the growling dogs yelped, howling for the attention of their master. Unafraid, Rebbe Shneor Zalman placed his hand on the gate, and slowly pushed it open. Suddenly, the howling stopped. The dogs, slinking toward the hedges, crouched timidly. Motioning to his friends to follow him, Rebbe Menachem Mendel, and Rebbe Layve Yitzchak walked confidently down the path leading to the mansion. They did not hesitate to knock loudly. Motel opened the door, for he was curious to know who could possibly escape his vicious dogs.

Dumbfounded, but recognizing the three rebbes, he stuttered: "Won't you come in? Sit down on these chairs." He pointed to softly tufted, overstuffed easy chairs. "What brings you here?"

"Well, Motel," began Rebbe Shneor Zalman in a kind voice, "we have come here on a very important mission. You see, the *arendar*, Hershko, the one that leases his inn from the local *poretz* and thereby earns his livelihood, has fallen on bad times. The *poretz* has chained him and thrown him into the dungeon until he can pay his debt. If he is chained, he can not work to earn the money that he owes. In addition, the *poretz* has hired a priest to instruct his youngest son in Catholic catechism. Motel, we appeal to you. This is absolutely a case of redeeming two human

Just One Kopeck

beings from a fate worse than death. Open your heart and help us in the most generous way that you can."

Rebbe Mendel Vitebsk and Rebbe Layve Yitzchak looked at Motel. The miser was sobbing.

"How much do you need, *rebbe*," choked Motel in between sobs?

"The *poretz* demands ninty one rubles to release the *arendar* and his son," gently whispered Rebbe Shneor Zalman.

"Wait one minute. I will help you," said Motel.

Quickly, he left the room. He was gone about fifteen minutes. When he returned, he held a rusty, bent kopeck in his hand.

[**Ed.** A kopeck is one-hundreth of a ruble.]

"Here," he said, looking at Rebbe Shneor Zalman, "I can give you this kopeck to help you with your work of rescuing the arendar."

Rebbe Shneor Zalman took the kopeck, and rose to leave. Rebbe Menachem Mendel and Rebbe Layve Yitzchak were ashen faced, but they followed him. As they reached the front door, Rebbe Shneor Zalman said: "Motel, I thank you for the kopeck that you gave me. I bless you to be able to give more and more."

They walked out the door and started for the path leading to the road.

Rebbe Mendel Vitebsk turned on Rebbe Shneor Zalman: "I don't understand you. After you pleaded with Motel for ninety one rubles to free the arendar, he handed you one rusty, bent kopek. You took the kopek, thanked him, and even blessed him. I don't understand. He acted disgracefully."

Rebbe Shneor Zalman did not reply. They walked ten steps along the path when they heard a familiar voice call: "Wait, wait!"

They turned to find Motel running after them, panting. "Please come back," he pleaded. "I want to give you more money."

The three rebbes turned around. Following Motel, they entered the mansion, sat down and waited. He disappeared once more. When he reappeared, he held two rusty, bent kopecks in his hand. He gave the money to Rebbe Shneor Zalman. Rebbe Layve Yitzchak found it difficult to hide his astonishment; Rebbe Menachem Mendel's face was creased with a deep scowl.

They rose to leave. Rebbe Shneor Zalman repeated his speech: "Motel, thank you for the two kopecks you gave me. I bless you to be able to give more."

They were not more than fifteen steps down the path when they heard the familiar voice shouting after them: "Wait, wait!"

When the panting Motel caught up with them, he invited them to return to his home once again.

The three rebbes returned a hundred times to Motel's home that afternoon. Hours and hours passed. First, he increased the amount of kopecks by fives and tens, then he produced single ruble notes, increasing gradually, until the rebbes had ninety one rubles in their hands.

Afterwards, Rebbe Layve Yitzchak turned to Rebbe Shneor Zalman and asked: "How did you know that Motel would finally give you the money we needed to ransom the arendar?"

"Truthfully, I did not know," he began. "I only know one thing. People generally want to do the right thing, for every person has a little spark of holiness within him. Many times the spark is covered by a barrier, making it impossible for that person to respond. I saw that spark in Motel's heart when he gave us the first kopek. Do you know how hard it must have been for him to do that? Then I blessed him to give more and more, to help him."

The three *rebbes* walked rapidly toward the *poretz's* mansion, happy that the money they carried with them would pay for the release of the *arendar* and his son.

༺

A Sacred Trust
— Commentary —
The Pintele Yid

Through the vicissitudes of exile, the Jewish people were often coerced to convert to a different religion. The choice was often convert or die. How many of these forced converts returned to their Jewish faith? We can not calculate the numbers, but we know that many returned to our people and to the God of Israel when the risk to their lives was removed.

The source of this loyalty is the *pintele yid*, a small fire that burns within the soul of every Jew.

There are those who believe that the Jew was exiled to teach the world by their example the meaning of One God. There are others who believe that the Jews were placed in difficult circumstances to alleviate the persecution of their brothers and sisters. This genre can be found in the story of Purim.

Esther is chosen queen of the Persian empire in a beauty contest that seems incomprehensible in a biblical book. Yet, because of her position, Mordechai was able to say to her: "And who knows whether it was just for such a time as this (to save the Jewish people from Haman's murderous plot) that you attained the royal position!" (*Megillat Esther* 4:14)

The same genre appears in the story of *The Jewish Pope,* (Volume 1, Chapter 11). When father and son discover each other, the Jewish pope says: "But, father, while I sit on the throne of Rome, I have the power to protect the Jewish people from evil decrees, from expulsion, from all sorts of false accusations that lead to acts of violence."

In this story, the *pintele yid* emerged because of an encounter with a holy *rebbe* who ignited the spark of *Yiddishkeit* within.

Avraham Yosef defends his people against the blood libel accusations "These blood libels are nothing more than a pretext to harm the Jewish people, who I must remind you, have been living peacefully in our country for more than four hundred years. I will stake my reputation, my title and my fortune on the truth of my words."

Being able to rise in the *Sejm* (Polish Parliament) to utter these words, he realizes that his conversion had not extinguished his *pintele yid*, and he sets out to try to re-ignite that which he thought he lost.

—*Authors*

The Silver Age of Polish Jewry: Chapter Forty-One

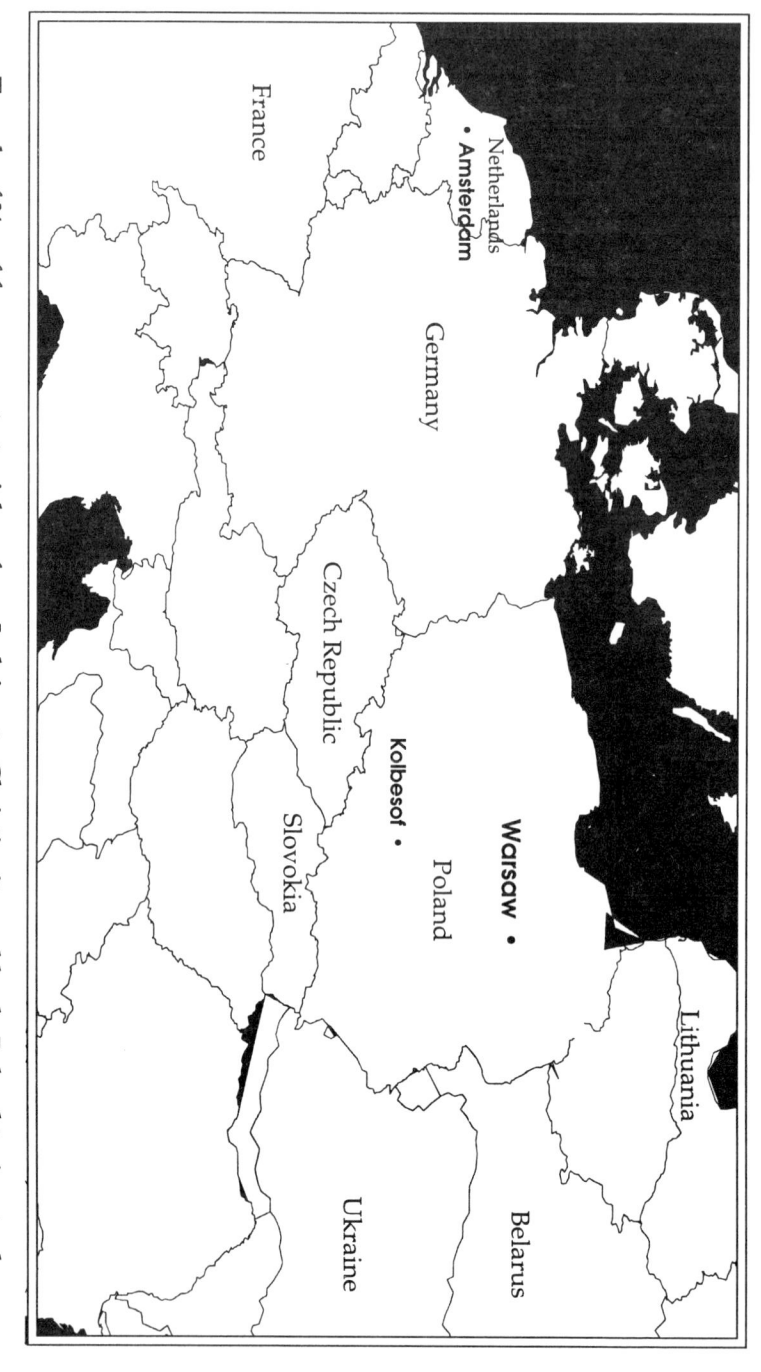

Travels of Yosef from poverty to riches, from Judaism to Christianity and back, Poland to Amsterdam

Chapter Forty One
THE PINTELE YID

Time Line

| 70 c.e. | 600 c.e. | 1000 c.e. | 1400 c.e. | 1600 c.e. | 1800 c.e. | 2000 c.e. |

Location: Poland

I am a *baal teshuva*.

> [**Ed.** A *baal teshuva* is a repentant Jew, one who had strayed but returned to Judaism.]

I've carried three names in my lifetime. My parents named me Yosef, but I became Tadeusz Korbonski/Pilce. Then, I changed my name again, to Avraham Yosef ben Avraham. I should really start my story from the very beginning; I am not seeking sympathy or understanding. Rather, I am telling this to you so that you will remember how easy it is for a Jew to lose his way in the world.

Because I kept a journal of all my business transactions, I knew that I began to change early in 1766.

I was a modest wheat merchant, a loving father, a devoted husband, a respected member of the *kahal*, the communal governing body.

I lived in one of the *shtetlach* owned by the Polish Duke Korbonski/Pilce. I bought wheat from the peasants and sold it to the townspeople. Because I was the intermediary between the peasants and the townspeople, I had to speak Polish fluently. I even dressed as a Polish gentleman.

Once, I thought I would try to enlarge the territory in which I was permitted to sell the wheat, so I made an appointment to see Stefan Karski, the overseer of the duke's property who lived on his estate.

When he asked me how he could help, I replied: "I have a proposition from which we will both benefit. Instead of all the peasant farmers in this entire region bringing their grain to your storage barns a little at a time, I will go to their farms and collect the grain. I will resell it to the townspeople in the marketplace. This service will save you much time and trouble. In essence, I am offering to become your distributor. You will have to pay me only a percentage of the profits."

Whether the overseer was astounded by my *chutzpa* or impressed by my manner, I shall never know, but he extended his hand to me in friendship.

"Somehow, I trust you. I think you're offer sounds reasonable. Let's experiment for six months. You are free to extend your territory, to collect as much grain from the peasants in the outlying vicinity, to sell it in the marketplace. After that time, bring me the profits and I will pay you your percentage. Then we will also reevaluate our arrangement."

I left the mansion heady with the promise of extended territory and great wealth, for I knew I could succeed in this daring endeavor ... and I was successful. The harvested wheat crop was abundant. The duke became richer, the overseer, more confident in my ability. I reaped the praise of my family and neighbors for my role as the peacekeeper between the nobility, the peasants, and the Jewish community.

This business arrangement lasted two years. During that time, I had free access to Stefan Karski's home, but I never met Duke Korbonski/Pilce, the Duchess Halina, or any member of their family.

In the spring of the third year, I heard that the duke had passed away. I went immediately to Stefan Karski's house to express my sympathy. He spoke to me gently: "I'm so glad you came to see me, even though this is not your usual time to report. I want to assure you, that our business arrangements will continue as in the past. I am satisfied with your performance. Before he died, the duke gave me the power to continue overseeing his vast estates, with the proviso that I care for his widow. He trusted me to treat her kindly."

I swore to him that I would be faithful. I left his house, certain that my future was assured.

A few months later, I returned to Stefan Karski's house to go over my accounts with him and pay him his share of the harvest's profits. When we finished, he said: "Before you leave, the Duchess Halina would like to meet you."

Curiously, I walked toward the mansion. It stood regally at the end of the path, crowning it in seeming majesty. I knocked gently on the door. A servant admitted me to a great hall and asked me to follow him to the drawing room. I had never had any direct dealings with Polish nobility, nor had I ever been invited inside any of their homes. I was awe struck by the luxurious furnishings. My knees quivered as I inched forward. My eyes blinked when I noticed the magnificent tapestries adorning the beige-colored walls, and the sparkling gold, silver and marble sculptures atop ornately carved wooden stands.

The Duchess Halina waited at the door of the drawing room. She realized how uncomfortable I was and tried to calm me. She spoke softly; her voice had a gentle musical tone. I had never met a more lovely lady.

"Please, do not be disturbed that I asked you to visit me. You see, I never met the people who were employed by my late husband, and I should like to do so. I want to learn a little about his employees and their families, and I want them to explain to me how they contribute to the continuing success of our fortune." She lowered her voice and extended her hand, pointing to the lavish furnishings that surrounded her.

"First, tell me about your family," she requested.

"I am married and I have three children, two sons aged five and nine, and a daughter aged seven. I live in a *shtetl*, not far from here," I whispered hesitantly.

"Now," she urged, "explain to me what work you do."

Patiently I detailed my arrangements with Stefan Karski. She seemed satisfied with my explanation, so I rose to leave. As I neared the door of the drawing room, she called after me: "Next time you come to report to Stefan Karski, why don't you stop in to see me?"

Her words echoed in my mind as I walked down the path leading from the mansion to the road where my carriage stood. I still recalled the lilting melodious notes of her voice as I climbed onto the driver's ledge of the wagon and set off for home.

Somehow, I invented excuses to see Stefan Karski five times that year, and each time temptation drew me into the presence of the Duchess Halina. During that fifth visit, Halina expressed her loneliness to me. "I enjoy your visits so much," she murmured. "I wish you would come to see me more often."

I became part of the Duchess' life. The servants, at first leery of strangers, accepted my coming and going without questions.

Two years passed. One day, during one of my visits, the Duchess Halina said: "I think you know that we have grown very fond of each other. Listen carefully to what I have to say. I would like you to marry me. You will have to convert to Christianity, but with our marriage you will acquire the family name of Korbonski/Pilce, my dead husband's wealth and his title in the Sejm.[1] You will sit in Warsaw with all the honored nobles of this land."

I was taken aback, shocked by her brash proposal. Unable to speak, I stood up and paced the floor. She repeated her proposal and added: "If you are worried about the welfare of your wife and children, I will provide handsomely for them. I certainly have enough money for you to give her a large enough sum that will enable her to live comfortably for the rest of her life. In the meantime, return home and organize your affairs. I will arrange for my priest to convert you. In two weeks time, I shall send my coachman and my coach to fetch you. He will have the money in his possession."

Her voice echoed in my head as I ran from her presence.

The thought of changing my religion abhorred me. Untold numbers of my ancestors had been given the choice of conversion or death, and they died with *Sh'ma* on their lips. Here I was one of the responsible members of the *kahal*, the Jewish community governing council. No one was standing over me with a sword. How could I even think these forbidden thoughts? What about my wife? What about my children?

I could not think clearly for two weeks as I struggled with the thought of luxury and title. I didn't eat or sleep. I imagined that I loved Halina, that I was comfortable with her, that we enjoyed talking to each other. I knew that I felt alive when I was with her. The more I struggled, the more temptation beckoned. After two weeks, temptation won.

The coachman arrived while my wife was in the marketplace with our daughter. Our sons were in *cheder*.

[**Ed.** *Cheder* was the early childhood and primary grade religious school.]

He handed me the money and I placed it on the table. I quickly glanced around my home for the last time, then I closed the door behind me, sealing that portion of my life.

The priest awaited me. He baptized me, renamed me Duke Tadeusz Korbonski/Pilce and married me to the Duchess Halina. She loved me very much. We lived contentedly together for four years in which time a son Piotor and a daughter Jadwiga were born to us.

I was welcomed honorably in Warsaw at the bi-annual meeting of the Sejm. Automatically, I occupied the seat of Halina's dead husband. King Stanislaw II August Poniatowski and the nobles respected me; on occasion, they even listened to my advice. I was included in the inner circle of the king's advisors. I was accorded more reverence than when I had been a member of the *kahal* in my former life.

[**Ed.** King Stanislaw II August Poniatowski was crowned the last king of Poland, with Russian help, in 1764. He tried to introduce political reform with the aid of his relatives, the Czartoryski family, but the Russian minister to Warsaw Nikolai V. Repnin sewed seeds of discord between the king and the nobility leading to the first partition of Poland eight years later. The king succumbed to Tzarina Catherine the Great's pressure and joined the pro-Russian Confederation of Targowica, which was formed to overthrow the new constitution and snuff out the liberalism that had flowered under his rule. After the third partition of Poland in 1795, the king abdicated and fled to Russia where he died in exile in 1798.]

In 1772, I attended my second session of the Sejm. Near the close of the proceedings, a duke that I had hardly knew arose.

"Before this session ends," he thundered, pounding his fists on the table for order, "I want to place a new piece of business on the agenda." Hushed silence settled in the room. He proceeded: "In one of the villages of my estate, two girlfriends went walking in the nearby woods. One was Jewish, the other was Polish. Only one girl returned, the Jewish one. The villagers told me that the Jewish girl lured her Polish friend into the woods so the Jews could kill her. They told me that the Jews needed her blood to bake matzot for their holy day, the one they call *Pesach*."

The dukes were not surprised with the story.

"That kind of thing happens in my duchy all the time!" one duke commented.

King Stanislaw II August Poniatowski had been daydreaming. Suddenly, his attention returned to the proceedings.

"What do you mean?" he demanded. "Are you sure that Jews murder Christian children? If this is so, I will have no Jew in my kingdom!

"Duke Wieniawski, is this true?"

"Yes, your majesty, I have heard this before," he muttered. "I thought it was only a rumor, your majesty, but if the subject is brought up on the agenda of this revered governing body, I guess it must be true."

"What have you heard," Duke Florian?

"What's you opinion," Duke Karlowicz?

All the dukes nodded in agreement.

"In that case," shouted the king, "I will draw up a decree immediately expelling all the Jews from my kingdom. All their property will be confiscated by the crown. No one must use the power of the *liberum veto* to delay the enactment of my decree.

> [**Ed.** The *liberum veto* was based upon political equality of every Polish gentleman who participated in the governmental process. Every proposed law had to be unanimously approved. If unanimity were lacking, the Sejm could be dissolved until its next meeting two years later.]

Scribe! Write this decree!"

The decree was written as dictated and passed from Duke Wieniawski to Duke Milewski to Duke Florian to Duke Karlowicz for their signatures.

I knew I could never sign such a decree. I had to think of a plan quickly. The whole thing was a pretext to disfavor the Jewish people in order to expel them from a country where they had lived in relative security for more than four hundred years. I sighed when I realized how deeply my feelings were identified with my people. My lips quivered, my hands shook; trembling seized my entire body.

My conscience screamed: "Get hold of yourself! You have something very important to do!"

When the parchment reached me, I shakily arose.

"Before I sign this decree, I should like to say something. Everyone here knows that I was born a Jew, and that I converted to Catholicism many years ago."

All the assembled dukes sat in rapt attention. No one had any idea what my next words would be.

"But," I continued slowly, "I have to tell you that you are making a terrible mistake. Jews are not murderers!"

"How do you know that?" interrupted Duke Milewski loudly.

"I'll tell you how I know," I continued, unabashed by his interruption. I tried to remain calm. I felt more courageous the longer I stood in my place. "I was raised a Jew. I was educated in a *yeshiva*, a school where young men learn Jewish law many hours a day. I know that their law prohibits them from murdering.[2]

In addition, the law prohibiting the eating of blood is clearly spelled out. 'For the life of every creature depends on its blood. Therefore, I say to the children of Israel: do not eat the blood of any creature, for the life of any being is its blood.'[3]

This decree is based upon false pretext. In all good consciousness, I can not and I won't sign it."

"Are you telling me," injected the king, "that these accusations are just that: they have no basis in fact?"

"Yes," I answered. "These blood libels are nothing more than a pretext to harm the Jewish people, who, I must remind you, have been living peacefully in our country for more than four hundred years. I will stake my reputation, my title and my fortune on the truth of my words."

"In that case," thundered the king, "I am rescinding the decree." He removed his sword from its sheath and sliced the parchment into pieces. Then he said assertively: "I adjourn this session of the Sejm."

When I returned to the Duchess Halina, I acted like a crazy man. I was angry, depressed, uncontrollable, confused. I didn't know who I was. Was I still a Jew or was I a Catholic? Days passed. Halina tried to make me happy, but I spurned her efforts. I raised my voice. I almost hit her. I could not stand to be in her presence. Our children disgusted me. My life was chaotic.

One night she said to me: "Since you returned from Warsaw, things are not the same. Maybe you are just overtired from the taxing trip. Why don't you ride around all the villages on our property and check up on the innkeepers, the woodchoppers, the fishermen, the millers, the peasants. You might return refreshed."

I thought her idea was good, so I accepted her advice, primarily because it would give me an opportunity to think. The next day, I loaded a wagon with supplies, and set off by myself for the neighboring villages.

I travelled around the area for days, trying to reconstruct my life, attempting to form a solution to my religious dilemma. After wandering for two weeks, I found myself in the vicinity of Kolbesof, the *shtetl* of Rebbe Avraham Yehoshua Heschel.[4] Knowing his reputation for helping people in trouble, I decided that I would talk to him. I made arrangements with the innkeeper in Kolbesof to take care of my wagon. I told him I had to see someone and that I would return in a few hours to spend the night under his roof. I unhitched one of the horses and rode toward the rebbe's house. It was almost midnight when I arrived there.

Only the glimmer of a candle flickered from a corner of the darkened house; the rebbe was the only one awake at this hour. He was studying. He opened the door when he heard the gentle rapping of my carved cane on the door. He was frightened by the appearance of a well dressed Polish noble on his doorstep.

"I have to talk to you," I whispered. "May I come in?"

He hesitated to open the door wider, but as his deep eyes penetrated mine, he seemed to relax a bit and beckoned me to enter. He led me to the room where he had been studying and pointed to a chair.

"You must be in terrible trouble to come here at this hour of the night," he whispered softly. "How can I help you?"

I started from the beginning. As I spoke, I noticed that every muscle in his face tensed. His eyes reddened, his lips trembled, his cheeks hardened. I realized that I had not alleviated his fear by telling him my story. I continued: "I have come because I honestly believe you can advice me how to return to my people. I admit I made a tragic mistake. I want to repent, to change my life. Please, tell me what I must do."

He arose from his chair and began pacing the length and breadth of the small study. Suddenly, he screamed.

"You have not come here to repent. You are a famous Polish prince. Your presence here will be a pretext for some sort of *pogrom* against my people. Please, go away before something terrible happens! Every minute you sit in my house, the danger increases."

I sat helplessly, refusing to move.

"Please," I pleaded, "I am a famous Polish prince, but I was born a Jew. I want you to tell me how to return to my people. I swear, no harm will come to you or to them."

The *rebbe* continued pacing. Then he noticed my carved cane. He lifted it roughly, waved it back and forth over my head and thundered: "I will not guide you back to Judaism."

"I will not move until you show me what to do," I whispered. My eyes pleaded for his help. Tears welled up within me and rolled silently down my cheeks. We sat facing each other all night. Finally, the rebbe relented.

He said: "I know now that I must help you. I know that the *pintele yid*—the spark of your Jewish soul—was never washed away from you when you were baptized. You proved it by saving your people from a tragic blood libel. This is what you have to do.

First, return to Duchess Halina. Tell her that in your wanderings you found out about some exciting business opportunities in Amsterdam and that you have to go there. Take enough money with you so that it appears that you are investing in them. Tell her you might be away for many months, that you will inform her about the progress of your dealings. I will give you a letter to Rabbi Shaul Levinshtam.[5] Take it with you to Amsterdam and give it to him. He will help you."

I thanked Rebbe Avraham Yehoshua Heschel for his advice and bid him farewell. I returned to the inn for the night. The next morning I started travelling toward my home.

It took a little time to rearrange my life, but I followed the directions of the *rebbe* explicitly.

Arriving in Amsterdam, I went directly to the house of Rabbi Levinshtam. I did not have to say too much after handing him the letter of introduction. He invited me to stay in his home until I could establish myself in the city.

I did not have to go through a ritual conversion, for I had been born a Jew. But as many converts have done before me, I took a new name. I renamed myself Avraham Yosef ben Avraham.

I spent the majority of my waking hours studying Torah. Occasionally, I went to the marketplace, buying and selling merchandise as a means of supporting myself; it was what I knew how to do best.

I was content to live among my people in Amsterdam for the remaining years of my life.

The Silver Age of Polish Jewry: Chapter Forty-One

A Sacred Trust
— Commentary —
Remember Who You Are

We often ponder, "What are the forces that kept Judaism alive for four thousand years?"

This story of Rabbi Yitzchak Isaac "Chaver" Wildmann may give us some answers. There is no doubt that we find here one of the most moving forms of pedagogy, which must have impacted upon Jewish youth, not only in the 19th century, but at many junctures of our history, particularly when the going got rough. When I finished reading the story I was actually in tears. I see this form of teaching as experiential education, which nurtures not only the intellect, but also the heart and spirit and also the body. How startled these youngsters were when they saw a rabbi who had practised that precious Jewish quality of *Mesirat Nefesh*, self-sacrifice - dressing up as a drunken peasant (and it wasn't Purim!), risking his well-being before these treacherous people. Perhaps by some spiritual osmosis he kindled their hearts with a desire to meet the challenge of remaining Jewish over a period of several years of attempts at conversion and peril to their physical survival. He modeled the attribute of *Mesirat Nefesh* in a manner their young minds could grasp without having reached an age of intellectual development. And the remarkable thing is that this type of teaching remained with them over a period of 31 years!

This concept of experiential education is most significant. It is introduced to the child early when he is given a bit of honey or candy as he begins *Aleph-Bet*, to associate Torah with sweetness.

Another intriguing phrase is the use of the expression 'holy sheep.' What an endearing way for the rabbi to express his deep love for these kidnapped children. In a different setting we used to use the same phrase on *Simchat Torah*, which turns the limelight on children, having them carry flags and little Torahs, giving them *Aliyot*, calling them to the Torah. At that time we used to call our children *Tzon Kedoshim*—holy sheep. Who could forget such a beautiful expression!

This story speaks to this confused generation of Jews, many of whom are searching for tools for continuity, but who do not know how to find them. One of the answers lies in charismatic teachers, whose greatest assets are their humanity and their ability to transmit Jewish values and our sacred heritage through the medium of spiritual love.

Rabbi Chaim Richter
Director of Chaplaincy and Practicing Psychotherapist
Jewish Federation of South Broward, Hollywood, Florida

The Silver Age of Polish Jewry: Chapter Forty-Two

The Pale of Settlement

Approximate area at the end of the 19th century

✡

Area names are of the 19th century.
Specific boundries are today's boundries.

Chapter Forty-Two
REMEMBER WHO YOU ARE

Time Line

70 c.e.   600 c.e.   1000 c.e.   1400 c.e.   1600 c.e.   1800 c.e.   2000 c.e.

Location: Poland/Lithuania, Russia, the Pale of Settlement

[**Ed.** The "Statute of Military Conscription," the Cantonist Laws, were promulgated by Tzar Nicholas I, the tyrant, in 1827, to force Jewish boys, beginning with twelve year olds to serve in the military. It was "a training school for producing a generation of de-Judaized Jews, who were completely Russified and Christianized...." Clinging with patriarchal devotion to their religion, estranged from the Russian people, and kept, moreover, in a state of civil rightlessness, Jewish parents ... were terrified ... over the prospect of military service for their sons for the duration of twenty-five years, which was bound to alienate them from their ancestral faith, detach them from their native tongue, their habits and customs of life, and throw them into a strange, often hostile environment. The law demanded that the years of preparatory training for the military, from ages twelve through eighteen, not be included in the mandatory term of active service, thereby effectively adding six more years to the twenty-five.

The duty of enlisting the recruits was imposed upon the *Kahal*, the leaders of the Jewish community, who were held responsible for supplying the quota imposed by the government. If the quota of twelve year old boys remained unfulfilled, the government employed kidnappers to hunt for fugitives, or seize boys as young as eight years old. The kidnappers perpetrated incredible cruelties upon the children. Raiding the houses during the nights of the autumn months, the children were torn from the arms of their mothers, taken to special holding cells where they were kept in confinement until their physical examination at the recruiting station, then deported to the eastern provinces and Siberia, distant from any Jewish community.

The children were religiously re-educated; many died of starvation, refusing to eat pork or cabbage soup cooked with lard; others were force-fed salted fish, denied water and tortured in other ways until they consented to formal baptism; some chose a martyr's death.]

Rabbi Yitzchak Isaac "Chaver" Wildmann[1] travelled through one of the small *shtetlach* in the northern part of the Pale of Settlement shortly after Sukkot.

[**Ed.** In the year 1792, in an official act of the Russian government, Tzarina Catherine the Great decreed that the former Polish kingdom, which Russia annexed, be called the Pale of Settlement. She prohibited Jews from venturing forth from this territory. The word "pale" is derived from the Latin palus, meaning a stake or pole, and it was an area surrounded by poles that restricted or confined people to a specific area. The Pale of Settlement was located between the Baltic and Black Sea from north to south, and by the surrounding countries of Russia, Prussia, and Austria on the east and west sides. The Jews were confined to small *shtetlach*, villages, in the Pale of Settlement, the western provinces of the Russian empire, to limit their living in other parts of the country. They were treated as a hostile population, different from other Russian citizens, unworthy of equal citizenship.]

As his wagon crossed through the main street of the densely populated area, he heard anguished cries.

Knowing that the Cantonist Laws were carried out during the autumn months, he calculated that the kidnappers must have struck the previous night. He knocked on a few doors; in each house the story was the same. The distraught parents could not even speak. It seemed to him that a child had been kidnapped from every house in the *shtetl*.

"I know that I can do nothing to comfort them. I can do nothing to alleviate their pain. I also know that I can not rescue the kidnapped children, but maybe I can find a way to see them, to strengthen them for the treacherous journey upon which they are about to embark."

Immediately, he put a plan into action. Jumping back into his wagon, he set out for the outskirts of the *shtetl*, where the peasants lived.

He rode around for a few minutes, then guided his horse

under the shade of a broad branched tree. Tying the wagon to the tree, he alighted and set out to find a peasant who would be willing to exchange his tattered clothing for his garments. It took only a few minutes. Walking over to the peasant, he said, "I need to exchange your clothes for mine. Since you, no doubt, will think this is an unfair exchange, take this money and buy yourself another pair of pants and a shirt."

Disguising himself in the peasant's clothes, he headed back toward the main street of the *shtetl*. Pretending to be drunk, he cursed and shouted, staggered and tripped, coughed and spit, shuffling from one side of the road to the other.

It didn't take long for the constable to notice the drunken stranger. The constable grabbed him by the shoulders and turned him forcefully around.

"Let me see your identity papers," he growled!

"Identity papers! What are identity papers?" sputtered the rabbi. "Why do you need my identity papers?" he laughed raucously.

"You don't live here. You must be the thief that is terrorizing the merchants who live in those big houses on the hill. You better come with me!" shouted the constable.

He dragged the rabbi to the jailhouse and pushed him into the same cell in which the kidnapped children were fearfully awaiting their fate. He slammed the door and stalked out.

When the children saw the drunken stranger, they huddled into the corner; they watched him suspiciously as he slowly approached them.

Calmly, he whispered: "Do not think that I am a drunken peasant. My name is Yitzchak Isaac. I am the rabbi of Volkovsysk. I happened to be passing through this *shtetl* when I found out that all the eight year old boys were kidnapped last night. I disguised myself so that I would be placed in the same jail cell with you. I wanted to talk to you."

The startled children gazed at the face of the rabbi. "I want you to know," he continued, "that all of you are fated for many years of living in an alien, hostile environment. I wish it was in my power to free you from this fate, but it is impossible to challenge the power of the Russian government. Nevertheless, whatever happens to you, remember who you are, children of holy forefathers, Abraham, Isaac and Jacob. Be as loyal to your faith as you possibly can; try to eat only that food which is permissible for a Jew to eat, remember to recite *Sh'ma* morning and night, do not speak evil words or think evil thoughts, care for and help each other."

He pulled them very close to him and told them the stories of the martyrdom of Rabbi Akiva[2] and of untold numbers of others who had preceded them by sanctifying the Name of God.

He told them one story after another. Neither the boys nor the rabbi slept that night.

"You are holy sheep," he murmured. Quoting a passage from the liturgy of *Rosh Hashana* and *Yom Kippur*, holy days that had just passed, he continued: "*K'va-ka-rat ro-eh ed-ro, ma-a-vir tzo-no ta-chat shiv-to,* As the Shepherd of Israel pastures His flock, making them pass under His staff, So He will ... (care) ... for the souls of all the living; and shall apportion the needs of all His creation...."[3]

"No doubt, I will be beaten severely for having tricked my way into this jail cell, but no matter. I don't know if I will still be living when you are released from military service. However, knowing that you will be loyal to our faith, I'm certain that our souls will meet in the eternal world. My precious, holy sheep," he cried, unable to control the tears that silently rolled down his cheeks. "I know that nothing you do will ever be embarrassing before the Heavenly Court. I know that you will always try to conduct yourselves like Jews!"

Thirty one years later, after having survived the most barbaric brutality, they returned to their *shtetl* and resumed their lives as Jews.

A Sacred Trust
— Commentary —
The Holy Shekel

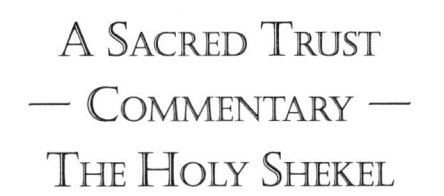

Twentieth century Jewish history has unquestionable taught us that to not see clearly the potential for evil that is present in human beings and not to guard one's self accordingly is to court disaster.

But along side that notion, the Torah also teaches us, "to see the good." Even if we observe a fellow Jew in an ambiguous, compromising situation, we should avoid a snap judgement and give him the benefit of the doubt.

How far should one stretch in order to extend the benefit of the doubt?

After you read this story, you may be ready to answer that question.

Rabbi Meir Fund
Rabbi, Flatbush Minyon
Brooklyn, New York

The Silver Age of Polish Jewry: Chapter Forty-Three

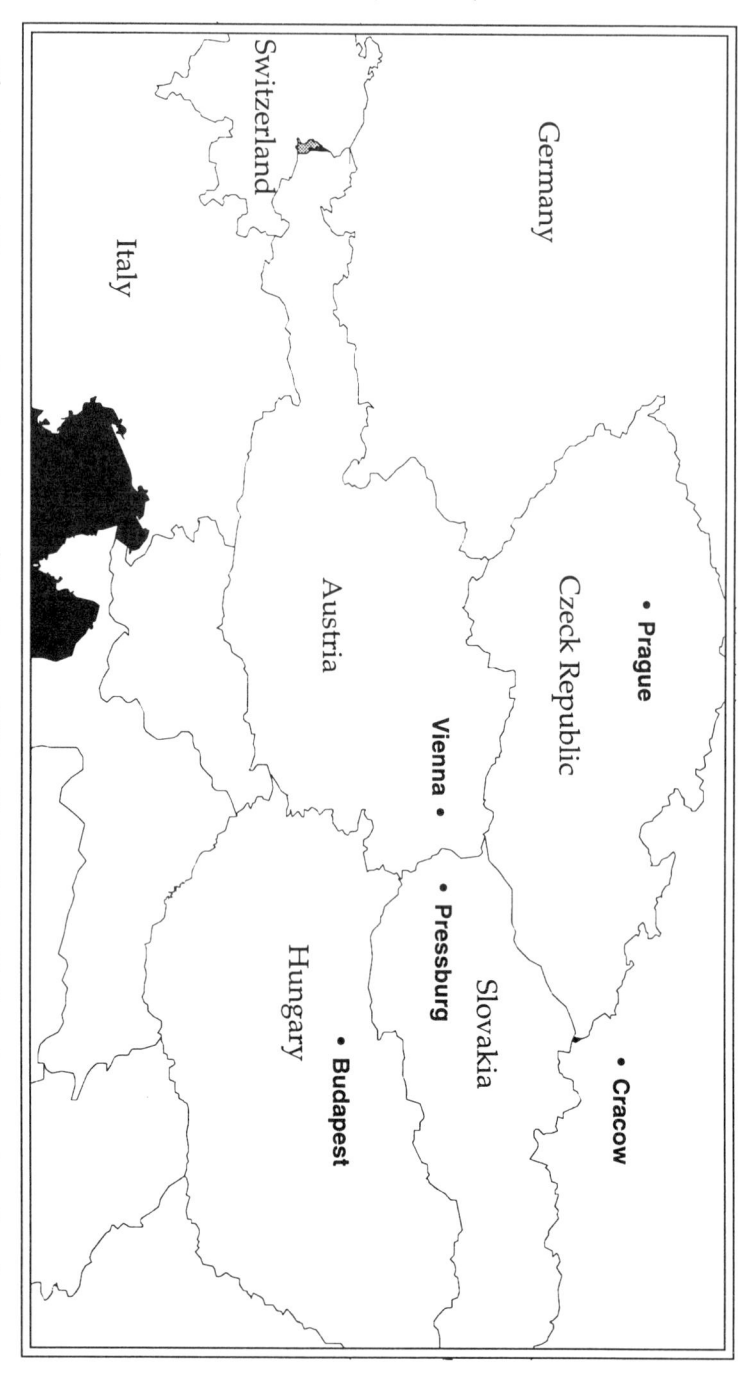

The Austria-Hungary Empire Area of the time of "The Holy Shekel" showing modern borders.

Chapter Forty-Three
THE HOLY SHEKEL

Time Line

70 c.e.   600 c.e.   1000 c.e.   1400 c.e.   1600 c.e.   1800 c.e.   2000 c.e.

Location: Austria/Hungary

The unified Austrian-Hungarian empire separated into two distinct countries in 1867. The large Jewish population that lived within the borders of the two countries were emancipated. The walls of the ghetto that had incarcerated them for a thousand years were broken down as the secular society opened to their full participation as citizens.

That autumn,[1] a Congress was convened to decide which roles the emancipated Jews could fill in the Hungarian government. The Congress deliberated for four months.

After that Congress concluded, Jewish leaders from Germany, Austria, Hungary, Poland, and Russia met to ponder specific religious issues effecting world Jewry. The agenda included the following questions:

1. Could emancipated Jewry survive in exile?
2. Should young Jews be encouraged to immigrate to *Eretz Yisrael*, then under Turkish rule, to begin the process of rebuilding the homeland?
3. Which language, Hebrew or *Yiddish*, should be recommended to combat assimilation?

It was at this convention that the "holy *shekel*" disappeared.

[**Ed.** *Shekels* were used for a variety of purposes among which were the ceremony for the redemption of the firstborn son; the means whereby Jews were counted during a census; purchasing sacrifices to be offered in the Holy Temple; refurbishing the Holy Temple.]

Towards evening, at the closing banquet of the convention, the assembled religious leaders were satiated with the joy of having shared Torah and Talmudic learning. They had formulated guidelines for the questions on their agenda. Rabbi Avraham Shmuel Binyamin Sofer, the Kesav Sofer,[2] stood up at his place at the head of the table and raised his hand for attention. He was smiling mysteriously.

Silence spread over the room as the delegates waited patiently for him to speak. "*Ra-bo-siy*, my honored colleagues," his voice echoed throughout the hall. "Tonight I want to show you something very special. That which I am about to show you was given to me by my father, of blessed memory, who received it from his father, who received it from his father. It is a family treasure that can be traced back for many generations, since the period of the Holy Temple. There is nothing in this world like it; it is the only one of its kind."

The rabbis sat on the edges of their chairs, breathing deeply, curious, unable to imagine what the Kesav Sofer was about to show them.

"This," he continued, putting his hand in his pocket and withdrawing a velvet pouch, "is ..." Slowly, he unwrapped it and laid it on the palm of his hand, holding it at an angle so everyone could see. "This is a *holy shekel* dating from the period of the Holy Temple. This *holy shekel* has been in my family ever since. I would like each one of you to be able to see it so I will pass it around beginning at my right. Please examine it and continue passing it until everyone has had a chance to see it."

Silence turned to animated excitement. The first Rabbi took the *holy shekel* from the Kesav Sofer, turned it over in his hand, examined it closely, and passed it to his colleague. The *holy shekel* passed from hand to outstretched hand, half way around the long banquet table. Suddenly, one of the rabbis seated on the opposite side of the table whispered to his colleague next to him:

The Holy Shekel

"Where is the *holy shekel*? It should have been passed to us by now!" They asked around, but it was nowhere to be found.

They hoped they could find it before the Kesav Sofer realized that it had been missing, but he could tell by their pale faces and their dumbstruck expressions that something was terribly wrong. Confusion gradually spread throughout the room.

How could the *holy shekel* have disappeared? It was simply being passed from one hand to another. It had to be in that room, on that table, in someone's pocket, somewhere. They searched the floor, around their chairs, under the table, on their dinner plates ... but it had disappeared.

The Kesav Sofer rose. In a quivering voice, he said: "I don't have to tell you how much that *holy shekel* means to me. I am not accusing anybody of stealing it. I beg you to please search your pockets or your wallets. Perhaps one of you confused the *holy shekel* with the coins of this land and put it away, by mistake. Please," he pleaded, "will everybody stand up and search themselves?"

Because everyone felt the anguished pain of the Kesav Sofer, each person stood up next to his place and emptied the contents of his pockets and his wallet on the table. But there was no trace of the *holy shekel*.

"With all due respect to you," the Kesav Sofer implored, "I will have to demand that each one of you search the man on his right. I must have it returned to me."

Suddenly, Rabbi Asher, the oldest delegate, spoke. "I have a suggestion to make. I would like to propose that each one of us search his own person one more time for fifteen minutes before we search each other." In deference to his being the elder of the convention, they agreed to wait.

The minutes dragged like a rock being pushed across a sand dune. Each person searched himself once again, but the *holy shekel* did not appear.

When the time passed, Rabbi Asher spoke again. "I am

pleading with you that we extend the time another fifteen minutes."

Most people present could not understand the reason for what appeared to be time delaying tactics. But when the Kesav Sofer acquiesced to an additional fifteen minutes in deference to Rabbi Asher who had been his father's contemporary, everyone agreed to wait. They were not prepared when Rabbi Asher asked for fifteen minutes more.

"This will be the last time I will ask you to wait to begin the body searches," his voice quivered. "I will not ask you to delay one more minute after the next fifteen. "

Some rabbis whispered, others shouted. Pandemonium! The room was ready to explode. Suspicion, doubt, nagged at the consciences of most everyone.

They wondered why Rabbi Asher wanted to delay the body searches. Two people suggested that they search him immediately for it seemed obvious that he was the one who had the *holy shekel*. But the Kesav Sofer stopped them.

"After all," he said, "Rabbi Asher promised he would not request any more time. Let us be patient meantime and continue to search the area around where we were sitting."

The hall was deathly quiet. Rabbi Asher sat alone, hollow cheeked, stooped back, his right hand shaking on the cane that supported him when he walked, tears streaming down his face, his lips mumbling a silent prayer.

Abruptly, a shriek rent the air. I have the *holy shekel!* I have the *holy shekel!* screamed a close friend of the Kesav Sofer. He ran to the head of the table and placed it in the palm of its rightful owner. Happily, the Kesav Sofer turned the *holy shekel* over and over.

Joy turned to tumult as the close friend tried to explain how he happened to find it.

"While we were waiting for the time to pass," he began, "I nervously played the folds of the tablecloth near my place. I

The Holy Shekel

noticed a roundish, dull silver shape. At first I thought it was the bowl of a spoon, but when I stretched the folds of the tablecloth, I realized that it was the *holy shekel.*"

All the rabbis were embarrassed that they had suspected Rabbi Asher. Sheepishly, they turned to him, begging forgiveness one by one, pleading with him to explain why he had requested delaying the body search.

Rabbi Asher pulled himself up to his full height. "*Ra-bo-siy,* my respected colleagues," he began. "I have lived longer than any one in this room, for I remember studying with Rabbi Moshe Sofer, the Chasam Sofer, the revered father of Rabbi Avraham Shmuel Binyamin who so ably follows in his father's footsteps. I was honored to be invited to this conference.

"I was very impressed when I saw the Kesav Sofer's *holy shekel.* But it is not true that it is the only one in the world."

He placed his hand in his pocket and withdrew a velvet pouch. Opening it, he removed a replica of the Kesav Sofer's *holy shekel.*

"This *holy shekel,* too, has been in my family's possession for generations, since the time of the Holy Temple. When Rabbi Avraham Shmuel Binyamin, the son of my revered colleague and teacher, told you that his *holy shekel* was the only existing one in the world, I decided not to show mine. I did not want to challenge his word. His *holy shekel* was passed around and mysteriously disappeared. I could not allow myself to be searched lest I be falsely accused of having stolen his *holy shekel.*

"I pleaded for time, hoping that his would be found. Can you imagine the disgrace of the Almighty's Holy Name, of my name, of the names of every rabbi in this room had you found it on my person? In my old age, I would have become a laughing stock, insisting that there were two *holy shekels.*

"Meantime, I prayed from the depth of my heart. Thank God, my prayer has been answered," Rabbi Asher concluded in an almost inaudible voice.

He replaced his *holy shekel* in its velvet pouch and sat down.

Immediately, the *Kesav Sofer* rose. "We have to publicly express our gratitude to the Almighty for the amazing conclusion of this episode. Can you imagine the *che-lul Ha-shem*, the disgrace of God's Name, that would have occured when the people would have found out that one of us had accused a colleague of stealing my *holy shekel*? Could there be any greater embarrassment for us, the religious representatives of the Jewish people?

"We have learned an important lesson from this experience. Even though we all know not to embarrass our friends publicly, we may never have had the opportunity to apply this to a real life situation.

[**Ed.** "One who humiliates his fellow in public has no share in the world to come." *Avot* 3:15][3]

"We have also learned that we must always judge our fellow man in a favorable light even though it is difficult not to assume a person's guilt.

[**Ed.** "Judge everyone favorably." *Avot* 1:6.][4]

"Had we learned nothing more during this conference than the application of this lesson, our conference could still be considered successful."

A Sacred Trust
— Commentary —
Quick Thinking

And the man grew and he went forward and grew until he was very great. And he had sheep and cattle and domestics, and the Philistines were jealous of him. For all the wells which his father Abraham's servants dug in his lifetime, the Philistines stuffed them and filled them with dirt. *B'rayshit, Genesis, 26:13, 14, 15*

The Torah describes the blessings that the Almighty bestowed upon Isaac when he lived in the land of the Philistines and the reaction of the Philistines to Isaac's wealth. The reason for this form of *sinat yisrael*, hatred of the Jewish people was for economic jealousy. Pharaoh enslaved the Jewish people because of xenophobia, fear of strangers. Haman wanted to annihilate the Jewish people because he perceived us to be different. Theological anti-Semitism was written into the Christian bible. It is therefore possible to trace the hatred of the Jewish people from time immemorial.

No wonder the Talmud states: "Rav Chisdah and Rabbah bar Rav Huna said: What is the meaning of Mount Sinai? The mountain where hatred came down to the nations of the world." *Talmud Bavli, Shabbat 89a*

What did these two sages mean? They were playing with the word *Sinai*. On the one hand, the name Mt. Sinai is the mountain of Revelation, the mountain upon which the Jewish people received the Torah. On the other hand, the same Hebrew root forms the word *sin-ah*, and means hatred.

—*Authors*

Polish Jewry: Chapter Forty-Four

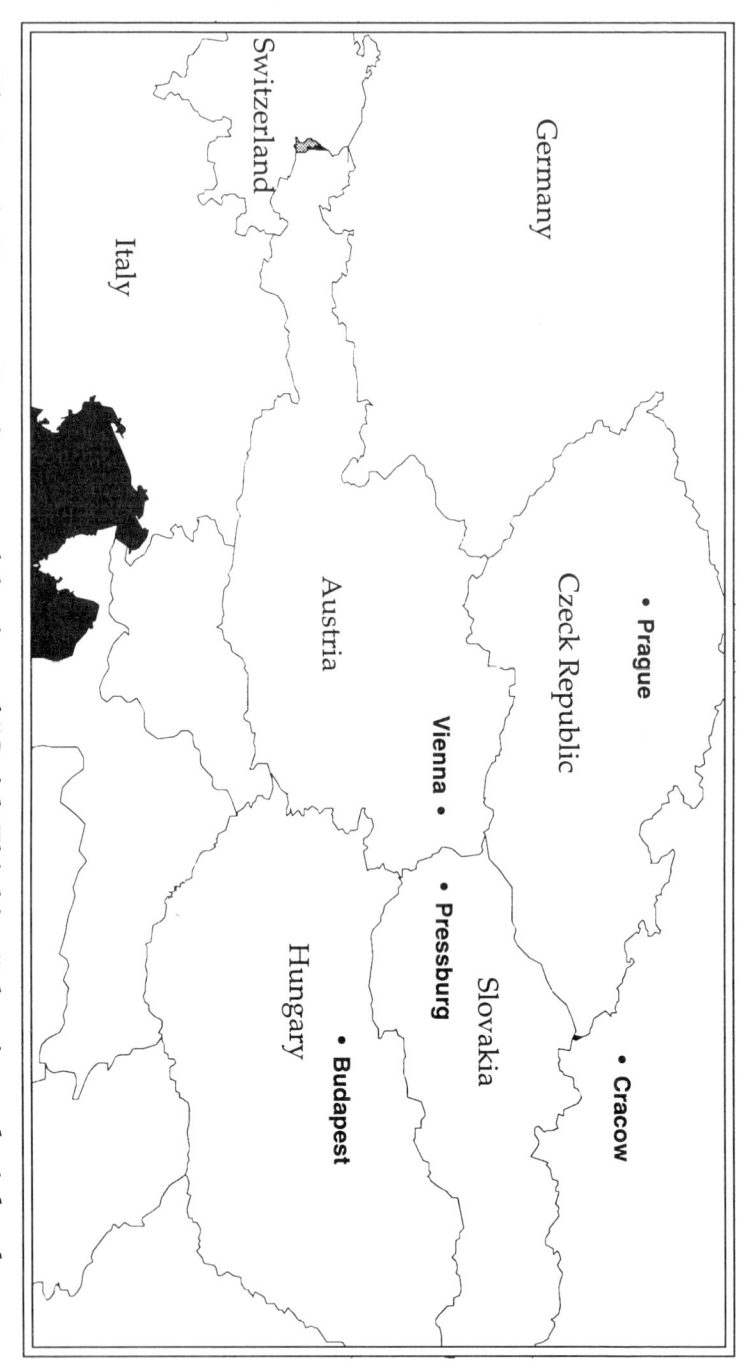

The Austria-Hungary Empire area of the time of "Quick Thinking" showing today's borders.

Chapter Forty-Four
QUICK THINKING

Time Line

| 70 c.e. | 600 c.e. | 1000 c.e. | 1400 c.e. | 1600 c.e. | 1800 c.e. | 2000 c.e. |

Location: Poland

Emperor Francis (Franz) Joseph[1] arranged a royal tour of his empire, accompanied by political and military advisors. Travelling within the province of Galicia, he decided one evening to stop in Cracow, and visit the main synagogue early the following morning.

> [**Ed.** The borders of Poland changed often, beginning with the first partition in 1772. Austria, Prussia (Germany), and Russia alternately annexed different provinces until Poland regained its independence in 1921.]

News of his majesty's visit spread rapidly. That night, two Jew-haters, determined to discredit the Jews. They broke into the synagogue and removed the portrait of the emperor that hung in the lobby. As the emperor marched up the steps of the synagogue, they whispered into his ear that the leaders of the congregation ordered the portrait removed to demonstrate their hate for him and their distrust of his rule.

When the emperor heard these spiteful words, he turned to Rabbi Shimon Sofer,[2] the chief Rabbi of Cracow and a delegate to the Austrian/Hungarian parliament and demanded an explanation. "Is it true that my portrait hangs here all the time, and that it was removed just this morning from the lobby as a sign of protest?"

Rabbi Shimon was stunned for a moment. He could not believe to what lengths Jew-haters would go to discredit the Jewish people. Searching for a plausible reply, he cleared his throat and whispered, "The emperor! May your majesty be exalted. Allow me to explain the mystery of your missing portrait with a parable.

"According to our religious tradition, we are commanded to wrap ourselves in *tefillin* each day as a sign of the Covenant between God and the Jewish people. However, on *Shabbat*, we are specifically commanded not to wrap *tefillin* because *Shabbat* is also a sign of the Covenant between God and the Jewish people. We do not need two signs in one day.

"The conclusion regarding your majesty's portrait is now obvious. Each day, your portrait is prominently displayed in the lobby of this synagogue as a sign of our gratitude for your majesty's caring treatment of his Jewish subjects. The portrait substitutes for your majesty's presence. Today, however, your exalted majesty honors us with his presence. Had we not removed the portrait, it would have insulted your exalted majesty, for why should we look at the portrait when we can honor your person face to face?"

A Sacred Trust
— Commentary —
A Woman Ahead of Her Time

There have always been individual women learned in Jewish texts and Jewish law. Most were taught by their fathers and protected by their husbands. Sara Schneirer was the first to envision a system whereby women as a class of people would have regular access to Jewish education. Her goals were modest and within the cultural expectations of her times: to educate women to teach their children and other women. Today, women are educated along side men to become rabbis and teachers of the entire Jewish people. Yet, without Schneirer's first steps, the right Jewish women enjoy today might still be a long way off.

The reference to *Yehudit* (Judith) makes this an excellent story for Hanukkah. The tale as told here is a European version of the Apocryphal book of Judith, written during the Hasmonean period (1st century BCE) although set in the days of Nebuchadnezzar (6th century BCE) and traditionally read as symbolic of the revolt led by Judah Maccabee. Sara might well have seen herself as a modern day Judith: a single woman, inspired by her faith, acting against all odds, surmounting danger and the apprehension of the Jewish establishment to save her people. Both Judith and Sara exhibit great personal courage and fortitude, teaching us that overcoming one's fear of failure is the first step in realizing any accomplishment of great lasting value.

This story is also appropriate for *Parshat Pinchas* in which the daughters of Zelophehad; Mahlah, Noah, Hoglah, Milcah, and Tirzah (Num. 27:1ff), actively pursue their rights as women. As Schneirer shows, rights are not given but won - by hard work, dedication, and overcoming all obstacles, even the lack of funds for basic teaching equipment when starting a school. Finally, *Parshat Beshallach* also comes to mind, as Miriam leads the women in song after their salvation at the Reed Sea (Ex. 15:20-21). The Sages note that Miriam and the women accompany themselves with instruments because Miriam had enough faith and prophecy to know that she would have good reason to lead songs in praise of God. With hope, vision, and faith one can accomplish great things, as did Sara Schneirer. We have reason, good reason, to celebrate her life and accomplishments.

—*Rabbi Susan Grossman*
Genesis Agudas Achim Congregation, Westchester, New York
Co-editor, **Daughter of the King: Women and the Synagogue**
Member of first class of Conservative women rabbis.

Polish Jewry: Chapter Forty-Five

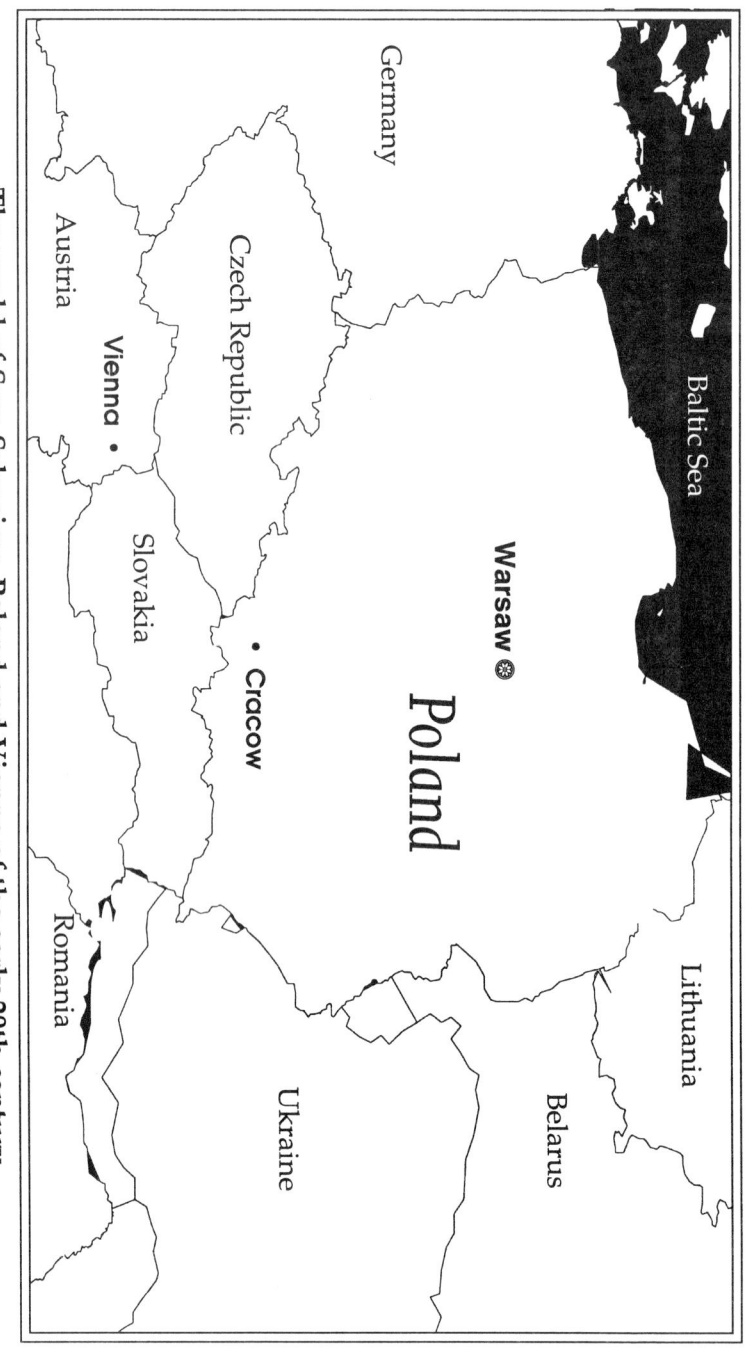

The world of Sara Schneirer, Poland and Vienna of the early 20th century

Chapter Forty-Five
A WOMAN AHEAD OF HER TIME

Time Line

70 c.e.   600 c.e.   1000 c.e.   1400 c.e.   1600 c.e.   1800 c.e.   2000 c.e.

Location: Poland and Austria

Until recently, Jewish girls received a minimum education, mostly from their mothers or older sisters. They were taught to read *Yiddish*, the vernacular language of the *Tzena U'Rena*, the translation of the Torah, how to keep a kosher home, how to sew, how to raise children, and other domestic chores.

What transpired during the past one hundred years that totally changed the methods in which women are educated? Today, young girls study side by side with boys in the same classrooms; they study Talmud in institutions of higher learning; the first class of women studying to be *poskot*, decisors of Jewish law has registered in a New York City *yeshiva*, and in Israel, *toanot*, women who plan to be lawyers, study Talmudic family law before entering law school so that they will be able to specialize in family matters in the Israeli court system.

Who was the charismatic woman who inspired her students to challenge the privileged domain of the male world?

Her name was Sarah Schneirer.[1] She dreamed that women would also understand the perplexities of Talmudic texts and appreciate the excitement of intense learning. She set her priorities to fulfill that dream.

She was a dressmaker by vocation. Returning home after an exhausting day at the shop where she worked, she felt excluded from the lively discussions between her father, her brothers, and their friends who were immersed in lively Talmudic debate. She knew that the men and boys would leave the *shtetl* many times during the year, before the holy days: *Rosh Hashana, Yom Kippur, Succot, Pesach, Shevuot,* and even for *Shabbat,* to spend the time with their *rebbes*. She saw the women waving goodbye from the platform, watching as the train pulled away, being left alone to fend for themselves during the festivals. The happy times of the Jewish calendar year were not times of celebration for the lonely Jewish women.

Many young girls wanted "out" of Judaism under these circumstances, for they were totally excluded anyway. The pull of the newly emancipated world tugged at their beings. They wanted the freedom of self-expression, to dress in modern fashions, to study science and mathematics at the university. They wanted to leave the *shtetl* for the big city, to find jobs and share the opportunities that the emancipation movement had opened for all. Truly, they believed that their mothers were fossils from a different century. Many of them were not interested in the responsibility of caring for or raising another Jewish "old-fashioned" generation. They wanted to be a part of the changing world.

Sarah Schneirer lay awake night after night wondering what she could do to change this situation. Men could immerse themselves in spirituality while women could discuss only new fashions. She became obsessed with the idea that the souls of the women were starving spiritually and could only be satisfied if they were exposed to the same educational opportunities as the men. Night after night, she asked herself how it was possible for little girls to grow up to be Jewish mothers if they were ignorant of Jewish law and tradition? How could they play a pivotal, influential role in their communities, if they did not understand the parameters of the *mitzvot,* of *gemilut chassadim* (unlimited acts of kindness), *bikur cholim* (visiting the sick), *hachnassat kallah* (providing a dowry for a bride), or of the permitted and prohibited laws of the dietary and marriage codes? She wanted the women to be able to preserve the mystery, the awe, the emotion of Jewish life, not the mundane which absorbed most of them when they entered her shop to buy new clothing, ready to exchange the gold of Torah study for the tinsel of mediocrity and gossip.

Fleeing with her family from Cracow in war-torn Poland to Vienna when World War I broke out, she perceived an opportunity to fulfill her dream. The first *Shabbat* after they arrived, she attended services at the *Stumperfergasse Shul*. It was the *Shabbat* of *Chanukah*, and Rabbi Fleisch sermonized about the accomplishments of Yehudit, one of the women who was responsible for inciting the rebellion against the Greek/Syrians. Sarah was impressed.

> [Ed. According to historical narrative dating from the period of the second *bayt hamikdash*, (the Second Temple) a young, beautiful, wealthy widow named Yehudit, daughter of Merari, a resident of the town of Bethulia, determined a plan to lift General Holofornes' seige of her city. She went into his camp. Attracted by her beauty, he invited her to a feast. When he fell asleep, she cut off his head with his sword. Deprived of the leadership, his frightened army fled. The *Book of Yehudit*, which continues this narrative includes two prayer poems, the first uttered before Yehudit sets out for Holofornes' camp, and the second, a thanksgiving song recited after the victory of the Jewish people over their enemy.]

Sarah pondered, "If Yehudit, so long ago, could turn the tides of Jewish destiny by setting a heroic example for the men to follow, so I, in this modern day, can set goals to accomplish my own objectives—to find a way to transmit what I love to the next generation of Jewish women."

She began by attending Rabbi Fleisch's weekly classes and writing the lessons she learned from him. Each week, after *Shabbat*, she meticulously recorded the ideas that she remembered from his sermon. She wanted to show the rabbi her work, for she understood that the notebooks in which she was recording the lessons might be the beginning of the accumulation of the additional knowledge that she needed to teach other women. She was shy, but her goals were so urgent, that one day, she gathered all her *chutzpa* and made an appointment to see Rabbi Fleisch. She wanted him to check her notebooks, to make certain that her notes were accurate.

He was very impressed with her almost total recall of his sermons and lectures. He suggested that she could further her knowledge if she would buy the book of commentaries on the Torah written by Rabbi Shimshon Raphael Hirsch, an eminent German Jewish thinker from the previous generation.[2]

She didn't have spare money, for her family and the other refugees who had resettled in Vienna lived just above the poverty line. So she scrimped and saved. She ate only one meal a day, dinner, and carefully put the money that she would have used to purchase food for lunch into a jar until she had saved the price of the Hirsch commentary. Once she had the precious books in her possession, she didn't stop reading. She understood that it was possible to attain spirituality through learning; the time she spent studying Torah was time of ecstasy.

She continued to record Rabbi Fleisch's lectures. She added notes from the commentaries that she was learning herself.

When the war ended, she returned with her family to Cracow. Her most prized possession was her precious notebooks.

Sarah set about the task of finding students, but found it very difficult to attract young women to her way of thinking. Most of them did not want to change their ways.

She was not discouraged. She knew that all new beginnings, all radical changes are difficult to accomplish.

Finally she assembled five sixteen year old girls who were committed to study with her. She used a simplified version of the inquiry method to plant concepts of belief and faith. She started the school year by asking her students: "How do we obtain bread?"

She did not want them to answer that bread comes from the baker and is purchased in a grocery store. She wanted them to understand that we express our gratitude to God by reciting blessings of thanksgiving; that all our blessings come from Him.

After the introduction to her first lesson, the eager girls were ready to delve into their formal studies. The only available texts were her handwritten notes and the Hirsch commentaries.

They copied her notebooks into notebooks of their own, for there was no blackboard, and no chalk. She explained and encouraged; they learned. Sarah Schneirer was training her first class of women.

Half of her small apartment was converted into her tailor shop, so she could always remain on the premises; the other half was converted into living quarters for herself and her five students. They loved her and she loved them; they thought of her as their second mother.

Her reputation as an inspiring teacher was known throughout Cracow. She attracted more and more students from all over Poland.

Finally, unable to house them in her small apartment, she moved into a large tenement house in the Jewish section of the city. #1 Catachina became Sarah Schneirer's teacher's training school. She knew she could not personally teach the hundreds of girls who sought admission to her school, so she decided that the graduates of each class would become her assistants. She planned to place them in every Jewish community in Poland. She wanted each one of her graduates to establish their own women's teacher's training school. She was on the way toward fulfilling her dream!

At first, she personally escorted her assistants to the small *shtetls* in the vicinity of Cracow. One by one, she introduced them to the leaders of the particular community. Usually, the leaders were impressed enough to undertake the responsibility of setting up and supporting a school for the girls who lived there.

By the outbreak of World War II, the Polish countryside was dotted with schools devoted to teaching Jewish girls the beauty of their Jewish heritage. The teachers had all studied under the guidance of Sarah Schneirer; the schools were called *Bayt Yaakov*.[3]

The *Bayt Yaakov* schools provided for the girls what the *yeshivot* provided for the boys: intellectual stimulation and total commitment, comradeship, organized recreational activities, complete devotion to the perpetuation of the Jewish way of life.

On her deathbed, she wrote an ethical will for her students: ".. I am turning to you, my dear students, who are going out into the great world to guide and train the daughters of Israel and to teach them how to establish Jewish homes. I am convinced that you understand well your great task. We have a good God in heaven, and He aids every person to walk in the way that He desires.... I should like to single out two grave dangers which threaten you, my daughters. Beware of the feeling of pride ... that persuades you to think that you are great in achievements and deserving of honor. On the other hand, keep away from the other extreme, the feeling of inferiority which whispers to you that you are nothing, without any value.... Your weapons of defense are fear of God, reverence, love and service.... Your task is to plant holy seeds in the souls of pure children. In a sense, the destiny of Israel is in your hands...."

Concluding the writing of her ethical will, she kindled the *Shabbat* lights. It was her last *mitzvah*. She was only fifty-two years old when she passed away. Her monument is tangible, for throughout the world, wherever *Bayt Yaakov* schools flourish, she is remembered as the founder, the inspiration, who dreamed the dream of educating Jewish women.

[**Ed.** Mrs. Helen (Hinde) Ostrovsky, now residing in Atlanta, Georgia, remembers Sarah Schneirer. "She was a diminutive woman, always dressed in black from head to toe, symbolic of the modesty she believed personified a Jewish woman. She was always clean as a **pin,** very neat. She talked to her students with her dark eyes. We all knew what she meant with her eye expressions. We students said that she had 'talking eyes.' She never became angry, she always smiled. The girls loved her, and she loved us. She was totally devoted to us. Her face was always shining, reflecting her happiness at seeing the fruition of her dream of creating a school for women. When she explained the biblical verses concerning creation, I believed that heaven and earth swayed under her feet. She taught us to understand the lesson of *Sh'ma*, that basic to Jewish belief is one God. She was such an inspiring teacher. No one ever had a complaint about or against her. She was a real *tzadeket* a holy and sincerely righteous woman. I was a student in Bayt Yaakov during the 1934-1935 school year. My mother perceived the rise of Nazism, and determined to move our family to Eretz Yisrael. I was very upset that I did not have the privilege of finishing the entire course of study, that I had to leave school before graduation. Nevertheless, Sarah Schneirer and the students made me a farewell party. When she bid me farewell, I silently vowed that I would never forget her 'talking eyes.'[4]

A Sacred Trust
— Commentary —
Don't Let the Lights Go Out

Heavenly stories are those that when we read or hear them for the first time, we know that we must tell them to our children. These holy stories tell us about our Jewish past and yet they really teach us how to assure a Jewish future.

The stories that came out of the concentration camps are more than tragic, and yet we rejoice in what they tell us about individual acts of heroism, love and self sacrifice.

In his struggle to kindle the Chanukah lights amidst the growing terror of darkness, Moshele the *Shammash* shows us how the spirit of self-sacrifice insures that the lights will never go out.

—*Authors*

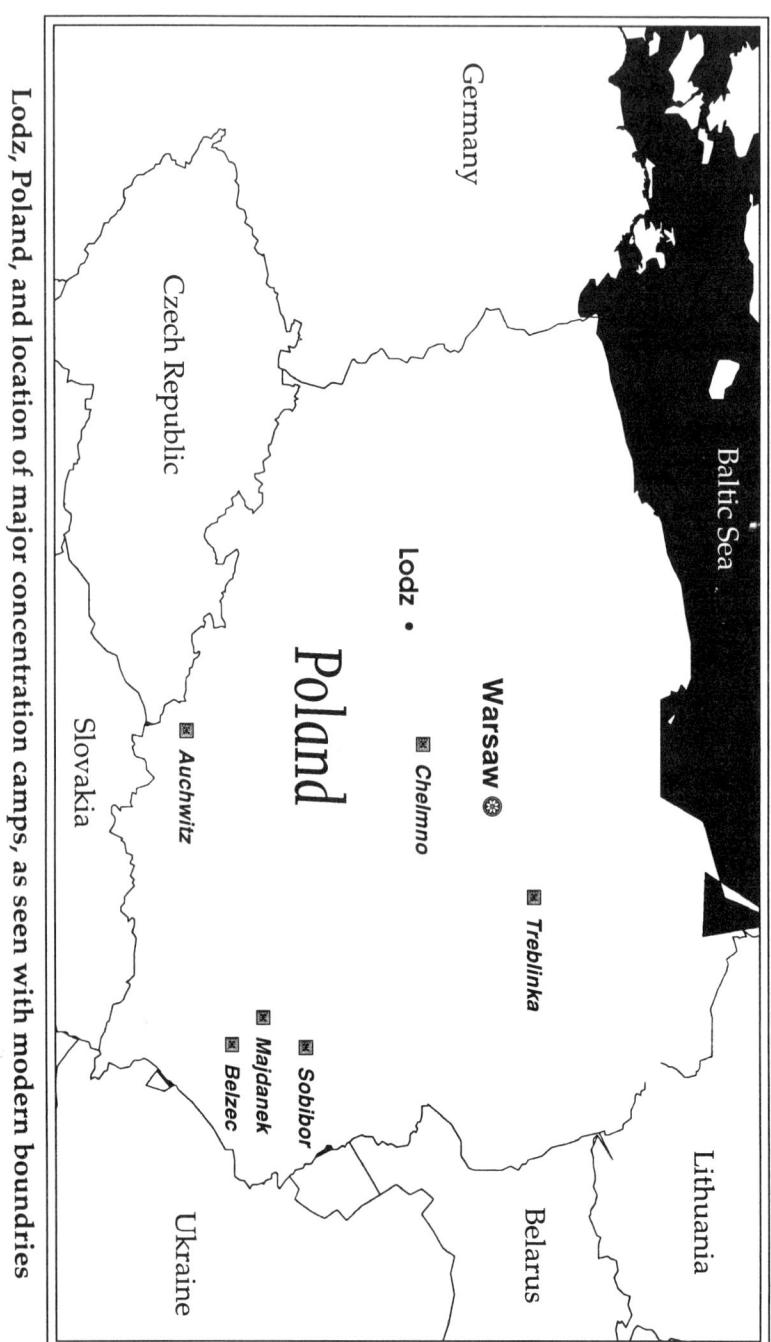

Polish Jewry: Chapter Forty-Six

Lodz, Poland, and location of major concentration camps, as seen with modern boundries

Chapter Forty-Six
DON'T LET THE LIGHTS GO OUT

Time Line

| 70 c.e. | 600 c.e. | 1000 c.e. | 1400 c.e. | 1600 c.e. | 1800 c.e. | 2000 c.e. |

Location: Lodz, Poland

It had been the home of one of the most important Jewish communities in eastern Europe.

Now, barbed wire, wooden fences and chained posts surrounded the ghetto shrouded in the frozen darkness of a fresh snowfall. Just a few months before, the Nazis had cordoned off the eighth district, mostly inhabited by Jews. They created two sections, separated by a thoroughfare that crossed through the ghetto but was not part of it. The Jews were not permitted to cross the thoroughfare that separated one section of the ghetto from the other. Families and friends were splintered.

To show how serious they were about implementing the *Final Solution to the Jewish Problem,* they rounded up Jews, confiscated their property, and deported them to Belzec concentration camp.

[Ed. The term *Final Solution to the Jewish Problem* is associated with the mass murder of Jews during World War II. It was officially formulated at the Wanasee Conference in January, 1942, by Henrich Heydrich. At that time, Adolph Eichman, his assistant, was appointed to design a plan to exterminate Jews more quickly and more efficiently.]

In the ghetto, meagre food supplies were rationed. Epidemics of dysentery, typhus, and typhoid were rampant amongst the starving Jews. One deportation followed another until the population of the ghetto was reduced by half.

The *shul,* built long before the Nazis came to power, was also excluded from both parts of the ghetto area. The remnants of its burned-out structure stood apart on the northeast side of the thoroughfare. Ferocious winds howled through the broken windows of the *shul's* charred structure which had once been the communal house of prayer. Singed curtains flapped boisterously, threatening to fly out the windows on their own. The scorched ark cover lay in shreds at the foot of the ark.

Where the conflagration had destroyed the roof, snow mounds piled on the broken floor. Over to one side, still protected by sections of seared roof, holy books and desecrated parchment sections of Torah scrolls lay strewn. Through the eery silence, the sacred letters howled to be lifted heavenward.

On the first night of *Chanukah,* December, 1939, Moshele prepared to do the job he had done for the past thirty years. Carefully, he inserted a box of matches and two small candles into his shirt pocket; one in honor of the holiday and the other for the *shammash.*

[Ed. The root of the Hebrew word for *shammash* is *shimesh.* It means to serve. The *shammash* candle is the serving candle, the one that is used to light the other candles. Another form of the word *shammish,* is also used to refer to the person who serves the Jewish community in the capacity of a messenger of the Jewish court, the Torah reader, a scribe, the caretaker of the synagogue, the caller who announces the start of *Shabbat* from the marketplace. A long time ago, he was the runner who knocked on doors to awaken people for the morning prayers.]

He put on his threadbare jacket, zipped it up, bid his wife good-bye, walked toward the barbed wire, stooped down and crawled through a hole near the ground, and slithered along the thoroughfare.

Moshele, the *shammish* inched his way, slowly, slowly, crawling stealthily through the frozen wasteland toward the *shul.*

"Ever since I became the *shammish* thirty years ago, I have lit the *Chanukah* candles in this *shul,*" he thought. "I will do it again this year, no matter what."

His thoughts impelled him to move forward, slowly, steadily through the wet snow. He raised his head, measuring the distance he had yet to crawl.

Don't Let the Lights Go Out

"Soon, soon, I will be there," he whispered, urging himself forward, "only a little farther, and I will be able to light the *Chanukah* candles in the *shul*."

Finally, Moshele pulled himself breathlessly into the charred structure, cautiously rolled over, and sat up in a corner still covered by the seared roof. Peering into the intense darkness of an almost moonless night, trying to accustom his eyes to the murky gloom, he saw the desecrated Torah scrolls and holy books. Tears welled up in Moshele's eyes. He sat for a long time, pondering. "What do they want from us? Why have they singled us out for such persecution? Are these beasts really part of the human race? How long will it last this time?"

Moshele pulled himself up to his full height. His shoulders heaved painfully, he sighed deeply, trying to control himself. He stumbled over to the uncurtained holy ark and prayed, "Master of the World! You swore, by Your Holy Name that the light of Jewish life would never be extinguished. The lights are dimming all around us. Please, don't let the lights go out."

Leaning on the holy ark, he bent his head into the crook of his elbow and wept pitifully.

Moshele stepped backwards. The snow mounds were on his right side and the desecrated heaps of Torah scrolls and holy books lay to his left. Wearily, he searched for a place to sit down. Out of the corner of his eye, he recognized an overturned stool, the kind used by mourners. He turned it upright and sat down to think.

"I risked my life to kindle the first *Chanukah* light. I have two candles and matches in my pocket, but where will I find the *Chanukah menorah* among this wreckage? The bookcases are overturned, bare wires hang in place of the chandeliers, even the upholstery on the special circumcision chair for the prophet Elyahu has been shredded."

[**Ed.** The prophet Elyahu (Elijah) is known as the "angel of the Covenant of circumcision" and the protector of children. A chair is reserved for him at the *brit millah*, the circumcision ritual.]

Looking around the carnage in the desolate *shul*, he noticed that the enemy had overlooked the brass *menorahs* which adorned the east wall, quietly glittering in the darkness. Walking toward them, he broke out in joyous laughter.

"They missed ripping the *menorah* from the wall. The candles I prepared to light last *Shabbat* are still in the *menorah*. It's a miracle! What a miracle. I will light one of the *Shabbat* candles from last week as my *Chanukah* candle. The light of the *Shabbat* candle will last much longer than the little flickering flame of the *Chanukah* candle that I have hidden in my pocket."

Moshele was ecstatic. He put his hand into his shirt pocket to withdraw the matches, but his pocket was empty. Beads of perspiration dotted his forehead. Hastily, he searched his pants pockets, his tattered jacket pocket, but he had no matches to light his *Chanukah* candle.

He stared at the candles, imagining that they pleaded with him to light them. He heard them sing, "*Nu*, Moshele, light us, light us. Tonight is the first night of *Chanukah*. Jewish life must never be extinguished."

The words and the melody were carried off in the wind.

"I came here to kindle the *Chanukah* lights," Moshele said to himself, "and I won't leave until I have done so, no matter what will happen. The light I will kindle tonight must reach the Heavenly Throne. It must bear witness that His children are suffering."

He turned all his pockets inside out. Moshele fell to his feet and crawled around the debris, lifting, turning over, feeling carefully for the dropped match box. He visualized the celebration of *Shabbat* in this *shul*, the sea of white *taletot (talit, singular)* covering the bent heads of men robed in white *kittels*, hundreds of children marching around the *shul* on *Simchat Torah*, the singing, the Torah reading, the joy. Determined, he screamed: "I must light these candles. Those memories must never be erased."

Don't Let the Lights Go Out

But, he could not find the matches. Still wet from having crawled through the falling snow an hour before, he pulled himself up in front of the *menorah* and forlornly prayed again. "Master of the World! You know that I have tried to fulfill Your commandment of kindling the *Chanukah* lights. Please accept my intention as if I had fulfilled the commandment."

> [Ed. Rabbi Assi said: "Even if one merely thinks of performing a *mitzva*, but is forcibly prevented from doing so, the Almighty ascribes it to him as though he has performed it." *Talmud Bavli, Kiddushin 40a*]

He moved toward the holy ark, kissed the remnants of the desecrated Torah scrolls that still stood within it, bent to lift the singed pages of the holy books to his lips. Hot tears rushed from his eyes as he said good-bye. "Please forgive me for not picking you up, for not taking you with me," he whispered, caressing the singed pages.

He turned to leave.

Moshele stooped and crawled along the same path on which he had traveled a short time before. He crawled as quickly as he could, trying to reach the break in the barbed wire before he was discovered. As he squeezed through the hole, his nearly frozen hands felt a small box. "The matches! The matches!" he cried joyfully.

Unhesitatingly, he turned, wiggled back through the hole once again, and headed toward the *shul*. Suddenly, it seemed he had the energy of a young man.

"I will be able to light the *Chanukah* candles. I will be able to light the *Chanukah* candles," he sang softly as he crawled.

Moshele stood in front of the *menorah*. His voice cracked:

Ba-ruch ... a-sher kid-sha-nu b'mitz-vo-tav v'tze-va-nu l'had-lik nayr shel Chanukah.

> [Ed. Blessed are You, our God, King of the Universe, Who has sanctified us with His commandments and has commanded us to kindle the *Chanukah* light.]

Ba-ruch ... she-a-sah ne-sim l'a-vo-tay-nu ba-ya-mim ha-haym baz-man ha-zeh.

[**Ed**. Blessed are You, our God, King of the Universe, Who has wrought miracles for our forefathers, in those days and in our time.]

Ba-ruch ... she-he-che-ya-nu v'ke-ma-nu v'he-ge-ya-nu laz-man ha-zeh.

[**Ed**. Blessed are You, our God, King of the Universe, Who has kept us alive, sustained us, and brought us to this season.]

"It is very dangerous to remain here now," he whispered to himself. "Surely, they will see the reflection of my *Chanukah* lights." He backed away from the *menorah*, from the uncurtained holy ark, saying good-bye again. Reaching the edge of the charred structure, he ran out of the *shul*, down the thoroughfare, toward the hole in the barbed wire. Locating it, he stooped and crawled through, breathed a sigh of relief, turned and looked back at the *shul*. The candlelight still flickered through the broken window pane of the desolate, burned structure. The wind had not extinguished the flame. He moved toward the protection of a tree.

"Maybe there is some hope in all this darkness. I will stand here until the last glimmer of light," he thought weakly.

Moshele leaned on the tree, staring at the flickering light. Snow continued to fall. The flakes covered him, head to toe. In a few hours, Moshele looked like another branch of the tree.

The wind howled. Pieces of desecrated parchment and singed pages whirled in the blistery squalls, crying as they ascended heavenward.

When the rays of dawn broke over the horizon, the people began moving about the ghetto. Soon the *minyon* gathered in the cellar that had replaced the *shul* for the morning prayers. They waited and waited for Moshele to appear, but he did not come.

A few men decided to go out and search for the *shammish* who had not missed a *minyon*, morning or night, for thirty years. They searched everywhere in the ghetto, but he was nowhere to be found. Looking toward the *shul*, they saw only the flickering light of the *menorah*.

Part Five
The Jewish American Experience

Time Line

| 70 c.e. | 600 c.e. | 1000 c.e. | 1400 c.e. | 1600 c.e. | 1800 c.e. | 2000 c.e. |

Location: North America in the "New World"

Introduction

America has always been a country comprised of multi-ethnic immigrant groups. The Jewish people comprised one of the earliest immigrant groups. The impetus for this Jewish migration was a response to persecution. The immigrants sought freedom, dignity, civil rights, and economic opportunity.

Four migration waves of the Jewish people to these American shores can be identified.

The first immigrants were Sephardic, refugees from the Spanish Inquisition. Some of the refugees who came to the "new world" with explorers on voyages of discovery settled throughout the Caribbean Islands. Others settled in Brazil, which, until 1654 was a Dutch colony and provided the Jews with a haven of refuge. When the Portuguese captured Brazil, they imported the dreaded Inquisition to the "new world." Twenty-three Jews who lived in Brazil fled with their meager belongings aboard the *St. Charles* to New Amsterdam (New York). Peter Stuyvesant, the governor of New Amsterdam, did not welcome them. He thought they would become public charges or compete with the local merchants. But the Dutch West India Company ordered him to accept them. (*The First*

Part Five: The American Jewish Experience

Jews in New Amsterdam: Excerpt from the Diary of Peter Stuyvesant, Chapter Forty-seven)

At the time of the American revolution a hundred and thirty years later, this small Jewish population had multiplied to about 3,000. (*The Light of a Small Candle Shines at Valley Forge,* Chapter Forty-eight)

The second migration were refugees from Germany who sought equal rights and economic opportunities. Many became peddlers or successful merchants. Others became bankers and founders of department stores. Some crossed the continent, hoping to prosper from the gold rush. Still others settled in towns along the way.

Sometimes, the only Jew in town was the owner of the general store. Because a structured Jewish community was almost non-existent in the interior of this country, it was very difficult for these Jews to maintain their Jewish identity. (*Rebecca and Judah,* Chapter Forty-nine)

Nevertheless, the Jews impressed their non-Jewish neighbors with their moral and family values. (*Concerning the Jews,* Chapter Fifty)

The third migration consisted of eastern European Jews who came to the "new world" to escape abject poverty and unrelenting persecution. They came in droves, more than two and a half million in the forty years between 1881-1921. Most of them settled in the lower east side of New York. Often, the first view they had of America was the Statue of Liberty. *(The New Colossus,* Chapter Fifty-one)

Others settled in cities in the northeast and the midwest, but the majority experienced similar adjustment problems. Many struggled to maintain their Judaism at any sacrifice. (*Rochel Leah's Parochet Comes to America,* Chapter Fifty-two)

Many of the immigrants wanted to acculturate, to become "Yankees." Some of them thought that the way to success was working seven days a week. *Shabbat* and *Yom Tov* became memories of the "old country." (*The Bintel Brief,* Chapter Fifty-three)

The second generation of the third migration immigrants acculturated; the third generation began to assimilate. The day school, a system of education that combined secular and Jewish studies each day, stands today in the forefront of stemming the tide of assimilation. (*Tuition,* Chapter Fifty-four)

The fourth migration were Holocaust survivors. They came to America with the hope of rebuilding their shattered lives. They were too stunned to talk about their experiences for at least twenty years after World War II ended. Then they revealed the truth. Since no one can fathom the immensity of the number six million, the story of one survivor describes what actually happened in the death camps of Europe, and how he has rebuilt his life in America (*One Survivor's Story,* Chapter Fifty-five)

Now, in the last decade of the twentieth century, a phenomenal *teshuva* (return) movement is occuring, attracting acculturated and assimilated Jews to learn about and explore their glorious heritage. (*In Memory,* Chapter Fifty-six)

We do not know the end of our American story. We are living the history of American Jewry every single day.

Part Five: The American Jewish Experience

A Sacred Trust
— Commentary —
The First Jews in New Amsterdam

Many readers will be surprised to know that Jews arrived in America well over 300 years ago. Our history here began with 23 immigrants who were considered problematic, and a threat to native life. They incurred the wrath of the ruling authority, and became the targets of immediate and baseless animosity.

In a period of history that echoes the first Jewish footsteps into biblical Egypt, complete with a Pharoah, New Amsterdam Governor Peter Stuyvesant is less than enthusiastic about the incoming Jewish population. He begins his diary entry by asserting he has nothing against the Jews, yet completes this excerpt by calling Jews deceitful and infectious, and admits to praying for their expulsion.

What began as the experiment of a few families trying to survive in New Amsterdam has become New York City, the third largest Jewish community in the world. And the secret of their success and growth can be found in the response Governor Stuyvesant received from the Board of the Dutch West India Company in denying him the authority to expel the "penniless Jews." The Board affirmed the right of the Jews to remain, provided "the poor among them shall not become a burden ... but be supported by their own nation."

Well, we didn't have a nation. But through an enviable network of emotional, financial and spiritual support, Jews are always helping each other. Everyone points to the Jews as a model community of care. We have a proud legacy of extending hands and hearts to family, friends and neighbors. It's something we are supremely honored to be known for, and something Peter Stuyvesant might have gotten to know about us, instead of resenting us.

Rabbi Elan Adler
Beth Tfiloh Congregation
Baltimore, Maryland

The American Jewish Experience: Chapter Forty-Seven

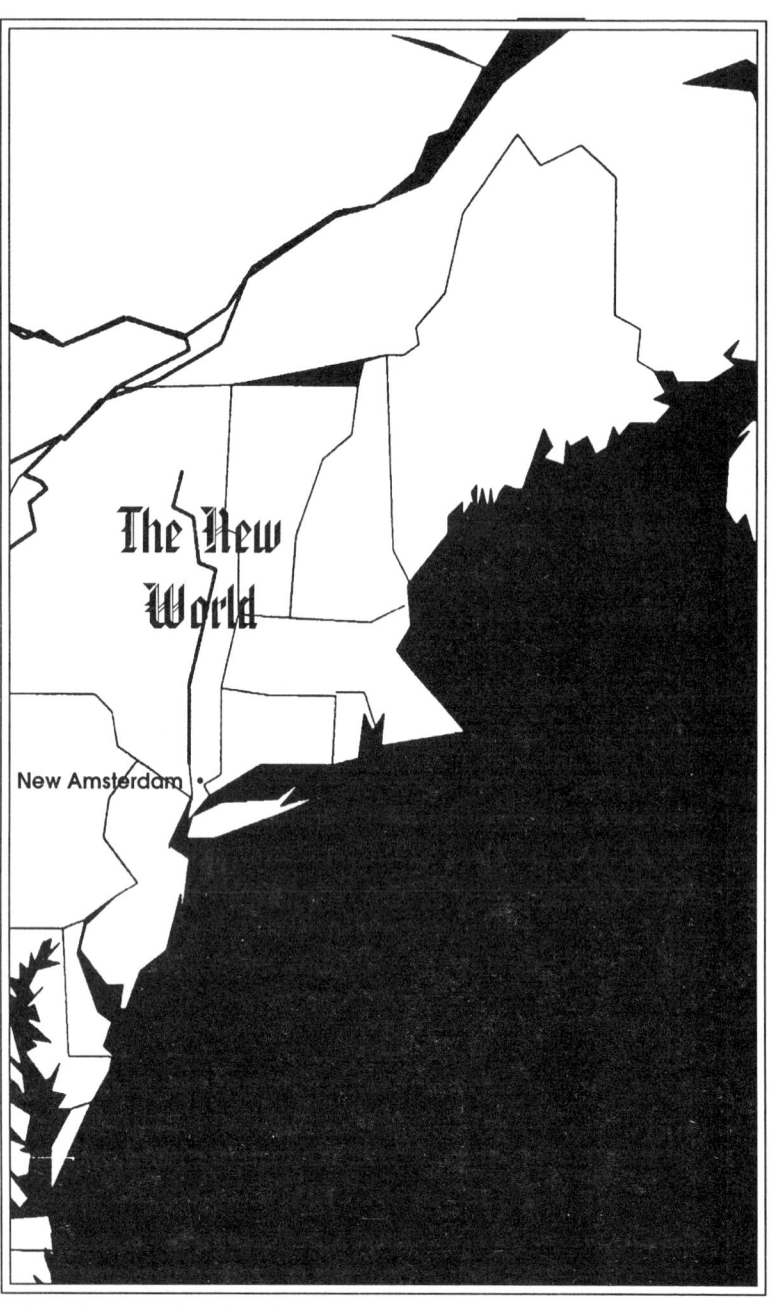

New Amsterdam in the New World with current boundries

Chapter Forty-Seven
THE FIRST JEWS IN NEW AMSTERDAM:
Excerpt from the Diary of Peter Stuyvesant

Time Line

| 70 c.e. | 600 c.e. | 1000 c.e. | 1400 c.e. | 1600 c.e. | 1800 c.e. | 2000 c.e. |

Location: New Amsterdam (New York City)

I, Peter Stuyvesant, governor of New Amsterdam, in the employ of the Dutch West India Company, am recording, for posterity, what I remember of the appearance of the first Jews on the North American continent.

I had heard that they were Spanish or Portuguese; that they had been living in Recife, Brazil, until the Inquisition was imported from the old world to the new. They decided to sail here, to New Amsterdam, to seek asylum.

I have nothing against Jews; I just don't understand why they can't remain among their own kind. There are none of them living in New Amsterdam at present.

Anyway, there were twenty three immigrants who disembarked from Captain Jacques de la Motte's small boat, the St. Catherine, on September 7, 1654. They had come via the West Indies. The captain submitted to the New Amsterdam court of Burgomasters and Schepens (city officials) a petition requesting payment of 2,500 florins for passage of these Jews from Cape St. Anthony in Cuba to New Amsterdam.

The Jews claimed that all their valuables had been stolen. They further stated that they expected that friends would be sending them money from Holland (Amsterdam, the Netherlands). The court decided to hold two of the twenty three as prisoners until the sum of their passage was paid in full.

They must have thought that I was hostile, or inhospitable. In truth, I did not want to have any problems. It was difficult enough keeping law and order in New Amsterdam without having to deal with penniless Jews. I petitioned the board of directors of the West India Company to "require them in a friendly way to depart...praying also most seriously ... that the deceitful race ... be not allowed further to infect and trouble this new colony." It took months for my petition to reach Amsterdam, be acted upon, and returned to me.

While waiting, the local court settled satisfactorily the problem of the debt of these Jews. Afterward, I offered them free farmland, not far from this settlement, which was plentiful. But they refused, and, as far as I know, there is little record of them or anything that they did.

While I waited patiently for a response to my petition from Amsterdam a problem erupted because I permitted those Jews to remain. Another group had arrived directly from the Netherlands. They were not poor. One of them, a man named Abram de la Simon, opened a little store. He engaged in business on our Christian Sabbath day.

Of course, when I investigated, he refused to admit that he had committed a crime. He could not understand why, if he closed his shop on Saturday, he couldn't keep it open on Sunday. He was arrested, and it was apparent from the outcome of his trial that he didn't even understand the charges that were brought against him. I really wanted to expel those Jews.

Imagine my surprise when the reply to my petition finally arrived many months later. It ordered me to permit them, and other groups of newcomers, who had requested permission to settle in the meantime, to remain in New Amsterdam. I will never forget the words in their response:

The First Jews in New Amsterdam

We would have liked to agree to your wishes and request that the new territories should not be further invaded by people of the Jewish race. We foresee from such immigration the same difficulties which you fear, but, after having further weighed and considered this matter, we observe that it would be unreasonable and unfair. This is because of the considerable loss sustained by the Jews in the taking of Brazil, and also because of the large amount of capital which they have invested in shares of this company. After many consultations we have decided and resolved upon a certain petition made by said Portuguese Jews, that they shall have permission to sail to and trade in New Amsterdam and to live and remain there, provided the poor among them shall not become a burden to the company or to the community but be supported by their own nation. You will govern yourself accordingly.

I think I know the best way to settle this new land. The only way to rule is with authority, not by obeying the pleasures and whims of the investors who don't even live here. I hear people whispering that I am stern, that they disagree with my rulings, but I still maintain that I know best how to govern this colony, so far removed from the motherland.

However, since I have been instructed otherwise, I must follow their orders.

A Sacred Trust
— Commentary —
The Light of a Small Candle Shines at Valley Forge

It comes as no surprise that great men or great events have the power to influence the everyday in our lives. But it is the subtle and profound message of both this story and the reminiscence in which it is found, that small acts have the potential to effect great men and influence great events.

No one would have expected that a single act of kindness by a Hessian mercenary would ultimately result in large scale aid to the suffering troops of General Washington. Likewise, no one would have expected that the General would be so deeply inspired by the quiet religious act of a solitary soldier.

In the end, that is the message of *Chanukah* as well. Devotion, dedication, commitment - these are the fundamental notions which can influence the everyday and the great alike. With the light of the *Chanukah menorah*, and with the light that each person brings, the world can be illuminated and enlightened!!

Rabbi Michael A. Weinberg
Temple Beth Israel
Skokie, Illinois

The American Jewish Experience: Chapter Forty-Eight

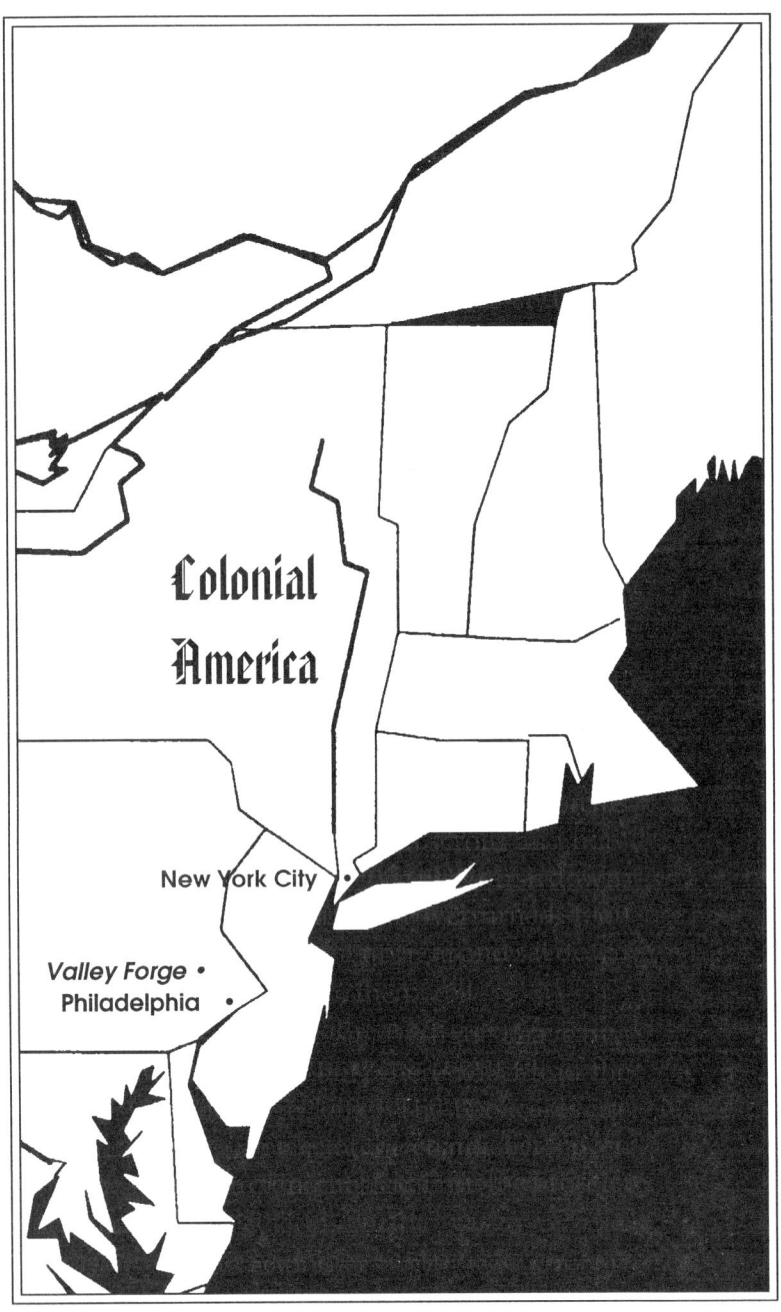

Colonial America

New York City

Valley Forge •
Philadelphia •

New York City, Philadelphia & Valley Forge

Chapter Forty-Eight
THE LIGHT OF A CANDLE SHINES AT VALLEY FORGE

Time Line

| 70 c.e. | 600 c.e. | 1000 c.e. | 1400 c.e. | 1600 c.e. | 1800 c.e. | 2000 c.e. |

Location: New York City, Philadelphia and Valley Forge

"I can't believe how I escaped from the Provost jail, a British prisoner, condemned after a court martial, to be hung for treason the very next morning," reminisced Haym Salomon. "If it hadn't been for the Hessian mercenary who accepted my watch, the last valuable thing that I owned, in order to leave the cell door open, I wouldn't be here. The Hessian also escaped from serving the British masters who hired him. I outwitted the British soldiers who used their dogs to pick up my scent when they found out that I had escaped ... but knowing that water destroys human scent, I swam through the ponds as I ran northward on Manhattan Island. At times, my pursuers were pretty close, but I evaded them. Then, this wonderful family sheltered me, provided me with new clothes, food, and rest. Afterward, I walked almost the entire distance from New York to Philadelphia where I finally found refuge.

It seems that I have been running most of my life; from Lissa, Poland, my birthplace, to Holland, to France, then Spain and Portugal. I easily learned the languages of the countries where I lived, so I was able to communicate with the natives. People said that I was friendly, that they trusted my word.

I am blessed with a certain talent for business, and I must turn these talents into helping the people who are now fighting for freedom against the British in this new land.

The final campaigns of this revolutionary war will be fought more in the marketplace than on the battlefield. Everyone that sides with the Continental Army knows that it is in dire need of financial support. There are shortages of food, inadequate clothing. Raging illness causes untold suffering for the troops loyal to General Washington. I even heard that the troops at Valley Forge are in desperate need of blankets. They would welcome additional bread. The morale of some is said to have shrunk to a low level.

I am determined to help the revolutionary cause. There is more than one way to serve one's country.

I will use my business know how as an experienced broker to supply the needs of the soldiers by stabilizing the bills of exchange on merchandise arriving aboard French and Dutch ships. This maneuver will enable the fledgling government to raise money. With the funds, they will be able to procure the supplies that they need.

I do this because my people have experienced persecution in every European country. In this new land, I am told that freedom will be accorded to all, regardless of religious beliefs. Here in America there is a glimmer of hope, a promise that my people will be able to live withour fear.

Here in America one can work and be free. Here in America a Jew has most of the same rights as a gentile. Here in America one can have all the land he wants. Here is an opportunity to be prosperous and to raise a family in peace.

I want this new government to succeed because there is no other place in the world that offers such hope and so much promise for my people. It is no small wonder that the majority of Jews who arrived here from Europe joined the revolutionary cause.

༄

A friend and I met a soldier at an inn one day who told us this inspiring story about himself and General Washington:

> I never doubted the outcome of the war, for men have always struggled against tyranny in the cause of justice. My father had told me about his personal struggle against tyranny, how he

fled religious persecution in Germany and migrated to the American colonies, how he hoped to build a new life in the new world.

When I joined the Continental Army two years ago, he gave me a *Chanukah menorah* and candles. I remember him telling me, "These candles are a symbol of man's struggle against tyranny. Light them each *Chanukah*. They will direct you toward the path of freedom."

I carried the *menorah* and the candles in my knapsack wherever I went.

On the first night of *Chanukah,* I removed the *Chanukah menorah* from my knapsack and walked away from where my comrades sat. I wanted to be alone when I lit my *Chanukah menorah*. I placed the menorah in the center of a small mound of snow. I inserted one candle and the *shamash* (candle used to light the other candles). I struck my one remaining flint, lit the *shamash* and the first candle, and recited the blessings. Tears welled up in my eyes as I imagined my father lighting his *Chanukah menorah* in front of the parlor window in our New York apartment.

I sat down in the snow to watch the little flickering light. From time to time, I cupped my hands over the flames, protecting them from the wind.

Suddenly, I felt that I was not alone. A man was standing over me. I looked up and recognized General George Washington. He spoke softly. "Soldier, are you lost? Why are you so far away from your comrades? I noticed the flickering lights of your candles, and I walked over here to see if you were in any kind of trouble. Why did you light two candles so far from the campsite?"

I could hardly speak. I hastily jumped to my feet. General Washington waited patiently for me to organize my thoughts.

"I am a Jew," I began haltingly. "Tonight is the first night of *Chanukah*, our festival of freedom. *Chanukah* celebrates the Maccabean victory over Greek tyranny more than eighteen hundred years ago. When I joined the Continental Army, my father gave me this *Chanukah menorah*. He told me to light the candles, that they would help me remember the cause of freedom. I wanted to be alone when I lit the candles, so I walked away from the campsite. I know that our soldiers will also win their freedom, just as my people did long ago. I hope that we will build a new land together."

I could distinguish a smile on General Washington's face in the soft glow of the candlelight. He stood with me for a few minutes, watching the reflection of the nearly extinguished candles. When the flames died out, he shook my hand and walked away. I sat down again near the mound of snow and remained there for a long time that night.

Years later, when the Revolutionary War ended, General George Washington was chosen to be the first president of the United States.

One day, sitting in the coffeehouse that I used as an office for my now successful brokerage business, my old friend joined me.

"Do you remember that story the soldier told us about the light of a small candle at Valley Forge?" he began. "Well, listen to the ending I heard recently."

> President Washington did not forget his encounter with that Jewish soldier. He searched for his identity for a long time, unsuccessfully. Then, on a recent trip to New York, during the week of *Chanukah,* he noticed the glow of the candles from the window of an apartment on Stone Street. He thought it might just be the home of the Jewish soldier who had inspired him years before. He knocked on the door. The door opened and there stood the veteran. He was speechless, so President Washington began:
>
> I was riding this way and I saw your *Chanukah* lights bringing hope to all passers-by. I remembered your *Chanukah* lights at Valley Forge, and I recalled your inspiring words. I took a chance, knocking on this door, hoping that you were the soldier who had inspired me. I have been searching for you all these years. I am glad that I found you, for I have carried this gift with me. Please accept it as a symbol of my thanks."
>
> The soldier extended his hand and accepted the box in which was a special Medal of Honor. Inside the box lay a small, engraved *Chanukah menorah* with the words, "Thank you for the light of a small candle."

When I heard this story, I swore that I would give back to my adopted country everything in my power for providing a new homeland for my persecuted people. ✡

A Sacred Trust
— Commentary —
Rebbeca and Judah

San Francisco has been called one of the most assimilated cities in America. Jews were accepted easily. Many gave up their Jewishness to reap financial gain and acceptance into the larger society. Had Rebecca and Judah remained in Philadelphia, or even Charleston, they and their family might have retained their Jewish identity, Both cities had organized Jewish communities, and that would have helped retain their identity.

The ethical will that Rebecca had was explicit about the Jewish values to keep. Her father was correct in stating that the refraining from work on Shabbat would help ensure their Jewishness.

Judah was ambitious and resourceful. The attainment of financial success seemed to blind him to the lasting values of Judaism. Their children changed their names and eventually married non-Jews. As the article states, "affluence and acceptance was a priority, not Judaism." As a result, they lost their Jewish identity.

Rabbi Arthur R. Oleisky
Congregation Anshei Israel
Tucson, Arizona

The American Jewish Experience: Chapter Forty-Nine

The Travels of Rebecca and Judah from Philadelphia, to Charleston, to New Orleans, to San Francisco

Chapter Forty-Nine
REBECCA AND JUDAH

Time Line

| 70 c.e. | 600 c.e. | 1000 c.e. | 1400 c.e. | 1600 c.e. | 1800 c.e. | 2000 c.e. |

Location:
Germany, Philadelphia, Charleston, New Oleans, San Francisco

Judah and I were married in Buttenhausen, Germany. We had decided that we would emigrate to the new world after our wedding. I couldn't believe that we were enroute. My father made me promise that I would read his ethical will three times each year, before *Pesach*, *Shevuot* and *Sukkot*. I wanted to see what he had written, so I removed the paper from the little purse I carried with me and clutched it in my hand.

[**Ed.** An ethical will is a document in which a parent underlines the values that are most precious to him.]

I was standing on the deck of the steamship. Judah was by my side. Gusty ocean breezes splattered specks of salt against my face. It was mid-winter, and I wrapped my coat tighly around me for warmth. The sun, almost directly overhead, sparkled on the water, its rays reflecting a bright, dancing sheen on the surging rippling waves.

I unfolded the paper carefully and started to read to myself: "When you reach the shores of the New World, you may regret that you have left your parents' house, your sisters and brothers, your native land. But have no regrets. You are fortunate to have the opportunity to leave this country where Jews have been deprived of civil rights and have been excluded from the society that other people take as their natural right. In the New World, you will find religious and civil freedom, and more important, you will be able to live with dignity. You have emigrated with mine and your mother's blessings.

Do not forget that you are Jews and never forsake God. Every evening and morning turn to Him in prayer. Follow the exhortations of the ten commandments, particularly refraining from work on *Shabbat*. Do not regard this day as another work day; on the contrary, let not the pursuit of financial reward blind you to violate both the law and the spirit of *Shabbat*. Rather, study the Torah reading for the week on this holy day.

When, as I hope, you will be blessed with material success, remember that acquiring goods does not guarantee happiness. All your blessings come from God. Use them to help your fellow Jews settle in that new land, for more and more of them will surely follow in your footsteps. If, on the other hand, you will not become wealthy, remember that wealth does not guarantee happiness.[1]

Even though you will be living in a far away land, remember to respect your parents. How will you do that from so distant a place? Write us letters often. Share your accomplishments with us. We will always be waiting for your letters.

Let the laws of the Torah be your guide through life. By following them, you will bring honor and respect to yourselves and to the Jewish people. Above all, trust in God: "In Your Hand, I commit my life."[2]

I read it aloud a second time. I wanted to share it with Judah. Then, silently promising myself that I would do my best to live up to my father's ethical will, I folded the paper, and replaced it in my purse.

Two weeks later, the boat docked in Philadelphia. The date was February 21, 1825.

We were immediately invited to spend a few days in the home of Hyman Gratz, one of the leaders of the Jewish community. He was known to be hospitable to newcomers, to help them become acquainted with America, to assist them in finding living quarters. He told us that there were approximately 500 Jews living in the city, divided between recent immigrants and original settlers.

There was so much excitement in his house, for the following *Shabbat* was the dedication ceremonies of the Mikveh Israel Synagogue.[3]

After *Shabbat*, I wrote my first letter home. This is what I wrote:

Dear Oma and Opa;

We have witnessed one of the most exciting events of our lives. Last *Shabbat*, we prayed in Mikveh Israel. Although, it was organized in 1747, it was just yesterday that the new synagogue building was dedicated as part of the services. In all of Germany, we have never seen such a magnificent edifice. It has a high domed ceiling, decorated with embossed, carved rectangles of oak wood. Ornate, finely chiseled balustrades circle both floors, a large lamp hangs from silver filigreed covered chains. The ark is curtained in rich crimson with fringed gold, and the *Ner Tamid* is suspended in front of it.

> [**Ed.** The Ner Tamid is the continuously burning lamp. "Command the children of Israel that they bring clear olive oil, to set up continuously burning lamps." *Vayikra*, Leviticus 24:2]

The services are conducted from the center of the synagogue. The dedication ceremony was solemn, truly a religious experience. A man named Mr. Keys, assisted by a *Chazan* Peixotto, invited from New York, officiated. Simon Gratz, the brother of Hyman, the one who made us feel welcome in his home, led the procession of the Torah scrolls. Nine people were honored to carry the scrolls and place them into the holy ark. To the accompaniment of a five-voiced choir singing appropriate *Tehillim* (Psalms) the people carrying the scrolls proceeded in seven circles around the reading desk. The congregation responded to the *Chazan* and the choir as the Torah scrolls were placed in the ark.

The people in Philadelphia have made us feel very comfortable. There is a benevolent society that helps newcomers find work and places to live, but we didn't have to ask them for help because Mr. Gratz offered Judah a job.

I will write again very soon.

Love, Rebecca.

Judah was a very good student; he learned a lot from Mr. Gratz. He was also very frugal. We saved as much money as we could. Within a few years, we opened a clothing store. We were also blessed with two children, a son Avraham and a daughter Leah. We prospered as Philadelphia grew because we were able to supply the needs of the immigrants who came mostly from Germany, and smaller numbers from England, Portugal, and Amsterdam.

I thought we would remain in Philadelphia, but Judah grew restless. He had heard about the Gold Rush and was excited about the possibilities of servicing the gold miners with clothes, tobacco, food, and other basic necessities. He wanted to sell everything and set out for California as soon as possible. Actually, the idea excited me too, so together we made plans to head south overland, to Charleston, then west, to New Orleans, and complete our journey by steamship. It seemed to be the safer way than crossing the continent by covered wagon.

At that time, Charleston was the largest, wealthiest, most cultured Jewish community in the United States, numbering about 700 people. The Jews owned land, some were planters. They participated fully in the arts; Penina Moise wrote Jewish poetry, Mordechai Manuel Noah and Isaac Harby wrote plays that were produced at the Dock Street Theater. Jacob Cardozo edited The Southern Patriot, one of Charleston's first newspapers. There was a Hebrew Benevolent Society, and a Hebrew Orphan Society. It seemed to me that the Jewish community was organized much the same as the one in Philadelphia.

We rested from our journey for a few days. On *Shabbat* we attended services in Kahal Kadosh Beth Elohim.

[**Ed.** This is the oldest synagogue in continuous use in the United States. It was originally built in 1794, destroyed by fire in 1838, and redesigned and rededicated in 1840.]

It is such a splendid synagogue. The entrance has six fluted Doric columns adorning the entrance portico that support the roof. The building is surrounded by a wrought iron fence. The interior is impressive, with a shallowly arched circular ceiling forming a truncated dome. The windows are decorated with pastel stained glass. The ark was built from Santo Domingo mahogany. The community welcomed us warmly. The president of the congregation wanted to know why we were heading for California. He thought that he would be able to convince Judah to stay. He told Judah that "in the wilds of America, living entirely among non-Jews, it would be easy to forget God and the Jewish religion." But he had his mind made up.

Our next stop was New Orleans, a commercial center and an important port. We hoped to be able to arrange passage for a paddle-wheel steamer to San Francisco from there. We found out that the next steamer would not sail for two weeks. As more and more people talked excitedly about the Gold Rush, our own excitement intensified.

New Orleans was the home of Judah Touro,[4] a merchant and philanthropist who donated generously to the establishment of synagogues, hospitals, and libraries. In fact, he was responsible for converting an old church building into a synagogue. His philanthropy was not limited to the United States. He established a fund for the poor in *Eretz Yisrael* to be administered by Sir Moses Montefiore, an English Jew who had great interest in the people living in the Jewish homeland.

We made arrangements for the four of us to stay in an inn. The cost of lodging and food for two weeks was exorbitant. Although we had plenty of money when we left Philadelphia, Judah was concerned that the steamer tickets between New Orleans and Panama, and between Panama and San Francisco would cost more than he had planned. He worried that we would not have any money left by the time we arrived in San Francisco.

Being very resourceful, he purchased three second class tickets for the steamer Panama City for me and the children, and paid for his passage by washing dishes and boot-blacking for the first class passengers during the trip. We arrived in

Chagris, on the east side of the Isthmus of Panama, in January, 1851. In the middle of winter, the heat was unbearable.

The Indians took us upstream in hollowed log canoes where they lived in huts made from sugar cane. We were exhausted from the journey and fell asleep under the broiling sun. We slept through that afternoon and the entire night. In the morning, we rented mules which cost eight dollars, for the mountainous trip to the western side of Panama, where we hoped to find a steamer waiting in the port. We were lucky this time. The steamer Golden Gate was scheduled to leave the next day. Judah did not think that washing dishes and boot-blacking were beneath him, so, in order to save money, he purchased three second class tickets for us again, and worked for the duration of the voyage. He provided such good service to the eighty first-class passengers, that they tipped him generously. He saved every penny.

We sailed north for three months, arriving in San Francisco on April 1, 1851. The sun glowed on the magnificent cedar covered mountains. We were very happy that we had reached our destination, albeit with very little money to spare. People walked around with determined looks on their faces; prospectors, merchants, adventurers, all in pursuit of riches. We were told that the population had increased tremendously since gold had been discovered, from 800 in 1848 to 25,000 when we arrived.

We rented one room for the four of us. Judah wanted to make our money last as long as possible. He wanted to pay cash for the merchandise he planned to stock in the clothing store he hoped to open. He wanted to supply the needs of the miners, just as he had supplied the needs of the new immigrants in Philadelphia.

He opened his store and decided to work seven days a week. He had tasted wealth and comfort in Philadelphia, and thought that he could recapture that life-style by working more days. On the first *Shabbat* that he worked, I reread my father's ethical will that I had been carrying with me all these years. The words about observing *Shabbat* as a holy day danced before my eyes. I wondered if *Shabbat* was not important to us, how important would it be to our children?

My father had instructed me to read his ethical will three times a year. Here it was April, the month of *Pesach*. I was reading his will, but wondering where would we obtain *matzot* for the holiday. Was it possible to be Jewish in San Francisco?

My conscience played the protagonist: I knew that few Jews lived here; that only thirty people attended Rosh Hashana services last year. But I had met Albert Sutro and Levi Strauss.

[**Ed.** Albert Sutro arrived in San Francisco in 1850. He emigrated from Westphalia, Germany. He was elected mayor of San Francisco in 1894.

Levi Strauss arrived in San Francisco around 1850, having emigrated from Bavaria, Germany. He began to manufacture pants from blue denim, reinforced with copper rivets, which under the "Levis" trademark became popular with the gold miners.]

They seemed to be accepted in every aspect of communal life. There was no prejudice against the Jewish people.

We didn't have to live in that rented one room very long. Lots of new houses were being built; it was the natural result of the economic stimulus of people settling in the region.

Jews did not live separately from other people. They lived in the neighborhood that they could afford.

Our children mixed with everybody. They became part of the affluent society. Judah made our son his partner. Our children changed their names. Avraham wanted to be called Albert; Leah changed her name to Lillian.

They could not find Jewish spouses. After a few years in San Francisco, they had so lost their Jewish identity, that they found no religious difference between themselves and the mates they chose. Affluence and acceptance was a priority, not Judaism.

When my father wrote his ethical will from the old country,

he had no idea how hard it would be to be Jewish in America. We really tried to raise our children with Jewish values. Maybe, it was not enough. We mistakenly sacrificed our religious principles for financial gain.

> [**Ed.** In the 1800's and 1900's Jews looked for acceptance and affluence. They fled to America from European ghettos in search of civil rights and dignified living, neglecting many of their Jewish religious practices.]

A Sacred Trust
— Commentary —
Concerning the Jews

By the time the Jewish people appeared in history, the ancient world had already been populated by many nations. Many of these nations, like the Babylonians and the Egyptians, were enveloped in splendor and greatness, yet they disappeared from the face of the earth. Even the Greeks and Romans, conquerors of the world in their time, are no more. Yet the Jews, who were subject to persecution and hardship, continue to develop, flourish and thrive in spite of all the ordeals they went through.

"What is the secret of Jewish immortality?" This question was raised, not by a rabbi or Jewish philosopher, but rather by the 19th century Christian American author Mark Twain, the author of *Tom Sawyer* and *Huckleberry Finn*. Had a Jewish author written the following essay, he would, no doubt, have been called a narrow-minded apologist. Mark Twain, who traveled to Jerusalem in 1869 and wrote an honest and most unflattering report about conditions in the city, in fact gives an answer to his own question about the secret of Jewish survival. In his essay, he enumerates the basic values that are important to Jews. Twain clearly believes that the world should learn and attempt to imitate these values.

The values Mark Twain describes are the same values Jewish educators are trying to pass on to future Jewish generations: strong family life, mutual respect, honoring the elderly, caring for the poor, strong community involvement and most important *Tzedakah*, or as Twain calls it, charity.

Is it possible that Mark Twain better understands the keys to Jewish continuity than many Jews do? With so much browbeating, with so much self-criticism among Jews, it is refreshing to read Mark Twain's essay. I have no doubt it will provoke thoughts and discussion.

Shoshana Glatzer
Director, Education Resource Center
Board of Jewish Education of Greater New York
Author of: **Coming of Age as a Jew-Bar/Bat Mitzvah**

Chapter Fifty
CONCERNING THE JEWS

Time Line

| 70 c.e. | 600 c.e. | 1000 c.e. | 1400 c.e. | 1600 c.e. | 1800 c.e. | 2000 c.e. |

Location: The United States

[Ed. The following essay was written by Mark Twain in the late nineteenth century.]

...The Jew is not a disturber of the peace of any country. Even his enemies will concede that. He is not a loafer, he is not a sot, he is not noisy, he is not a brawler nor a rioter, he is not quarrelsome. In the statistics of crime his presence is conspicuously rare—in all countries. With murder and other crimes of violence, he has but little to do: he is a stranger to the hangman. In the police court's daily log roll of "assaults" and "drunk and disorderlies" his name seldom appears.

That the Jewish home is a home in the truest sense, is a fact which no one will dispute. The family is knitted together by the strongest affections; its members show each other every due respect; and reverence for the elders is an inviolate law of the house.

The Jew is not a burden on the charities of the state nor of the city; these could cease from their functions without affecting him. When he is well enough, he works; when he is incapacitated, his own people take care of him. And not in a poor and stingy way, but with a fine and large benevolence. His race is entitled to be called the most benevolent of all the races of men. A Jewish beggar is not impossible; perhaps, such a thing may exist, but there are few men that can say they have seen that spectacle.

The Jew has been staged in many uncomplimentary forms, but, so far as I know, no dramatist has done him the injustice to stage him as a beggar. Whenever a Jew has real need to beg, his people save him from the necessity of doing it. The charitable institutions of the Jews are supported by Jewish money, and amply. The Jews make no noise about it; it is done quietly; they do not nag and pester and harass us for contributions; they give us peace, and set us an example—an example which we have not found ourselves able to follow; for by nature we are not free givers, and have to be patiently and persistently hunted down in the interest of the unfortunate.

These facts are all on the credit side of the proposition that the Jew is a good and orderly citizen. Summed up they certify that he is quiet, peaceable, industrious, unaddicted to high crimes and brutal dispositions; that his family life is commendable; that he is not a burden upon public charities; that he is not a beggar; that in benevolence he is above the reach of competition. These are the very quintessentials of good citizenship....

If the statistics are right, the Jews constitute but one percent of the human race. It suggests a nebulous dim puff of star dust lost in the blaze of the Milky way. Properly, the Jew ought hardly to be heard of; but he is heard of, has always been heard of. He is as prominent on the planet as any other people, and his commercial importance is extravagantly out of proportion to the smallness of his bulk. His contributions to the world's list of great names in literature, science, art, music, finance, medicine, and abstruse learning are also way out of proportion to the weakness of his numbers. He has made a marvelous fight in this world, in all the ages; and has done it with his hands tied behind him.

He could be vain of himself, and be excused for it. The Egyptian, the Babylonian, and the Persian rose, filled the planet with sound and splendor, then faded to dream stuff and passed away; the Greek and the Roman followed, and made a vast noise, and they are gone; other peoples have sprung up and held their torch high for a time, but it burned out, and they sit in the twilight now, or have vanished. The Jew saw them all, beat them all, and is now what he always was, exhibiting no decadence, no infirmities of age, no weakening of his parts, no slowing of his energies, no dulling of his alert and aggressive mind. All things are mortal but the Jew; all other forces pass, but he remains. What is the secret of his immortality?

The American Jewish Experience: Chapter Fifty

A Sacred Trust
— Commentary —
The New Colossus

This *midrashic* story is one of *teshuvah*, a tale of the great American Jewish poet, Emma Lazarus, and her spiritual return to the Jewish People. Born in America, blessed with wealth, nurtured in the bosom of a good family and given a fine classical education, Emma moved from her Sephardic Jewish roots towards assimilation. As a poet, she explored foreign gardens, pursuing and expressing her ideas through Greek themes.

Then, two mysterious incidents profoundly affected her and her work. She met a stranger who asked her a seemingly simple question; later, she attended a particular *Purim* party, one of hundreds held within the city of New York, where a particular people and a particular rabbi's words, influenced her. So moved was she, Emma began contemplating her own Jewish roots. And, finding them, she composed her most famous poem, *The New Colossus*.

Among the verses, she wrote, "..... *I lift my lamp beside the golden door,*" immortal words engraved upon a plaque which now graces the base of the Statue of Liberty. With this declaration, Emma became like that great statue, a lady with a beacon, holding aloft a 'light unto the nations,' beckoning to those who yearned for the *Goldena Medina*. With those words, Emma Lazarus began her own journey home.

And to Emma, and to each Jew who takes the first steps back to Judaism, we say, "Welcome home, *Baal Teshuva*. Welcome home!"

Norma Harris
Author, **Trumpets of Silver**

Chapter Fifty-One
THE NEW COLOSSUS

Time Line

70 c.e.   600 c.e.   1000 c.e.   1400 c.e.   1600 c.e.   1800 c.e.   2000 c.e.

Location: New York City

THE NEW COLOSSUS
by Emma Lazarus (1883)

Not like the brazen giant of Greek fame,
With conquering limbs astride from land to land;
Here at our sea-washed sunset gates shall stand
A mighty woman with a torch, whose flame
Is the imprisoned lightning, and her name
Mother of Exiles, from her beacon hand
Glows world-wide welcome; her mild eyes command
The air-bridged harbor that twin cities frame.

"Keep, ancient lands, your storied pomp!" cries she
With silent lips. "Give me your tired, your poor,
Your huddled masses yearning to breathe free,
The wretched refuse of your teeming shore,
Send these, the homeless, tempest-tossed to me.
I lift my lamp beside the golden door.

Emma Lazarus was minimally identified with her people, until two incidents changed her life.

The first incident occurred at the New York Museum of Art, which was housing an exhibit of Greek statuary. People walked through the exhibit, admiring the representation of ancient Greek culture.

A young man commented to his companion that the exhibit reminded him of the poetry of young Emma Lazarus, who wrote about Greek subjects. At that moment, she entered the exhibit hall. The young man walked over, anxious to meet the famous American poet.

"I am delighted to meet the admired American Jewish poet who writes on ancient Greek culture," he said, "But, I have often wondered why you have never written anything with a Jewish theme. I should think that the living saga of our people would be much more interesting subject matter than dead Greek statues."

"I have nothing to write about my people," she responded. "You see, I've traveled too far from home."

The conversation greatly disturbed her. Arriving at her apartment, she groped for some book that would connect her to her Jewish roots. The first book that she pulled off her shelf described the pogroms in Russia and the incessant persecution of her people. She read about the throngs of immigrants who sought refuge on American shores. She placed a fresh sheet of paper on her desk and began writing:

Wake, Israel, wake! recall today

The glorious Maccabean rage...

This was her first effort at incorporating Jewish themes into her poetry. Others followed.

Shortly thereafter, she attended a Purim party being held on Ward's Island in New York Harbor for immigrants waiting to be admitted to the United States. She attended the party because of an editorial she had read a few weeks before.

The New Colossus

[The Article:
"This year the Purim festival will have peculiar significance for American Israelites, owing to the few thousand refugees who are celebrating for the first time on American shores. The helpless victims of Russian persecution, exiles from home and kindred, how can they obey the traditional behest to be glad and joyful? It is the duty of the American Jew to inspire them with olden merriment and make the festival a day of joy for those tempest tossed emigrants, by prompt and cheerful assistance. Let no sacrifice be deemed too costly, if it secure for the refugee a happy home and enable him to become a useful and independent American citizen."]

She arrived with the Rabbi of Temple Emanuel, and he urged them "to maintain their religious beliefs, live as Jews, and keep a name which was bright and unstained.

After the Purim party, Emma Lazarus wrote her famous sonnet *"The New Colossus."* It was her way of describing the plight and hope of the immigrant masses. It was also her contribution to a fund to pay for a base for the planned Statue of Liberty.

Twenty years later, part of her sonnet was inscribed on a bronze plaque and placed in the pedestal of the Statue of Liberty, the symbol of America, the land of liberty.

Much of Emma Lazarus' poetry, written after these incidents demonstrate how she "returned home" to her Jewish heritage.

A Sacred Trust
— Commentary —
Rochel Leah's Parochet

Rochel Leah carried with her to America the most precious thing she possessed—the *parochet* that bore her name and her jewels. The two-and-a-half million Jews who came to America from Eastern Europe carried with them few possessions, but each one did bring valuable gifts. They, our great grandparents, brought their determination and dedication to hard work and education. They brought dreams of a better life in the New World for their children, a life of freedom and opportunity in this Golden Land.

They brought with them the hope and faith that their children and children's children would be good Jews in this New World, worthy heirs of the four-thousand-year-old tradition. So they built here their synagogues and established their Hebrew schools, trained teachers and ordained rabbis to teach the *Torah* and the Jewish way of life.

The stories we are now reading about our ancestors are their legacy to us. We can make our lives a "Thank you!" to them.

Professor Abraham J. Karp
Jewish Theological Seminary
of America

The long travels of Rochel Leah's *Parochet*—from Poland to Ellis Island to Chicago

Chapter Fifty-Two
ROCHEL LEAH'S PAROCHET COMES TO THE "GOLDENE MEDINAH"

Time Line

| 70 c.e. | 600 c.e. | 1000 c.e. | 1400 c.e. | 1600 c.e. | 1800 c.e. | 2000 c.e. |

Location: Poland, Ellis Island and Chicago

[**Ed.** Much of this story parallels the experiences of the authors' grandparents and many other immigrant families who fled from persecution and poverty in eastern Europe, arriving in America between 1881-1921.]

[**Ed.** A *parochet* is the curtain of the holy ark.]

Shlomo Zalmen and Rochel Leah stood under the *chuppah*. Their cousin, Rebbe Moshe Mordechai had just concluded the recitation of the seven blessings of marriage.

"I have one more blessing to add to these," he said softly. "I bless you with long life, a life in which you will dance at the weddings of the children of your children's children."

Shlomo Zalmen worked in a tobacco factory in Stazow, adjacent to Bulgria, a tiny *shtetl* where they lived. Because he was a diligent laborer, he was promoted to manager in a short time. With the promotion came a higher standard of living. He provided comfortably for Rochel Leah, bought her some jewelry, and distributed ten percent of his earnings to charitable causes.

For *Rosh Hashana* and *Yom Kippur*, Shlomo Zalmen and Rochel Leah traveled to Lodz.

[**Ed.** Lodz was a large textile center, with a Jewish population of 160,000.]

They liked to *daven* in the magnificent Italianante *shul* on Lutomierska Street.[1]

The people respected them because they always knew how to do a favor. In addition, they were philanthropic beyond their means. But most important to them was the excitement of saving *kopeks* and *zlotys* the entire year to be able to bid for the honor of Shlomo Zalmen opening the ark for *neilah*, the concluding service of *Yom Kippur*.

When they were first married, Shlomo Zalmen bid one *zloty*. The next year, he bid two *zlotys* as Rochel Leah held their first child and watched the bidding from the ladies' gallery. Each year, as he earned more money, as his family grew, he increased his bid. Rochel Leah and the children lovingly watched him stand next to the open ark. After a few years, no one in the congregation bid against Shlomo Zalmen. Unquestionably, his was the honor of opening the ark for *neilah*.

Then, Shlomo Zalmen lost his job in the tobacco factory. Knowing that he had to make a living for his family, he decided to venture into a partnership with the local chicken farmers. He offered to become their distributor. He arranged to buy their eggs and their chickens at their price. Each farmer would be alleviated of the problem of selling his own eggs and chickens. He sold the chickens and the eggs to the people living in the adjacent *shtetlach* of Bulgria and Stazow.

He barely made ends meet, but, nevertheless, each week he put away a few *kopeks*, so that he could pay for the honor of opening the ark at *neilah* on *Yom Kippur*.

That year, Leizer arrived in the *shul* just before *neilah*, just as the bidding had begun. People exchanged curious glances, for Leizer had not made an appearance in the *shul* for years; in fact, most Lodzers considered him a social outcast. The bidding started, and he raised Shlomo Zalmen's bid by ten *zlotys*. The *shammish* called out: "I have eleven *zlotys* for opening the ark. Who will bid more?"

Shlomo Zalmen bid twelve. Leizer bid fifteen.

The *shammish* called out again: "I have fifteen *zlotys* for the honor of opening the ark. Who will raise their bid?"

Rochel Leah's *Parochet* Comes to the *Goldene Medinah*

Shlomo Zalmen stood up in his place. "I bid sixteen," he said.

Leizer jumped up. "I want the honor of opening the ark for *neilah*. I bid twenty."

The congregation commiserated with Shlomo Zalmen, for they knew how difficult it had been for him to save sixteen *zlotys*, in order to be able to bid for the honor. Rochel Leah knew that he could not afford to bid one *zloty* more.

Shlomo Zalmen pulled himself up to his full height. "I bid twenty-one," he announced.

Immediately, Leizer countered: "I bid thirty!"

Suddenly, Rochel Leah, cradling her youngest child, shouted from the ladies' gallery: "My husband has bid for this honor for the past ten years; it rightfully belongs to him!" All eyes turned upwards.

She handed the baby to the lady sitting next to her. Then she unfastened a jeweled pin, her necklace, bracelet, earrings, and her wedding rings. She wrapped them in her handkerchief, knotted it, and tossed them over the railing.

"Here," she shouted. "These will pay for my husband's honor."

The *shammish* picked up the handkerchief.

The congregation accepted Rochel Leah's jewelry as payment for the honor. But they did not redeem the jewelry for money. After *Yom Kippur*, they voted to permanently honor Shlomo Zalmen with the opening of the ark.

"A wife who defends her husband's honor in such a way is truly courageous. She is the matriarch of this family," announced the *parnas* (president) of the congregation. "Instead of selling her jewelry, we will sew it on the *parochet*, and we will call it Rochel Leah's *parochet* forever."

About a month after Sukkot, winter weather began to take hold. Shlomo Zalmen waited for Stefan, the farmer who supplied him with the most eggs, to bring his daily delivery. As the hour grew late, Shlomo Zalmen instinctively knew that something was wrong. About eleven o'clock, Stefan's cart rumbled into Shlomo Zalmen's yard. It was empty.

"I came to tell you," Stefan moaned, "that somehow a fox stole into the chicken coop. I have no eggs today. Most of my hens are dead."

Shlomo sympathized with Stefan. He worried about his own livelihood. Days passed. He became very despondent.

"I think I will go to seek the rabbi's advice," he decided.

The rabbi lived in Stazow. He knew Shlomo Zalmen well.

"I feel your pain," said the rabbi. "I want you to know that you must never despair, that you must never give up. Be patient. Things have to improve. Whatever hits bottom, must eventually rise."

Shlomo Zalmen felt a little better after seeing the rabbi, but his despair returned when a fire destroyed Peter's chicken coops. He had no more suppliers.

"That's it!" he decided. "I can't take the poverty here anymore. I am going to emigrate ... to America. I work very hard but I don't earn enough money to live. In America ... I hear the streets are paved with gold. The letters that my friends send me describe America as "the *Goldene Medinah* (the golden land)." Besides, I have three daughters and a baby son. One day, I will need money for the girls' dowries. What should I do? My mind is made up."

He pushed his right hand into his pants pocket, felt something, and pulled out a *zloty*.

"I didn't remember that I had this *zloty* in my pocket. It must be a sign. I am going to use it to buy a lottery ticket! Even though I never bought a lottery ticket before ... one never knows...."

One month later the shammish ran helter skelter through Bulgria's one street.

"Did you hear the incredible news? Did you hear the in-

Rochel Leah's *Parochet* Comes to the *Goldene Medinah*

credible news? Shlomo Zalmen, the one who has three daughters and a baby son ... he won the lottery. He is sitting in that run-down house he calls his home. Tears are running down his cheeks. He doesn't know whether to laugh or cry."

Finally, Shlomo Zalmen said to Rochel Leah: "I have won a lot of money. Some of it has to be used to obtain a forged passport for me, since I was a soldier in the Russo-Japanese War,[2] and I am still considered a reservist by the Tzar. Reservists are not permitted to leave this country.

Passports for you and the children should not be a problem. We will use some of the money to purchase tickets to the *Goldene Medinah*. The remainder will help us settle in Chicago, in America, where we have relatives and *landsman*."

They left Bulgaria before *Pesach*, and went to celebrate the holiday with their friends in Lodz. Word spread very quickly through the Jewish community that Shlomo Zalmen and Rochel Leah had won the lottery, that they had come to say good-bye, that they were on their way to America.

On the last day of *Pesach*, just before the conclusion of the services, the *parnas* (president) of the *shul* stood before the *shtender* (pulpit).

"I have an important announcement to make," he began. "When the members of this congregation heard that Shlomo Zalmen and Rochel Leah are leaving for America, they voted to give them Rochel Leah's *parochet*. It rightfully belongs to her. She should take it with her to America."

From Lodz to Warsaw by train ... from Warsaw to Danzig. They sailed on the *British Prince*, two weeks later. The passengers were all Russian immigrants, most of them traveling third class, steerage. They slept in bunks, arranged fifty to each dormitory room. Their diet aboard ship consisted of bread, tea, and sometimes a piece of herring. The drinking water was so horrible, that they could not drink it even if they were very thirsty.

The weather was fair during most of the two week journey. Temporary bouts of seasickness occurred only when an occasional storm rocked the boat.

Before being permitted to enter America, they were processed in the great hall on Ellis Island, located in New York's harbor. Inspectors who had manifest sheets in front of them, asked questions to which Yiddish speaking immigrants could only shake their heads.

"According to my records, your point of origin was Lodz."

Shlomo Zalmen and Rochel Leah shook their heads.

"Are you older than thirty? Is your wife twenty-eight? Your baby looks like a big boy. He must be almost two years old." Again, they shook their heads. No matter their real ages, the inspector wrote down what he guessed their ages to be, and handed them the documents.

Shlomo Zalmen voluntarily showed the inspector the money that he had brought with him. He was a proud man, and wanted to prove that he would not be a public charge.

Just then the inspector glanced down again at his manifest sheet.

"I have information," he said, "about the person whose name appears on your passport. It seems that you have been in prison in Russia."

Shlomo Zalmen didn't understand, but from his expression, it was obvious that he was frightened. He couldn't understand all the questions, all the delay.

"Is it possible that he knows about my forged passport," Shlomo Zalmen wondered.

The inspector kept repeating the word prison. He wanted to know how many times he had been imprisoned. He assured him that he would not send him back to prison; he only wanted to know the truth so he could correct his records.

Shlomo Zalmen looked furtively around for someone who understood Yiddish to help him. He didn't understand what

Rochel Leah's *Parochet* Comes to the *Goldene Medinah*

the inspector wanted to find out and he was very nervous. The children tugged at his pants leg. Rochel Leah tried to reassure them that she was not afraid. She pulled her shoulders back and stood tall, her dark eyes staring at the inspector.

She prayed a silent prayer: "We only wanted to be admitted to the *Goldene Medinah*. Please help us!"

HIAS (Hebrew Immigrant Aid Society) representatives circulated through the great hall, trying to help the immigrants. Mr. Lipsitch, a *HIAS* representative, must have seen them standing in front of the inspector longer than usual, trying to make themselves understood. He rushed to their aid. He "discovered" that Shlomo Zalmen's passport had indeed been forged. He explained to him that the name on the passport, Zama Kotin, did not match his identity papers.

He talked to them very calmly, in Yiddish. Shlomo Zalmen told him that he had purchased the forged passport for a lot of money because he was a reservist in the Tzar's army, and the Russian government did not release its citizens so easily. He assured him that he did not know the person whose name appeared on the passport; and that he had never been in prison.

Mr. Lipsitch repeated to the inspector what Shlomo Zalmen told him. The inspector was a kindly man, and he cleared them to enter America.

The *HIAS* representatives took them to the railroad station. They were on their way to Chicago in America! It was springtime, and the world was wonderful! The railroad station was walking distance from Maxwell Street, so the immigrants naturally gravitated toward that neighborhood. It was filled with small ground floor shops underneath two and three story tenement buildings. Push carts lined the streets.

Shlomo Zalmen still had some money left, but he wanted to save it for emergencies. He rented a small, ill-ventilated, third floor tenement apartment near Maxwell Street for his family and went out in search of a job immediately. He did not want to be a burden to his relatives nor did he want to depend on the money he had left over to sustain him.

He found a job as a baker in Mr. Shultz's bakery and began to work in the back of the bakery shop the following Sunday. He worked long hours, and learned to bake white, pumpernickel and rye breads and rolls. Each evening, Mr. Shultz gave him fresh rolls for his family.

On Friday afternoon at five o'clock, he washed his hands and removed his apron. "I am going home, now, Mr. Shultz," said Shlomo Zalmen. "I will see you Sunday morning."

"What do you mean, Sunday morning," sputtered Mr. Shultz. "Who will bake tomorrow?"

Shlomo Zalmen shrugged his shoulders. "Tomorrow is *'Shabbos'*. I do not work on *'Shabbos'*."

"If you don't show up for work tomorrow, then don't come back on Sunday," he said angrily, and stomped away.

Shlomo Zalmen thought about his predicament. Finally he decided: "It will be impossible to observe Shabbat and work for someone else. I will have to go into business for myself."

He found a vacant store where Halsted crossed Maxwell Street. One side of Halsted was Jewish, the other side was Italian.

"This is a perfect location. I will stock housewares and groceries. Hopefully, both Jews and Italians will become customers."

With the remaining money, he paid two months rent in advance, purchased merchandise, and opened for business. He displayed the housewares on a pushcart directly in front of the store, and the groceries inside. Each morning at daybreak, he moved the pushcart outside, arranging the pots, pans, and cutlery neatly. He displayed the food attractively and swept the floor until it was immaculate. Very late at night, when he closed, he moved the pushcart inside.

Rochel Leah's *Parochet* Comes to the *Goldene Medinah*

He worked very hard. Rochel Leah brought him lunch and dinner. She spent a few hours in the store each day, while the children were in school.

One customer came into the store, then another. They were friendly merchants and supplied their customers needs. The customers recommended the new grocery store to their neighbors and friends. When the customer returned the second time, Shlomo Zalmen and Rochel Leah knew their name.

On Friday afternoon, Shlomo Zalmen hung a sign on the door of his store. "This store will be closed until after dark tomorrow night. When it opens, fresh lox will be available."

He walked out of the store, locked the door, and went home to celebrate Shabbat with his family. He had no idea how many people saw the sign, but on Saturday night, when Shlomo Zalmen arrived at the store, a long line of people waited to buy lox. He happily worked past midnight.

Weeks flew into months, months to years. Shlomo Zalmen and Rochel Leah prospered. They set aside ten percent of their profits to help settle the immigrants who followed them, and saved what they did not need.

They decided to buy an apartment building in the Lawndale area, the "new" Jewish neighborhood, filled with *shuls*, kosher butcher shops, *cheders* (religious schools) and many other immigrants who had prospered like themselves. They planned to use one apartment for themselves, and rent the others. They even thought about opening a second grocery store in the new neighborhood.

Their baby son had grown into a fine young man. According to his birth record, documented at Ellis Island, he was almost *bar mitzva* age. Shlomo Zalmen and Rochel Leah hired a tutor to supplement his *cheder* education and to prepare him for the *bar mitzva* ceremony which was celebrated at the *Polishe Bikkur Cholim Shul*, where they had started *davening* regularly.

After the *bar mitzvah,* Rochel Leah wrote about the event to her parents, who were still living in Bulgaria. Four months later, she received a response to her letter. Her mother wrote: "You celebrated his *bar mitzva* too soon. Our grandson is just celebrating his twelfth birthday. You have almost another year until his *bar mitzva!*"

The following *Yom Kippur* afternoon, before *neilah,* Shlomo Zalmen asked the rabbi if he could say a few words. He was holding Rochel Leah's *parochet* in his hands.

"My *landsman,*" began Shlomo Zalmen, "most of us have shared similar experiences. We arrived from the old country, some of us penniless, some of us with money we had saved. Some of us peddled, some of us sold used clothing from pushcarts, some of us opened businesses. We have prospered. We have rebuilt our Jewish lives in this blessed land.

"The last *Pesach* that Rochel Leah and I spent in Lodz, the congregation decided that we take this *parochet* with us to America. The reason that they gave it to us is not important. However, they called it Rochel Leah's *parochet* because they felt it belonged to her. Rochel Leah has worked by my side all these years that we have been in America, in addition to raising our children and caring for our home. Every Thursday night, she kneads dough, lets it rise overnight, and bakes fresh *Shabbat challah* for our family and for a dozen other families. She has helped new immigrants settle; she has cooked meals for the hungry, and comforted the bereaved. In every sense of the word, she truly is the matriarch of our family.

"I want to honor her. I would like the permission of this congregation to hang her *parochet* in this *shul,* in Chicago, in our new homeland, in America."

When Shlomo Zalmen and Rochel Leah celebrated their golden wedding anniversary, one of their great granddaughters, who was nine years old wrote:

Rochel Leah's *Parochet* Comes to the *Goldene Medinah*

Bubbie and Zadie are one of a kind
Yiddishkeit is uppermost in their mind.
Zadie is a man of conviction
Bubbie is a clever woman
They hold each other in high esteem
They are a perfect team.
Throughout the long and trying years
They stood side by side
Building a Jewish home
In which they take great pride.
Zadie never missed a *minyon*
Bubbie sits in the upstairs front row
The *parochet* that they donated
Makes their faces glow.
Their cousin, the rebbe, had blessed them
Many years ago
Truly their life is that fulfillment
As we, their great grandchildren, know.

∽

A Sacred Trust
— Commentary —
A Bintel Brief

Judaism always adapted to the culture of the various lands where Jews have lived throughout the centuries. Nonetheless, few lands offered the challenge of America, where 2-1/2 million Jews arrived at the turn of the century. Although anti-Semitism was prevalent until the late twentieth century, America was a land built on religious freedom. Jews were able to create synagogues, schools, and charitable institutions on a level unknown in Europe.

With religious freedom came a culture of individualism and autonomy which Jews had never known in their previous habitations. The rugged individual, particularly moving out west, was a cultural icon in America. In classical Judaism the community dictated to the individual such questions as where to live, who to marry, or what to eat. America emphasized autonomy, the right of the individual to decide for himself or herself how to live. This presented an enormous challenge to classical Judaism.

We see this tension clearly in *A Bintel Brief*. The editor answers a question, but ends with such statements as "you should act according to your own convictions," or "decide for yourselves." Such answers would be unheard of in any previous generation of Jewish history.

This tension between community values and personal autonomy remains the most vexing issue for the future survival of the American Jewish community.

Rabbi Michael Gold
Temple Beth Torah/Tamarac Jewish Center
Tamarac, Florida
Author of **And Hannah Wept: Infertility, Adoption and the Jewish Couple** *and* **Does God Belong in the Bedroom**

Chapter Fifty-Three
SNIPPETS FROM "A BINTEL BRIEF:" THE ACCULTURATION PROCESS

Time Line

70 c.e.   600 c.e.   1000 c.e.   1400 c.e.   1600 c.e.   1800 c.e.   2000 c.e.

Location: New York

Most Jews who came from the eastern European *shtetlach* struggled to adapt to the American way of life. They had to learn a new language, new social mores, and deal with a society in which Christianity was the dominant religion. Cultural confusion reigned during the forty years 1881 - 1921 when 2-1/2 million eastern European Jews arrived in America.

They wanted to become American in order to feel proud and free. They wanted to lose the self-consciousness of being "greenhorns," and become totally integrated into this new way of life. They wanted to be part of a democracy, to make their own decisions, believing that it was not necessary to ask questions of the rabbi or scholar, as they did back in their *shtetl*. They developed new customs, and they called it *Minhag* (custom) *America*.

Because the Yiddish language united these immigrants, the Yiddish press became a vital force in the process of Americanizing them. A famous feature of the *Jewish Daily Forward* was *A Bintel Brief*, an ongoing column of reader questions and writer reponses, presented to help the readers become "more American." The column, excerpted here, continued for sixty years.

Snippets from *A Bintel Brief*

Question - I am the oldest of five children. I go to school, where I do very well. But times are hard, and I want to give up my studies and go to work. My mother will not hear of it.

> **Answer** - You should stay in school, because you will be able to give your parents greater satisfaction than if you went to work.

(**Ed.** The hunger for education was very great among the eastern European Jewish immigrants.)

Question - I have been in America almost three years. I came from Russia where I studied at a *yeshiva*. My parents were proud and happy at the thought that I would become a rabbi. Before I left I gave my father my word that I would walk the righteous path and be good and pious. But America makes one forget everything.

Here I became a sewing machine operator. At night I went to school. I began to notice that the (gentile) teacher paid more attention to me than to the others. She wants to tutor me privately.

She says that she is in love with me, and wants me to marry her. She says that she will support me. She told me that she believes that all men and all nations are equal. I am in despair when I think of my parents. What heartaches they will have when they learn of this!

> **Answer** - We can only say that some mixed marriages are happy, others unhappy. Therefore, we cannot take it upon ourselves to advise the young man regarding this marriage. This he must decide for himself.

Snippets from a Bintel Brief

Question - I was observant in Russia, but when I arrived in America, I developed spiritually and became a freethinker. But the nature of my feelings is remarkable. Every year when Rosh Hashana and Yom Kippur approach, my heart grows heavy and sad. My memory goes back to my childhood years.

> **Answer** - No one can tell another what to do with himself on Yom Kippur. Naturally, a genuinely sincere freethinker is not drawn to the synagogue.

Question - The owner of the shop accused us of ruining the work. He threatens to throw us out of his shop. I wanted to pick up an iron and smash his head in, but I saw before me my wife and five children who want to eat.

> **Answer** - The worker cannot help himself alone. There is no limit to what must be done for a piece of bread. He must unite with his fellow workers and fight for their honor as men. The workers must be organized.

༄

Question - My husband and I were married for nineteen years and we have two sons. We were divorced three months ago because we hadn't been getting along. Now we have reconsidered, and we want to remarry. But we have difficulties. My husband is a *kohen* (of the priestly tribe) and no rabbi will perform a religious ceremony for us. The rabbi we went to explained that a *kohen* is not allowed to marry a divorcee.

> **Answer** - Handling this problem in a way that would be proper and suit everyone is impossible. You don't have to ask anyone's advice, but you should act according to your own convictions.

༄

Question - We live in a small town in the country where we are the only Jewish family, and we earn a good living. But we have four daughters of marriageable age, and they don't want to go to the big city without mother or father. We do not want to break up our home and leave our good life.

Answer - We can only tell you that many Jewish families are in the same position and they leave the small towns for the sake of their children. Others remain where they are. In such circumstances it is better not to rely on the advice of others but to decide for yourselves.

Question - Should religious parents be forced to eat non-*kosher* meat when they visit their children's home?

Answer - We cannot imagine that children would demand of their religious parents that they eat their non-*kosher* food. Not the children, but the parents would feel insulted when they come to visit and are served a non-*kosher* meal.

⁂

Question - I am the grandmother of a twenty-one year old bride to be. She is marrying a boy from an Orthodox family and she has adopted his way of life. She wants her parents to make their home *kosher*. My daughter-in-law will not hear of making any changes. She would prefer to break up the match. My granddaughter is considering moving out of her home. How do I handle this situation?

Answer - We feel that the religious beliefs of your granddaughters fiancee need not be a hindrance to marriage, rather you should consider her new beliefs a virtue, not a fault. When your granddaughter marries, she will be able to run her own home as she pleases, but she should not demand of her parents that they should change their way of life. This is the time for tolerance, and you must all be understanding.

⁂

A Sacred Trust
— Commentary —
Tuition

In the many years since my *Bubbe* sparked my Jewish soul with love, laughter, stories and real live *mentchlichkeit*, I have been "finding my way." I am one of the lucky ones. I really cut my teeth on Jewish values. However, knowledge of our history, heritage, ideas, or the "why's" of our tradition was a mystery. This, I believed, was for scholars, not the average Jewish citizen.

Involved in Jewish community for some 60 years, one becomes a "learner". It comes with the territory. I learned that there was no Jewish educational opportunity for serious adults seeking quality, not satisfied with the occasional course or lecture series.

Now, at 83, I am still a learner, but very happy to play the role in re-kindling the *Ner Tamid* in thousands of Jewish souls throughout the world. Through our 5,000 graduates of The Florence Melton Adult Mini Schools, we have learned that there is a hunger for Jewish knowledge. These serious learners, who commit 2-1/2 hours per week for two years to study, tell us that their lives have changed. They are now on a lifelong spiritual journey with Jewish values permeating their lives with family, synagogue and community.

There are many examples and programs that tell us there is a re-awakening to the values of our precious Jewish heritage. Many young parents have discarded empty materialism, investing more time in meaningful Jewish life. However, with the median income of a Jewish household being $39,000, most of our population is shut out of the mainstream of Jewish life because they cannot afford it. Most of these people will not come begging.

It is our responsibility to establish adequate funding mechanisms through special endowment funds from the 30% of our more wealthy families. This will provide comfortable entry for all who wish to fully participate in Jewish living and learning in our home communities. We shared in the rebuilding of Israel. Now, let's do our share to assure Jewish continuity here at home.

Florence Z. Melton, Ph.D.
Founder, Florence Melton Adult Mini Schools, Columbus, Ohio

Chapter Fifty-Four
TUITION

Time Line

70 c.e. 600 c.e. 1000 c.e. 1400 c.e. 1600 c.e. 1800 c.e. 2000 c.e.

Location: The United States

"Hurry, Binyamin, Yaakov, Chaim. I am going with you to school this morning. And I want you to dress in your *Shabbat* clothes," Mr. Goldberg called to his three sons.

The boys wondered why their father asked them to wear their *Shabbat* clothes on Thursday, why he was going with them to school, but they obediently did as they were told.

They walked together along the tenement lined streets toward their *yeshiva*, a large five floor stone building that had once been an orphanage. Entering the high ceilinged vestibule, they raced up to the third floor *bayt midrash*, where the morning *minyon* was just beginning. Tables, chairs, and *shtenders* (small pulpits) were scattered throughout the large room. In a few minutes, the sing song melody of the prayers floated through the open windows, heard by neighbors living on both sides and across the alleyway.

Breakfast followed the *minyon*. The boys sped to the basement dining room, where they shared the first meal of the day.

After breakfast, Mr. Goldberg asked his sons to go with him to the business office. They looked at each other, perplexed, for they did not want to be late for class.

The treasurer looked up, surprised, when Mr. Goldberg entered with Binyamin, Yaakov, and Chaim at his side.

Mr. Goldberg removed a folded manila envelope from his pocket and placed it on the treasurer's desk. "Open it, count the money inside," he said.

The treasurer opened the envelope. Mr. Goldberg and his sons stood quietly while he counted $352.23. Then he looked up, puzzled.

"You see," Mr. Goldberg explained, "during the latter part of the depression, around 1937-1938, I nearly lost everything that I owned. Somehow, I had faith that I would be able to improve my financial situation. For many years, I barely managed to feed my family even though I worked very hard. I had to educate my children, but I had no money to pay tuition. You took them into this school. You provided them with an intense Jewish education, for which I and their mother are very grateful. When you found out how I was struggling financially, you never asked me for one penny. But, I kept a record of all that I owe.

"During the last few years, my financial situation has improved, and I was able to save some money. The first debt I am repaying is the debt for my children's education. I calculated that for educating my sons for the past five years, I owe you the sum that I have just placed on your desk. It is a privilege for me to be able to pay their tuition."

Then he turned to his sons. "I'm sure you still want to know why I asked you to wear your *Shabbat* clothes today. I want you to know that when a father is able to pay the tuition he owes for his children's education, that day is *Shabbat*, it is *Yom Tov*, it is truly a holy day worth celebrating."

[**Ed.** Fifty years later, almost every Jewish community with a population greater than 5,000, has at least one day school. Many day school graduates continue their education in Jewish high schools and *yeshivot*. It is estimated that there are more students studying in *yeshivot* in North America and Israel today than studied in the *yeshivot* of eastern Europe during the nineteenth and twentieth centuries prior to the Holocaust.[1]]

A Sacred Trust
— Commentary —
One Survivor's Story

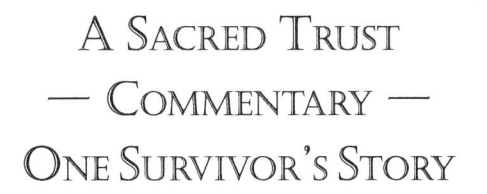

An event as overwhelming as the Holocaust teaches us so much about what it means to be a Jew.

The most awesome lessons are:

✡ that a Jew is incapable of doing to the world what the world has done to him.

✡ that religious observances which were not necessarily required under those horrendous circumstances were adhered to by many.

✡ that unbelievable heroism and acts of kindness were a source of strength for those who struggled to survive.

✡ that underground resistance movements in forests, ghettos, and concentration camps attempted to provide a thread of hope to those who perceived there was no hope.

✡ that torture, hunger, and inevitable death was not the most terrifying fear that was experienced; but rather the fear that they would not be remembered.

—Authors

The American Jewish Experience: Chapter Fifty-Five

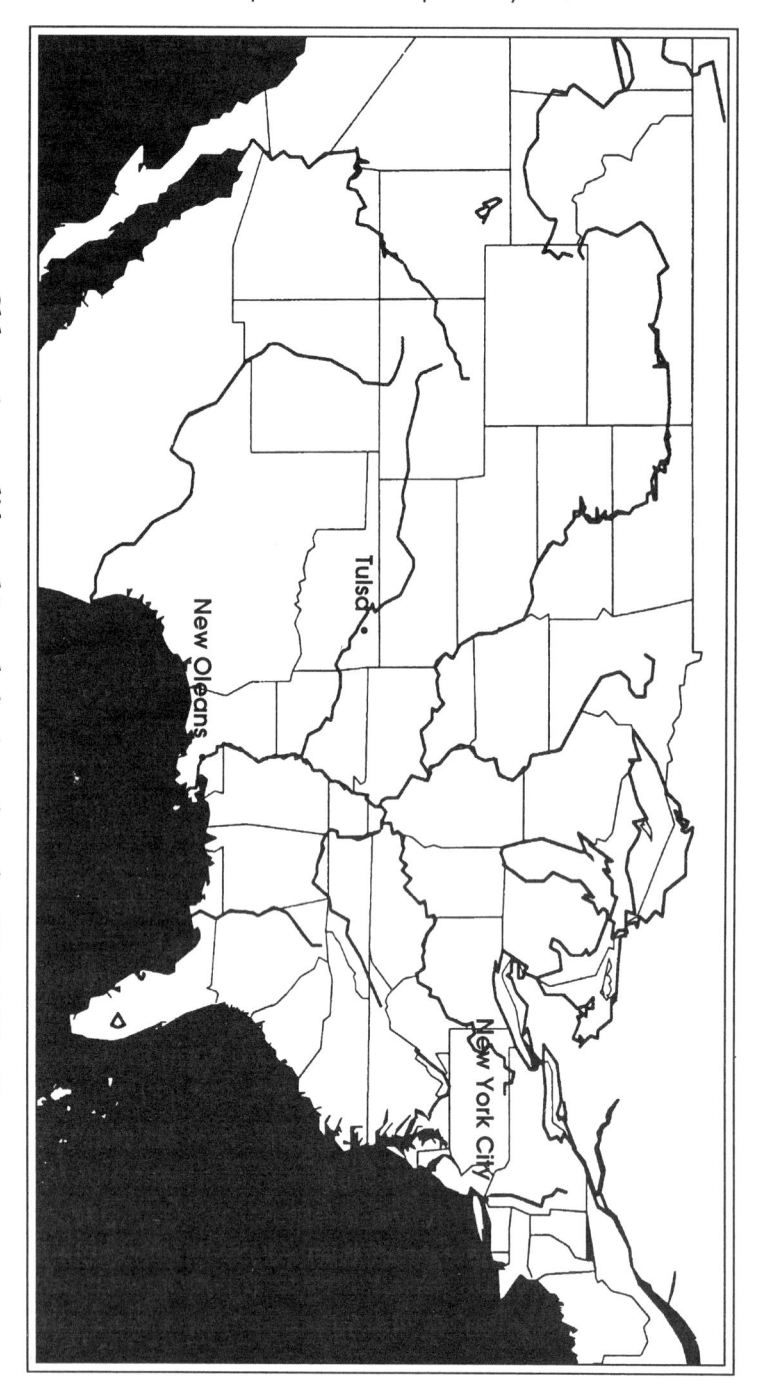

Shlomo's new life and travels in America after World War II

Chapter Fifty-Five
ONE SURVIVOR'S STORY

Time Line

70 c.e.   600 c.e.   1000 c.e.   1400 c.e.   1600 c.e.   1800 c.e.   2000 c.e.

Location: Europe & The United States

My name is Shlomo ben Moshe and Shifra. My grandfather's name was Berel. My grandmother's name was Gitel.

I have borne my personal pain in silence for the past forty-three years. However, I can no longer contain my silence. I feel compelled to speak, to give credence to the stories of the survivors, thereby counteracting the vicious lies of the people who say that the *Shoah* was a Zionist plot or that the *Shoah* did not happen.

So many words have been written about the *Shoah*. Yet, it is impossible to fathom the number "six million," which staggers the imagination. Only through the personal story of a survivor, such as myself, can one magnify the monstrous proportions of the tragedy.

I have to start my story by describing Jewish life during the 1920s and the 1930s, in order for the reader to fully appreciate the devastation that followed the blitzkreig, Germany's swift and furious attack on Poland in September, 1939.

During those years, Jewish life flourished; it was obvious that Jews were Jews. The life-style that was totally consumed in the conflagration will never return to eastern Europe, where it had existed for hundreds of years.

I was born in 1921 in a *shtetl*, Gniewoszow, located about fifty miles east of Warsaw. The *shtetl* provided a framework of religious security, for the young people were raised with the words: "The Lord is my light and my salvation, whom shall I fear...." This verse always meant that the source of our real, true being, our guide through life, our yearning for perfection, came from faith in God.[1]

Some of the people in my *shtetl* were, by today's standards, middle class businessmen, but none were rich. Most of the others earned their livelihood as craftsmen; shoemakers, butchers, tailors, furriers, dairymen, small grocers, distributors of wheat brought into the *shtetl* by the peasants who lived in the surrounding area. Some worked on the farms they leased from the wealthy landowners. Jews were prohibited from owning land; this was one of the manifestations, among many, of Polish anti-Semitism in those years.

But the religious life ... it was so beautiful! It was so beautiful to be a Jew in the *shtetl*. I not only knew I was born a Jew, I felt it. I experienced it. I dressed it. Jews with *payot* and beards, dressed in *bekashes* and white stockings, tied at the waist with *gartels*, going forth to *shul* ... of course, only the Rabbi and the *shochet*, the ritual slaughterer wore *shtreimels*.

[Ed. The Jews dressed in this fashion, wearing long black coats, special fabric belts, and fur hats because they wanted to make a statement about the difference between themselves and the Polish people.]

I was friendly with the *shochet's* son. He taught me to sound the *shofar*. On *Shabbat* and *Yom Tov* you could see the *Shechina*, God's presence hovering over the streets.

Like all the observant boys in the *shtetl*, I was sent to study in Pulawy, about twenty kilometers from Gniewoszow, at a branch of Yeshiva Chachmay Lublin just before I became *bar mitzva*. I remember those days so clearly. We studied very long hours. We ate our meals in different homes each day.

[Ed. This was known as the tag system, whereby meals were served to *yeshiva* students in different homes in the *shtetl*. Many *yeshivot* were unable to provide board for their out-of-town students, so people in the community took turns inviting them for meals. Students would eat at a different home each day. This system permitted students to devote their energy to study without worrying about providing for themselves.]

We slept on hard benches in the *yeshiva* building each night when we returned from dinner.

> [**Ed.** Today the building which housed the main branch of Yeshiva Chachmay Lublin is a medical school. The broken, chipped, overturned weed covered grave markers in the cemetery are testimony to hundreds of years of a Jewish presence in Lublin.]

Of course, not everyone in the *shtetl* was so observant. There was room for differences of opinion because our *shtetl* was home to ten thousand Jews. Some young people joined Labor Zionist groups and prepared themselves for *aliya*, learning to be soldiers, scouts, farmers, for the time when they would reach the holy land.

The British, however, had issued a series of White Papers, restricting Jewish immigration in order to appease the Arabs. Do you know that in 1936, '37, '38, thousands of Jews waited for visas, but only one received permission to make *aliya* from our entire *shtetl*? Hitler wanted to make the world *Judenrein* (free of Jews) while civilized governments refused refugees immigration visas. There was no place to go, especially after the Evian Conference.

> [**Ed.** Evian, on the shores of Lake Geneva, was a conference site where Britain, the United States, and thirty-two other nations representing the international community, met, on Wednesday, July 6, 1938, to discuss the problems of those Jews who tried to escape from Nazi persecution. Most delegates expressed sympathy, but none were willing to finance resettlement of refugees or increase their immigration quotas. World powers effectively slammed their doors against the Jews. On Friday, the headline of the international *Herald Tribune* blared: "Jews For Sale! Who Wants Them?"[2]]

The leading Nazi newspaper chortled over the conference's failure. The editorial of the Voelkischer Beobachter observed: "They weep crocodile tears over the Jews, but nobody is willing to make any sacrifices for these unfortunates since everyone knows what the Jew means within a national community. Those countries who themselves refuse to take any Jews merely justify the German Reich's defensive measures against them, measures which in any case are not yet sufficiently far reaching."[3]

I remember Vladimir Jabotinsky's electrifying announcement after The Evian Conference: "we will organize an army to walk all the way to *Eretz Yisrael!*"

Those words shook up young Jews from their reverie. It seemed that he had announced it from the rooftops, and his message reverberated all over Europe.

I want to share with you my most tender memory of our *shtetl*, before I tell you about the war.

Gniewoszow was located in the heart of *chassidic* territory, and Rebbe Ahron (Ahrele), the last Koshnitzer Maggid was a close friend of our family.

Once, my mother told me, she had passed Otwock, renown as a health resort, on her way to Warsaw. The *rebbe* stayed there in a villa from time to time. She was going to the big city to sell skins and horsehair for export. She usually went to the market instead of my father. He could not leave the *shtetl* because the peasants who sold the skins and horsehair would deal only with him. She stopped to see Rebbe Ahron. The *shammish* told her to write a *kvittel*, a note on a piece of paper requesting an appointment. "I don't have time to wait. Tell the *rebbe* that Shifra bat Bezalal wants to see him."

The *rebbe* immediately came out of his private room to greet her. When he would visit our *shtetl*, he would stay in a big house, not far from where we lived. My mother supervised the *kashrut* in that house the entire time the *rebbe* stayed there. He honored my father in *shul* because of my mother.

It was Friday morning, just before *Rosh Hashana*, 1939, when the Nazis stormed into our *shtetl*. I had been swimming in the Vistula River which flowed past our summer cottage. It was made from straw, more like a hut than a cottage. It was only one and a half kilometers from the center of town. Apple trees grew on the property which my father rented with the agreement that he could harvest the fruit. My father sent me to pick the apples that had ripened, so that they could be sold in the market before the holidays. I wanted to cool off a bit before I started to work.

Suddenly, floating on my back, looking skyward, I saw five low flying airplanes swooping across the treetops. The German planes had shot a Polish plane out of the sky. I noticed the wreckage in the distance. As I ran toward it, I realized that the downed plane had landed belly up. I drew closer, only to hear faint moans from the cockpit. One of the pilots seemed badly wounded, the other was dead. I dug around the wreckage and pulled out the wounded man. I looked around for a way to transport him to the hospital in town.

Polish peasants worked the fields apathetic to the situation. I waved frantically, trying to get their attention, but they ignored me. Finally, I ran over to where they were working and demanded to borrow their wagon. They refused my pleas until I threatened to inform the Polish police. They were just as scared of the Polish police as of the Nazi invaders. They could not think in human terms. I took the wagon back to the wreckage, lifted the wounded pilot and laid him gently in the back. Then I lifted the body of the dead pilot into the wagon. I wanted him to have a decent burial. I covered them with grass and weeds so they would not be visible from low flying German planes.

I managed to reach the police station. The captain praised me for my courage. Solemnly, he wrote my name down in his record book. He said he wanted to maintain contact with me, that he would find me after the war and reward me. I never heard from him.

The Nazis brutalized the Poles, and the Poles turned Jews over to the Gestapo for a bottle of liquor, a kilo of sugar, or a salami. The Poles were commissioned to operate the trains that careened over miles and miles of endless tracks going seemingly nowhere, destined for the concentration camps. Sometimes, during the last kilometer, when the words above the gates, *Arbeit macht frei,* were visible, German conductors were substituted for Poles.

[**Ed.** *Arbeit macht frei* means labor makes you free.]

The stories of meagre, scarce rations, smuggling food to survive, sickness, overcrowded ghettos, roundups, merciless selections separating families are all true, believe me. My nightmares, till this day, erase the beauty of Jewish life as it was before Hitler and his Nazi SS marched into Poland.

How did I survive? I was strong, young, and I had unlimited energy. I think I was a bit daring too, now that I recall the facts. Since I was raised to do *mitzvot,* I dared to smuggle a little more food into the ghetto, I dared to hide a child, I searched for an extra blanket; everything I did was for the purpose of saving life, for a *mitzva.* I fled just as I perceived that the Nazis discovered what I was doing. I lived in stables, slept on straw, fled from one place to another to avoid detection; hid in the forests, attempted to sneak back into the *shtetl* to see my family with two different sets of forged identity papers, one with the name of Jan Koral, the other with the name of Roman Zagurski.... Yes, all you've heard and read is true.

When the Gestapo finally caught up with me, I was sent to a slave labor camp in Suleyev/Sadlovitz. I had to weave baskets from the willows that grew nearby to camouflage the transportation of grenades.

Once, I was on an open transport truck. I still had a few cigarettes that I smoked as we rode. I waited for a good strong wind and flicked the ashes into the eyes of the Nazi guard, then I jumped. He didn't chase me for some reason. I guess the other prisoners would have followed my lead had he moved his rifle from pointing directly at them. I hid in the silo of Wladislow Wolesik's farm. It faced the cemetery. He was married to a decent Polish women who knew *Yiddish* from her

One Survivor's Story

dealings with the Jews who lived in the nearby *shtetl*.

She provided me with potatoes, bread and water. On moonlit nights, I rummaged around other fields, trying to find more food, more potatoes, more carrots which grew all over the area. When I found anything that needed to be cooked, she prepared it for me and brought it to the silo. She always pleaded with me not to approach the house. She feared that someone would see me and report to the Gestapo that she was harboring a Jew. Sometimes, I felt the silo was not secure; then I hid in the cemetery, among the gravestones.

My family had been moved to the Zworllin ghetto by *Rosh Hashana* of 1942. Despite the fact that it was completely controlled by the Gestapo, I smuggled myself inside to bring my parents some extra potatoes and carrots for *Yom Tov*. I decided to stay through *Yom Kippur* because my father pleaded with me not to return to the silo.

That *Yom Kippur*, the holiest day of the Jewish calendar year, Dumijen, a very tall, thin Gestapo commander ordered the Jews to surrender all their money, jewels, gold, anything of value. Then he announced a round up for five days later. That day was the first day of *Sukkot*. Mercifully, my mother passed away before the round up.

I stood together with 25,000 to 30,000 people all day under the grueling sun with no food or water. A few SS officers, accompanied by their savage, ferocious dogs marched back and forth from the head of the line to the end, keeping order with a minimum of effort. Occasionally, the SS guards shot bullets randomly, just for the fun of it, further terrorizing the people who stood in line. Any person who moved was shot.

Towards evening, the people were forced to march to Garbatka, a railroad station fifteen kilometers from Zworllin, and from there they were crammed like cattle into airless boxcars and transported to Treblinka. Ten members of my immediate family were among those transported that evening.

Seventy-five young adults were selected to clean up the Zworllin ghetto after the people were marched off. My brother and I were among those selected for the clean up crew. It was there, in Zworllin, while I was cleaning up the ghetto, that I started reciting *Kaddish*.

The job we were selected to do was to bury the dead in communal graves in a nearby cemetery. We had to locate the bodies of those who had been indiscriminately shot by the SS, carry them to the edge of the pit and throw them in. I recognized the face of a neighbor from my home town; he still breathed, but knew he was dying. He whispered my name, and as I turned to face him, he uttered a heart-breaking question, "Are my parents still alive?" Those were his last words. The SS were watching the work crew. I could not stand over him any longer.

I had noticed a little blond girl, about four or five years old, darting aimlessly between the work crew. She was crying bitterly for her mama, her papa. The SS left her alone until our task was almost complete, then one of them aimed his rifle carelessly, purposely missing, in order to frighten her more. He played his game for a while, finally killing her. I was told to throw her body on top of the mass grave.

I found out who that little girl was. Her name was Rachel. Her parents were wealthy Jews. Before the roundup they had given all their material possessions—all their wealth—to a Polish couple to pay for her keep and hide her until after the war. They kept the money, but turned the child over to the Gestapo.

Yiskadal v'yiskadash sh'may rabah! The words of the ancient *kaddish* filled my being. I could only mouth them, I could not speak. "Master of the World." I thought, "how much longer?"

My thoughts were interrupted by the snarling shouts of the SS commander. "Cursed Jew! Return to work!"

For about a month, I remained on the ghetto clean up crew.

During that time, I methodically moved from one apartment to another, gathering anything of value, clothing, jewelry, silver, precious stones, money, sorting it into boxes that were placed in a shed near the town square. I knew all of it would be confiscated for the Nazi war effort.

After the job in Zworllin was finished, I was taken to Skarzysko Kamjenna, the largest Polish ammunition factory. I lived in a stable with about one thousand other people. The food ration was so meagre that it was impossible to survive on it more than two weeks, but the Nazis did not care. They always had other replacements for the dead.

The people in my group had to produce 360 grenades each day. Not fulfilling the quota was cause to execute everyone on that production line. I knew I had to find a way to survive. Quite accidentally, I found out that the Polish engineer, Mr. Sobieszclk, who was in charge of the technical functioning of the machinery, had a son who looked like me. His son had been killed fighting with the Polish army during the blitzkreig at the beginning of the war. I hoped that he might have a little compassion on young people who were the age his son would have been had he lived, so I tried to speak to him. I knew that I had nothing to lose.

Surprisingly, he responded to my overtures, resulting in his teaching me how to repair the furnace used for smelting the iron for the grenade cases. I worked to gain Mr. Sobieszclk's confidence. I realized that if I knew how to repair the furnaces, I also knew where to crack the brick linings. Once, when he was too ill to work, I found myself in charge. In a few unguarded moments, I secretly sabotaged one of the furnaces. In order to repair it, the furnace had to be shut down for twenty-four hours to cool. I was the only one who could repair it, since I knew exactly where the cracks in the brick lining were located. I became an expert, a specialist in furnace repairs, and this insured my safety for awhile. Being so important to the technical operation of the factory, my rations were increased slightly.

By the fall of 1944, we thought it would be impossible to survive another winter.

As the Russian army closed in on Germany's frontier lines, I was moved to different ammunition factories; to Shleiben, a rocket factory, to Drezien, to Bautzen, to other slave labor camps. I found myself in Thresienstadt and in Buchenwald concentration camps. My arm number was 84-99-33.

I was moved again and again, sometime by train, sometime forced to march tens of kilometers. As the Allies closed in on the Nazis from all sides, they did not give up their fiendish plans to liquidate ghettos, to annihilate all the Jews. They worked feverishly, intensifying their efforts to carry out their nefarious schemes.

∽

I don't know why or how I survived. But I've heard that a number of studies have been done describing how survivors rebuilt their lives in America. I'll continue my story. I believe one living person with a name, a home, a family has more meaning than all the statistics and surveys.

I was liberated by the Russians at Nicksdorf, Sudentenland, Czechoslovakia on May 8, 1945. It was not a well known camp, rather an army barracks. I had spent sixty-six months and seven days under the Nazi regime. My world was barren; like the barren boughs of trees in the dead of winter.

On that May day, airplanes flew all over the skies, and we heard shouting from the surrounding villages. The war was over.

Our Russian liberators provided food and told us that we were free. But we had no place to go. We wandered into the nearest village to seek shelter where we found plenty of additional food and clothing in the abandoned houses. A few days later we heard that survivors were gathering in Prague. We all wanted to find out who had survived, and if anyone knew the whereabouts of family, relatives and friends. When a group of us arrived in Prague, we found that all the survivors were struggling to return to normalcy, to find jobs and shelter. We were helped by JDC.[4]

I didn't remain in Prague very long. I decided to go to Landsberg, Germany, with five friends. Landsberg was near Munich, and many survivors had gathered there. When the Nazis fled, they had left homes completely stocked with everything needed for comfortable living, including money.

With some of the found money I was able to open a little grocery store which supported me for about four years. But the organizations that were working to resettle the survivors in Palestine, Austrailia, Canada, South Africa, succeeded during these years, and many people left. I followed the crowd, and registered as a displaced person, adding my name to the list of survivors who waited to resettle in America.[5]

I never dreamed of America, but there I was standing in line to register for a visa. It took four more years for my visa to be processed. Then, one autumn morning, I stood on the deck of the SS General Sturgis, a refitted military boat, determined to put the past behind me. There was plenty of food on the boat, but I wanted to feel useful, so I performed whatever chores were necessary during the two week voyage: I mostly painted and scraped, painted and scraped.

As we approached New York, the boat anchored in the harbor. New York City was just turning on its lights. The Statue of Liberty glistened and the tall buildings glowed. I had never seen anything so beautiful. I watched this scene the whole night, not believing that I was in America.

But to everyone's disappointment, we were not permitted to disembark in New York. The next morning, the boat continued its voyage toward the Mississippi River port city of New Orleans.

I did not know that arrangements had been made for each of the survivors in various cities around America. I was to be met at the boat, and placed on a train for Tulsa, Oklahoma, where "my sponsor" would meet me. The Tulsa Jewish community had accepted the responsibility of sponsoring newcomers, much as many other Jewish communities across the length and breadth of America were doing.

My sponsor met me at the train station. He held up a placard in Yiddish with my name on it. As we drove to the house that already had four survivors living in it, he told me wonderful stories about what it was like to live as a Jew in America. Thinking I had come from a primitive country, he told me that a locomotive car could pull fifty trains, and that by turning a faucet one could have hot or cold water. I laughed at his stories.

The people were wonderful. My physical needs were immediately taken care of. I had shelter, food, clothes, and a job working in a laundromat for $16 per week.

[**Ed.** Even in those days, this was a meagre salary.]

But I was very lonely. Not many people in the community could speak Yiddish, and I yearned to be with *landsleit*, friends that I knew from the camps and from Landsberg, that had been permitted to settle in the New York area.

I confided to my sponsor. He told me that New York had too many newcomers. If I left Tulsa, I would lose the support of the local community. I would be totally on my own.

I worked very hard, determined to save every penny for train fare to New York. In the meantime, I located a friend who was living in New York. He informed me that there was a factory owner named Kramer in Trenton, NJ, who had immigrated years before the war, and had become very successful in the air conditioning business. My friend told me that he hired newcomers, and that he had available jobs.

I left Tulsa for Trenton, and I worked for Mr. Kramer for $60 per week. That immediately made a big improvement in my lifestyle. I noticed one thing about Mr. Kramer. He never used the words immigrants, refugees, or survivors. He always called us newcomers.

Each weekend and on most holidays, I travelled to New York to be with my friends. Because I had no surviving relatives, these people, with whom I had shared common experiences, were as close to me as kinfolk.

I knew I had to learn the English language in order to succeed, but I didn't have the time to go to school. By deciding that I would not speak Yiddish until I learned English, I became so attuned to other people speaking, that I was able to make myself understood. I guess I have a pretty good ear for languages, for it didn't take too long to speak and understand my new country's language.

Eventually, I had saved enough to join my friends permanently in New York. I found a job in a factory which manufactured leather coats and jackets. I was able to learn the process, and was promoted very soon to a managerial position. But I didn't want to be responsible for the livelihood of the people who worked under me. I simply did not have the physical stamina to work from early morning to late at night, as the job required.

One day I noticed that the irregular coats and jackets were being discarded. Sometimes, there was only an unnoticeable flaw. I saved money and proposed to the owner of the factory that he sell me the seconds and the irregulars. I resold them to smaller shops at a fair price. I became a merchant, doing what Jews had done for thousands of years before.

I guess the goal of becoming self sufficient had been implanted in me before the war. I worked hard and eagerly toward achieving that goal. Most of my friends were also ambitious and optimistic. We did not want to be a burden to anyone. We knew that America was the land of golden opportunities. If we worked hard, we could become successful.

I saved every penny that I did not need for my sustenance.

In those days, forty years ago, America was sprouting suburbs. I invested in a construction company as a silent partner. The site of the building was two hours from New York City. I would travel there often, to watch my investment grow. Eventually, I was able to retire comfortably.

During those years, I was very confused about God. I struggled with the concept of the Jewish people being the "Chosen People." After living through the hell of the concentration camps and after burying Rachel, I wasn't sure what "Chosen People" meant. I was angry at God, but I couldn't turn Him off. I told my rabbi that I didn't ever want an *aliyah* to the Torah.

But a few years ago, my friend's son was married. The Shabbat before, their family celebrated in the synagogue. The groom was called to the Torah. Many friends also received an *aliyah*. I was among them.

My teeth virtually shook in my mouth, when I recited the blessings on the Torah. *Blessed are You ... You Who has chosen us from all the nations of the world!* But I realized that I had no choice. It is better to believe in God, than not to believe. I don't ever again want to be left to the mercy of man.

Recently, I started kissing the *mezuzah* again when I entered and emerged from my house.

The first years that I spent in New York, I gave no thought to marrying. I had a girlfriend before the war; we promised each other that we would wait, in the event that we survived. I never found her.

I had rebuilt part of my life, but I felt incomplete. When I married, I decided that bringing children into this world was a sign of faith; faith that is possible to believe, even after Auschwitz. I believe that children are our arrows into the future.

I heard Elie Wiesel speak at an event soon after the Yom Kippur War. He said:

We owe it to our past not to lose hope. We must show our children that three thousand years of history cannot end with an act of despair on our part. Do not permit the enemy to rob us of our joy and our hope; to give up would be his victory and he does not deserve it.[6]

I was blessed with one daughter—what joy she is! Do you know that the reason that I sent her to a Jewish day school is because I wanted her to follow in my mother's footsteps. I hope that she will be a better Jew than I am. Some day, I want her to be able to supervise the *kashrut* for a holy man, just as her *bauby* had done. I hope she will continue to fill her *bauby's* shoes.

I've learned that a Jew must never despair. We must never give up.

A Sacred Trust
— Commentary —
In Memory of Shlomo

Our friend Rabbi Shlomo Carlebach, of blessed memory, was one of the architects of the *keruv/teshuvah* (outreach/return) movement, long before others became involved in awakening young Jews to the beauty and holiness of our heritage.

The geographical distance between South Florida, where we live, and Shlomo, whose address was the airline which carried him around the world to awaken our people, was great. Nevertheless, we spent as much time as we could with him, learning with him and from him.

He confided one of his dreams to us: "I wish I could stand on top of the Empire State Building to announce to the world how holy and precious it is to be a Jew."

We saw him last in October, 1994. It was two weeks after *Sukkot*. Somehow, he felt he had to tell us this story from many years ago. His stories usually were about the holy *chassidic rebbes* of eastern Europe. Occasionally, he would tell us of his encounters with the scions of those rebbes who are rebuilding their dynasties in New York and *Eretz Yisrael*. This story, however, describes the relationship he had with his *rebbe*.

—*Authors*

Chapter Fifty-Six
IN MEMORY OF SHLOMO:
RABBI SHLOMO CARLEBACH (1925-1994)

Time Line

| 70 c.e. | 600 c.e. | 1000 c.e. | 1400 c.e. | 1600 c.e. | 1800 c.e. | 2000 c.e. |

Location: New York City

"I went to see my rebbe, during the years I was learning in the *yeshiva* in Lakewood. Do you know what he told me? He told me I should go out into the world to talk to Jews. I wasn't sure what he meant. I hadn't yet picked up my guitar to compose my first *niggun*. I wasn't sure what I was supposed to talk about to "Jews in the world."

I did not understand the parameters of reaching out to my fellow Jews. I thought that if I kept his instructions in mind, I would learn what he wanted me to do from experience. So, I decided that whenever I had to ride the subway, I would find a Jew, sit next to him, and try to teach him some *Torah*.

One Wednesday night, the night before *Shavuot*, I was returning from a private session with my rebbe at 4 a.m. I entered the last subway car and sat down next to a young man. He looked Jewish, but I wasn't sure. If he was Jewish, I wanted to teach him some *Torah*. Besides, happiness was written all over his face, so I started the conversation by asking him why he was so happy.

"I'll tell you," he spoke excitedly. "In three day, this coming Saturday, (which was *Shabbat*, the second day of *Shavuot*) I will be married to a most wonderful girl. I am Jewish, and she is not. We will be married in a church in the Bronx. This is a very special weekend for me, and I am trying to visualize the ceremony This is why I am so happy."

I could see how happy he thought he was. I told him that marriage was a very serious business, and that before he was married, he should seek a blessing from a holy man. I told him that, coincidentally, a holy man lived only a few stations back, and I would be happy to accompany him. I assured him that although it was late, he needn't worry about the hour, for the holy man received visitors at all hours of the day and night.

The young man must have been curious, for he agreed to go with me. We left the subway at the next stop, crossed over the walkway to the other side, and took the next train back two stops.

My *rebbe* himself opened the door to my knock. He was a bit surprised to see me so soon. I told him that this young man was looking forward to a special weekend when he would be married to a non-Jewish girl in a church. I explained that I had convinced the young man to seek his blessing.

It was past 4:30 a.m. My rebbe put his arm around him, and led him into his office. I waited for three hours, reciting *Tehillim* (Psalms).

When the door opened, I heard him thanking the *rebbe* for teaching him who he was. When he turned around to face me, I saw that his eyes were red. My *rebbe* had washed his soul. It was not that his soul was covered with a little bit of dust. He didn't even know that he had a Jewish soul.

My *rebbe* had performed surgery on his soul. He emerged from his study and told me to take him to the *mikveh*, (ritual bath) and then to put *tefillin* on him.

The young man spent Shavuot with my *rebbe*, and indeed had a very special weekend.

I hadn't thought about that story for a long time," concluded Shlomo. "Somehow, I needed to tell it to you."

∽

In Memory of Shlomo

Making it mean something, making every action, every prayer, every bit of learning, have meaning ... what a mammoth task! That's why learning with Reb Shlomo, hearing his lessons or his beautiful stories helped so often. He was the prescription for augmenting joy, buffering sadness, or filling emptiness. As if to say, "Take two songs, repeat these stories and call me in the morning — you'll feel better."

—Dr. Alan Singer, Edison, New Jersey

Rabbi Carlebach put the words of Jewish prayer and ceremony to music that is heard at virtually every Jewish wedding and bar mitzvah, from *Chassidic* to Reform ... (At his concerts) most of his songs seemed to have no ending, but would keep going and going until the crowd was exhausted. The rabbi would rise and tell an elaborate *Chassidic* tale or a bit of *Torah* wisdom until he began another song.

—Ari L. Goldman., The New York Times.

Rabbi Shlomo Carlebach—"Shlomo," as he was known to tens of thousands around the world — was far more than the century's greatest composer of popular Jewish music, the man who provided the Jewish soundtrack for our time. He was this generation's great devotee of *ahavat Yisrael*, love for the Jewish people, seeking out lost Jews from Haight-Ashbury to Moscow and inspiring thousands to "return" to a Judaism they never knew. With a hug and a kiss on the forehead and a half-ecstatic, half self-mocking roll of the eyes, he turned strangers into instant friends, and symbolized a Judaism that embraced rather than repulsed.

—Yossi Klein HaLayve. The Jerusalem Report.

The damaged and the dispirited, the scarred and the searching, all wended their way to the doors of Reb Shlomo. Homeless souls, broken souls, yearning souls, lost souls, but ultimately what mattered most for Shlomo was that they were Jewish souls. If they didn't seek him out, he went out to hunt them down himself, a brave, lonely crusader. Shlomo Carlebach was in fact the true father of the *keruv rechokim* (outreach) movement, and long before other organizations jumped belatedly unto the bandwagon, he, singlehandedly, began pulling them out, one by one by one.

—*Yitta Halberstam Mandelbaum. The Jewish Press.*

PART SIX
OUR PEOPLE RETURN TO OUR LAND

Time Line

| 70 c.e. | 600 c.e. | 1000 c.e. | 1400 c.e. | 1600 c.e. | 1800 c.e. | 2000 c.e. |

Location: Eretz Yisrael

INTRODUCTION

From the time of the destruction of the first Holy Temple (586 B.C.E.) by the Babylonians, the Jewish people have prayed:

> *How shall we sing the song of the Lord*
> *In a foreign land?*
> *If I forget you, O Yerushalayim*
> *Let my right hand forget her cunning.*[1]

Many returned from exile and rebuilt the Holy Temple, but it was destroyed again by the Romans in 70 C.E. Since that time, Jewish tradition emphatically strove to keep awake our faith in the sanctity of Zion through prayer.

> *And to Yerushalayim, Your city,*
> *May You return with compassion, and reside in it,*
> *And rebuild it soon in our days....*
>
> *May our eyes behold Your return to Zion...*[2]
>
> *Rebuild Yerushalayim, the Holy city,*
> *Soon in our days....*[3]

But the reality was that the Jewish people wandered from country to country, searching for a relatively secure place to live, always praying to return to Zion, but remaining in the *diaspora*.

Part Six: Our People Return to our Land

During the eleventh century, Rabbi Yehuda HaLayve, the poet laureate of the Golden Age in Spain wrote:

> *My heart is in the east,*
> *And I in the uttermost west*
> *How can I find savour in food?*
> *How shall it be sweet for me? ...*
> *A light thing would it seem to me*
> *To leave all the good things of Spain*
> *Seeing how precious in mine eyes to behold*
> *The dust of the desolate sanctuary.*

At the age of sixty, he packed his belongings and made *aliya* (moved to *Eretz Yisrael*). Others followed in his footsteps.

Rabbis encouraged their disciples to settle in *Eretz Yisrael,* or at least, to visit. (*Be Careful How You Speak,* Chapter Fifty-seven; *When Will the Messiach Come?* Chapter Fifty-eight)

Through the centuries, a steady stream of Jews returned to our ancestral homeland. Some settled within the walls of the Old City of *Yerushalayim*. Others settled in *Tzefat* and Tiberias, others along the coastal plain. Slowly, the desolate land, having lain fallow under almost two thousand years of foreign domination, began to blossom and flourish.

Rabbi Shmuel Salant witnessed the dedication of the first railroad in the middle east. (*Once He Cried,* Chapter Fifty-nine) Even though he made *aliya,* some of his family remained in Russia.

Rabbi Yosef Chaim Sonnefeld emigrated from Hungary to *Eretz Yisrael*. Once he arrived in the Old City, he hardly ever walked outside its walls. (*The Determination of a Yerushalmi,* Chapter Sixty)

After World War II, thousands of survivors from Hitler's concentration camps, made their way "home." (*A Fragment of Torah,* Chapter Sixty-one; *The Afikoman that Restored Life,* Chapter Sixty-two)

Introduction

While immigrants flocked to *Eretz Yisrael* with the hope of rebuilding their lives, the settlers who had immigrated during the previous generation, struggled to build the country, to provide housing, jobs, counselling services, security, for the newcomers. (*Let Our Work be For Peace,* Chapter Sixty-three)

During the War for Israeli Independence (1948), the emerging Jewish state lost control of the Old City. Jews were not permitted to pray at their holiest shrine, the *Kotel,* (the Western Wall) until the Old City was recaptured during the Six Day War. After that war, young married couples returned to rebuild what their fathers had died defending. (*Kfar Etzion,* Chapter Sixty-four)

And then Russian Jews, Iranian Jews, Ethiopian Jews—Jews from the four corners of the world—came by the hundreds of thousands. (*From Moscow to Yerushalayim,* Chapter Sixty-five; *The Iranian Connection,* Chapter Sisty-six; *Why Did You Come To Israel?* Chapter Sixty-seven).

So much of Israel's population are children of survivors. Each has a unique story to add to the history of the Jewish people. (*Don't You Think Its Time?* Chapter Sixty-eight)

And the future? We pray it bring years of peace and security. (*I Have A Dream,* Chapter Sixty-nine)

These are the stories of our Israeli brothers and sisters.

Part Six: Our People Return to our Land

A Sacred Trust
— Commentary —
Be Careful How You Speak

Elyahu Hanave's disguise in common every day encounters teaches us the profound lesson that in the very simplicity of life one can find the deepest expression of Divine Revelation. The tragedy in most *Elyahu Hanave* stories stems from our inability to hear the message of redemption spoken to us amidst our mundane life experiences. The brilliance and uniqueness of this story shows how ultimate redemption requires us not just merely to hear the sounds and words but their purest expression.

The inner recesses of every human soul remains untarnished within and such sacredness can be expressed only with utmost care and sensitivity. The Baal Shem Tov's advice to his disciple about being careful how to speak to everyone is the path we must take if we are to reveal our real selves in order to achieve the great final redemption. We must also pray as we speak, with the purest and most honest simplicity.

Our lives have become so complicated that our natural higher yearnings are covered up with so many lower layers of resignation making us indifferent to the harshness that surrounds us. We need to address each other by learning how to apply the spiritual language of prayer.

It is honest to admit that the status most acceptable to us can be the earnest yearning for a new day. This is neither depressing in its candor nor is it fantasy in its hope.

Rabbi Samuel Intrator
Interim Rabbi,
The Carlebach Shul

Our People Return to our Land: Chapter Fifty-Seven

Zalman traveled from Poland to *Eretz Yisrael* and back

Chapter Fifty-Seven
BE CAREFUL HOW YOU SPEAK

Time Line

| 70 c.e. | 600 c.e. | 1000 c.e. | 1400 c.e. | 1600 c.e. | 1800 c.e. | 2000 c.e. |

Location: Poland to *Eretz Yisrael*

The Baal Shem Tov[1] set out for *Eretz Yisrael* many times, but each time his plans were thwarted by some unforseen circumstance. Once the axle of his carriage cracked, once the boat upon which he traveled encountered terrible storms on the high seas and the captain refused to continue the voyage until the weather subsided. Eventually, he came to the realization that it was not destined for him to see the Holy Land. Nevertheless, he encouraged his disciples to make the trip, so they might be privileged to walk where Abraham and Sarah, Isaac and Rebecca, and Jacob and Leah had walked.

[**Ed.** Rachel died as Jacob and his family returned to *Eretz Yisrael* from Laban's house in Padan Aram. She was buried on the border, in Bethlehem. B'rayshit, Genesis 35:19]

The Baal Shem Tov had a special blessing for each of his students who journeyed to *Eretz Yisrael.*

Once, Zalman approached the Baal Shem Tov. "Rebbe," he announced, "I have decided to go to *Eretz Yisrael*. I have come for your blessing."

The Baal Shem Tov responded: "My blessing to you is: be careful to whom you speak and what you say!"

Zalman thought this blessing a little bit strange, for he knew that one of his friends was blessed with an easy journey, another was blessed to be able to pray fervently at the holy wall, a third was blessed to pray for the barren women at matriarch Rachel's grave. But he knew that he couldn't question his *rebbe*, so he set off still wondering the meaning of the blessing.

On the long and hazardous route between Mediziboz and *Eretz Yisrael*, Zalman met many interesting people, among whom were pilgrims, merchants, and beggars. Before he spoke to any of his traveling companions, he whispered the words to himself, to be sure that he followed his *rebbe's* instructions.

Once he arrived in *Eretz Yisrael*, he immediately went up to *Yerushalayim*, to the *Kotel*, the remaining western wall of the Temple Mount, where he prayed with fervent devotion. He was overwhelmed with the beauty of the living stones that were a visible remnant of Israel's ancient glory.

During many months in *Eretz Yisrael*, he walked the length and breadth of the land, comparing it to biblical and prophetic passages. He visited *B'er Sheva*, where Abraham planted his famous *ayshel* (tamarisk) trees;[2] Beth El, where Jacob annointed with holy oil the stone upon which he had slept after his dream of angels ascending and descending the ladder;[3] Shechem, where Joseph was sold;[4] Anatot, the suburban area just north of *Yerushalayim*, which Jeremiah purchased before the destruction of the first holy temple;[5] Tiberias, the gravesites of Rabbi Akiva, Rabbi Mayer, and Rambam (Maimonides);[6] finally ending his pilgrimage back in *Yerushalayim*, to bid farewell to the holy city. Wherever he went, to whomever he spoke, he consciously heeded the instructions of the Baal Shem Tov.

While he was standing in front of the *Kotel*, he noticed a white-robed, bearded, gentle eyed old man scavengering around the ruins of the Holy Temple. He followed him for a time, fascinated with the agility with which he climbed up and around, in and out all the ruins. Suddenly, their eyes met. The old man beckoned to Zalman.

Be Careful How You Speak

Unhesitatingly, Zalman walked over to where he stood. He spoke: "It seems to me that you are from *chutz la'aretz* (the *diaspora*), aren't you?"

"Yes," responded Zalman, carefully. "I am from Medziboz, the city of the Baal Shem Tov."

"Tell me," insisted the old man, "how are my people faring in the *diaspora*?"

Wanting to be very careful how he answered, Zalman said slowly: "Life is very difficult for our people in the *diaspora*. We live in *shtetlachs*, scattered throughout the Pale of Settlement. Because it is very difficult to earn a livelihood, most of us are very poor. The government enacts many harsh decrees against our people. However, we are managing to survive."

"Tell me more," persisted the old man. "Are my people studying much Torah?"

Zalman still felt a little uncomfortable speaking to him, so he answered cautiously: "We have a few *rebbes* who teach us, and a few *batay midrash* (plural of *bayt midrash*) scattered throughout the Pale of Settlement. Some Jews set aside specific time to study before going to work or in the evening when they return from work. However, most Jews do not have time to study, because it takes so many hours to earn money to put bread on the table. Truthfully, under the circumstances, we are doing the best that we can.

> [Ed. In the year 1792, in an official act of the Russian government, Tzarina Catherine the Great decreed that the former Polish kingdom, which Russia annexed, be called the Pale of Settlement. She prohibited Jews from venturing forth from this territory. It was located between the Baltic and Black Sea from north to south, and by Russia, Prussia, and Austria on the east and west sides. The Jews were confined to small villages in the Pale of Settlement, to limit their living in other parts of Russia. They were treated as a hostile population, different from other Russian citizens, unworthy of equal citizenship.]

"And," the old man whispered, "are my people yearning for redemption?"

"We yearned so much after the Chmielnicki pogroms,[7] that many Jews followed Shabbetai Zevi, the false messiah. They wondered how long this bitter exile would continue, how long their prayers would go unanswered. But when he converted to Islam, we knew we had been disillusioned, that he had perpetrated a hoax upon us. So we continue to yearn and to pray, and in the meantime, we are managing to survive."

Then the old man disappeared.

Zalman did not think this meeting had any special significance, for he had met many people in the course of his travels. He returned to Medziboz.

As soon as he arrived home, the Baal Shem Tov summoned him. Zalman could tell from the tone of his *rebbe's* voice that he was deeply perturbed.

"Tell me, Zalman, did anything unusual happen to you while you were in *Eretz Yisrael*?" asked the Baal Shem Tov in an anguished voice.

Zalman thought a minute, and then answered carefully. "No, I don't think anything unusual happened. I met some very interesting people, some scholars, some beggars; I visited the gravesites of some of our great teachers; and I heeded your warning to be careful to whom I spoke and what I said."

The Baal Shem Tov probed further: "Didn't you meet anyone who discussed the plight of the Jews living in the *diaspora* with you?"

Zalman thought for a few moments:

"Rebbe, do you mean the white-robed, bearded, gentle-eyed old man that I met at the holy wall just before I returned home?"

"Tell me about him," insisted the Baal Shem Tov. "Tell me what he asked you. Tell me what you told him."

"Well, he was digging around the ruins of the Holy Temple. He climbed above and over, in and around the ruins. It seemed he beckoned to me, so I walked over to him. He wanted to know how the Jews were faring in the diaspora."

"What did you tell him?" prodded the Baal Shem Tov.

"I told him that it was very difficult to earn a livelihood, that our people were always in danger of government decrees being enacted against them, but that we were managing to survive."

"*Oi vey*," moaned the Baal Shem Tov. "What else did he ask you?"

"He asked me if we were studying much Torah?" Zalman answered.

"And what did you answer to that question," continued the Baal Shem Tov.

"I told him that we have a few rebbes who teach us in their *batay midrash*. I told him that most of us don't have too much time to study Torah because it takes so much energy to eke out a living. And I told him that we were doing the best that we can."

The Baal Shem Tov had tears in his eyes. "Didn't he ask you anything else?" sobbed the Baal Shem Tov.

"Yes , he asked me one more thing. He wanted to know if our people are yearning for the coming of the *Messiach*."

"How did you answer that question?"

"I told him that we prayed every day for redemption, that we are yearning for the coming of the *Messiach*, but even though he tarries, we will manage to survive."

The Baal Shem Tov's shoulders heaved with pain.

"Zalman, my son, you didn't heed my instructions. I warned you to be careful what you said and to whom you spoke. That old man was *Elyahu Hanave*. He was on his way to bring the *Messiach*. Had you told him that we were desperate, that we were yearning every minute for his coming, that we couldn't manage another second, he would have told the Heavenly Court that it was time to bring the *Messiach*. But since you told him that we could wait, that we are managing to survive, the decision was made by the Heavenly Court that the *Messiach* could also wait."

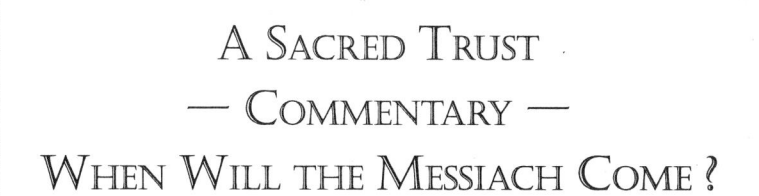

A Sacred Trust
— Commentary —
When Will the Messiach Come?

Three days before the *Messiach*, *Eliyahu* the prophet of peace and redemption will appear and proclaim:

> "Mountains of Israel! How long will you remain desolate and waste. Peace has come to the world. This is the coming of the age of redemption. This is the beginning of the great day!"

Pesikta Rabati 36:4

We do not know when the *Messiach* will arrive. But until the arrival of that great day, we must work together in a process of *ti-kun o-lam,* to fix the world and prepare it for redemption.

—*Authors*

Our People Return to our Land: Chapter Fifty-Eight

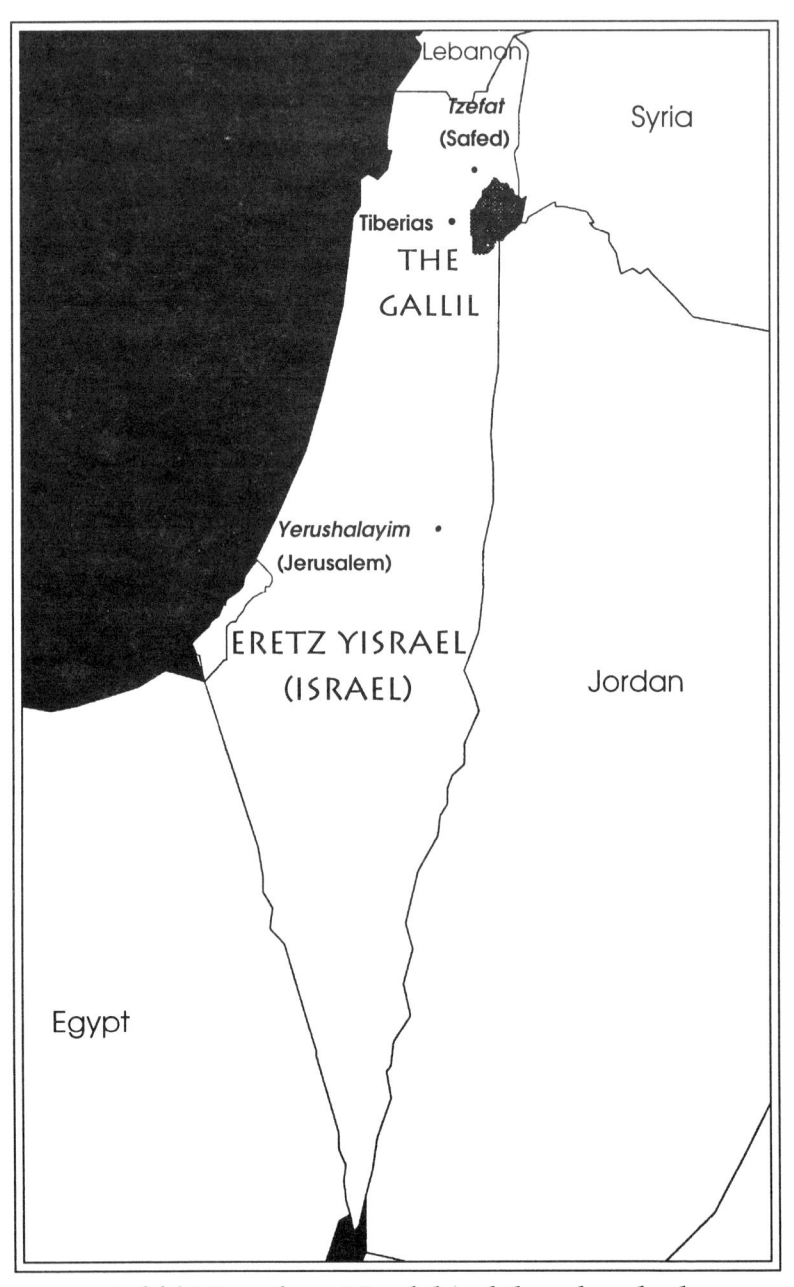

Rabbi Menachem Mendel and three hundred chassidim and their families settle in the *Gallil*.

Chapter Fifty-Eight
WHEN WILL THE "MESSIACH" COME?

Time Line

| 70 c.e. | 600 c.e. | 1000 c.e. | 1400 c.e. | 1600 c.e. | 1800 c.e. | 2000 c.e. |

Location: *Tzefat, Eretz Yisrael*

Tired of battling for the legitimacy of the chassidic movement against the *mitnagdim*, Rebbe Menachem Mendel Vitebsk[1] decided to make *aliya* in mid-life, to live his remaining years in *Eretz Yisrael*.

[**Ed.** The *chassidim* believed that the unlearned could approach the Heavenly Throne through prayer and good deeds. Serving God with joy, song, and dance in addition to the study of Torah created an emotional environment of love and caring. The *mitnagdim* insisted on intensive Torah study and the strict interpretation of *halacha*. They believed that the performance of the commandments was the ladder to reach the Heavenly Throne. Although their styles were different, oftentimes creating animosity between the leaders of the two movements, both *chassidim* and *mitnagdim* ultimately had the same goal; namely, to elevate the Jewish people to the highest possible level of holiness.]

Three hundred *chassidim* and their families accompanied him. They settled in the towns of Tiberias and *Tzefat* (Safed) in the *Gallil*, (the Gallilee) the northern part of the country, and were followed by many others, setting the foundation for *chassidic* life there.

Rebbe Menachem Mendel concluded his daily morning prayers with *Anee Maamin*, (I believe)[2] and waited patiently for the arrival of the *Messiach*.

One day rumor spread through the Gallilee that a man had

ascended the Mount of Olives in *Yerushalayim* and had blown the *shofar*, to announce the arrival of the *Messiach*. The followers of Rebbe Menachem Mendel were in a frenzy; for if in reality the *Messiach* had arrived, they considered themselves totally unprepared. Confused, they rushed into his study to consult him.

"Wait, one minute," he told them calmly. "I will go out into the street and try to find out if the rumor is true."

It did not take him long to return.

"I want you to know," he sighed, "that the *Messiach* has still not come!"

"How do you know?" asked one student. "Why did you have to go outside? Further more, if you had to go outside, how could you find out any information in the few minutes you were there?"

"I'll tell you," whispered Rebbe Menachem Mendel, sadly, "I had to go outside because inside, in this study hall there is always so much love, so much caring, it feels like the *Messiach* is among us always. On the other hand, when I walked around outside, I had no such feelings. I saw that the majority of the people still haven't changed, so I assume that the *Messiach* still hasn't come."

∽

A Sacred Trust
— Commentary —
Once He Cried

From the destruction of the Second Holy Temple and the ensuing *Diaspora*, the Jewish people have always yearned to return to their ancestral homeland. From time immemorial, our eyes, our hearts, and our faces have been turned toward the *Kotel*, the Western Wall, the one remaining symbol of the glory of ancient Israel.

This story profoundly illustrates that connection. The grandfather of the family has made *aliya*. His children and grandchildren remain in Russia. Trying to cope with the reality of forced army service, the father of the would be soldier, having no power to protest against the government, opts for the only choice he perceives to be a solution to his dilemma. He begs his grandfather to place a *petek*, inscribed with a prayer, in the crevices of the *Kotel* because he believes that his prayer will not go unanswered.

Besides the spiritual component of this story, we are also privy to the political situation as the 19th century came to a close. We meet Emperor Franz Joseph and Kiaser Wilhelm when they visit *Yerushalayim*. We see how Jewish leaders struggled to pave the way for the rebuilding of the Jewish homeland by their encounters with European royalty.

This year (5758/1998) marks the 50th birthday of the independent State of Israel. It also marks the 3,001th anniversary of King David making *Yerushalayim* the eternal capital of the Jewish people. We have never abandoned the Holy Land. From wherever we happen to live, we reiterate the words of the eleventh century Spanish Golden Age poet laureate:

My heart is in the east, and I in the uttermost west.
How can I find savor in food? How shall it be sweet for me?
How shall I render my vows and my bonds, while yet Zion lies beneath the fetter of Edom, and I in Arab chains?
A light thing it would seem to me to leave all the good things of Spain.
Seeing how precious in mine eyes to behold the dust of the desolate sanctuary.

—*Rabbi Yehudah HaLayve*

Our People Return to our Land: Chapter Fifty-Nine

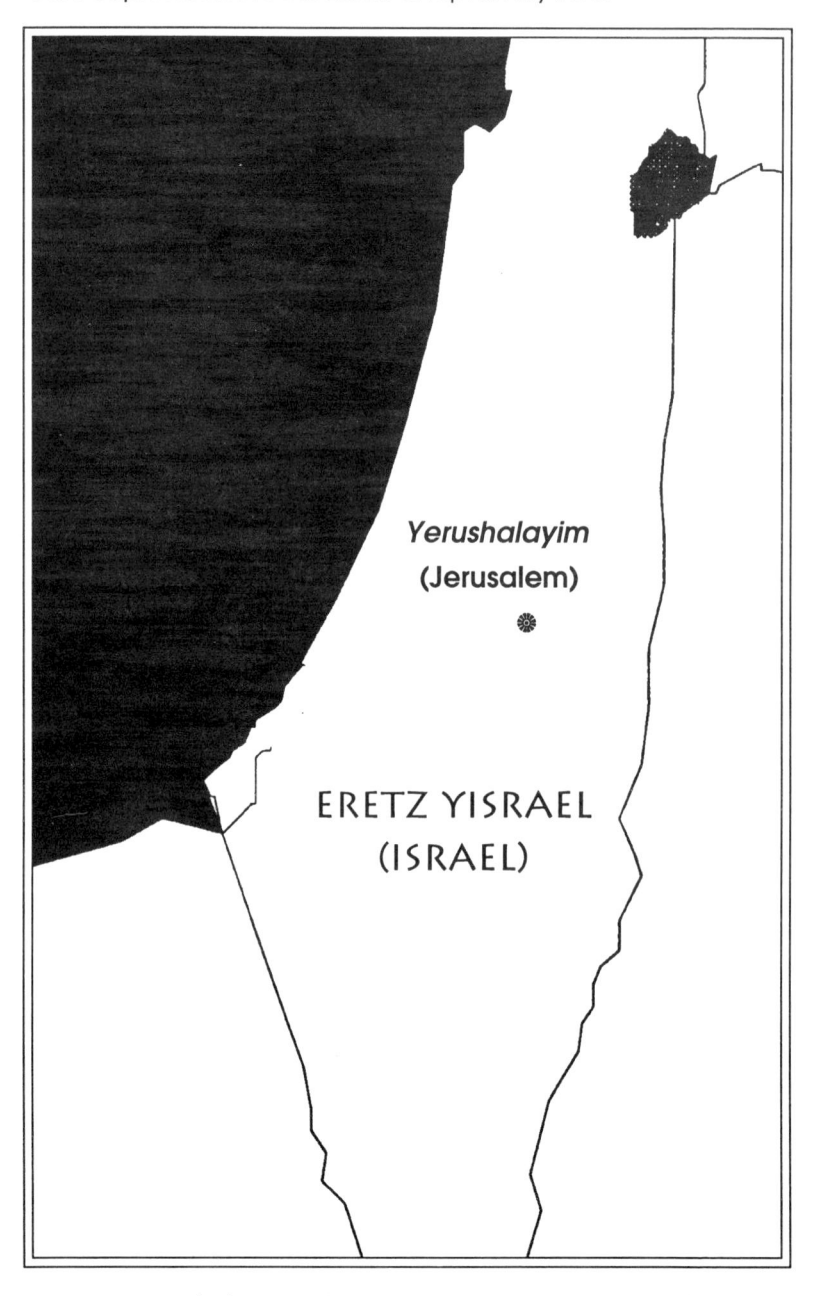

Yerushalayim (Jerusalem)

ERETZ YISRAEL (ISRAEL)

Yerushalayim, **the Holy City, in** *Eretz Yisrael*

Chapter Fifty-Nine
ONCE HE CRIED

Time Line

70 c.e.   600 c.e.   1000 c.e.   1400 c.e.   1600 c.e.   1800 c.e.   2000 c.e.

Location: *Yerushalayim, Eretz Yisrael*

Rabbi Shmuel Salant,[1] Ashkenazi chief rabbi of *Yerushalayim* immigrated to *Eretz Yisrael* from eastern Europe as a very young man. When he reached the walls of the holy city, he was totally overcome with emotion. Trembling, he kissed the stones of the *Kotel*, his eyes filled with hot tears in thanksgiving for the privilege of having arrived in the city for which his heart yearned. He settled in a small two room apartment, in the courtyard of the Churva *shul*, that had no windows; the only natural light that filtered in was from a door whose top half was glass.

[**Ed.** When Rabbi Moshe ben Nachman made *aliya* in 1267, he found only two Jewish clothes dyers in the entire city of *Yerushalayim*. The Holy City had been decimated by the Crusades. He located a house that had been almost totally destroyed, the remnants leaning on marble pillars supporting a beautiful dome. He consecrated that house as a synagogue. About four hundred forty years later (1700), Rabbi Yehuda Hechasid, who led the first organized Ashkenazic immigration to *Eretz Yisrael* with approximately 1,000 followers, arrived and bought that land from its Arab owners. Ownership of the land changed hands many times. Eventually, the Churva (destruction) *shul* was built on the ruins of the original tract of land bought by the followers of Rabbi Yehuda Hechasid. The *shul* was built and later destroyed. Today, it has been rebuilt and is an integral part of the *Rova Hayehude*, the Jewish section, of the old city of *Yerushalayim*.]

He lived in this apartment for fifty two years, eating, learning, receiving dignitaries like Sir Moses Montefiore, and deciding points of Jewish law at the same table. People that sought his help did not need an appointment, for he was always available. He often said that God didn't make appointments either. He strove to develop communal institutions such as *yeshivot* and hospitals under unified administration. He encouraged the building of new areas outside the walls of the Old City to accommodate the increasing number of immigrants who made *aliya.* He lived an exemplary life, both as a scholar/teacher and as a role model of devotion to the needs of the community.

He had a rare personality; a superior knowledge of Torah and Jewish law combined with burning love for the people he served. He was a model of kindness, humility, simple sincerety, and patience.

"I want to tell you what I remember about Rabbi Shmuel Salant," said Rabbi Ahron Cheyus, "so that his deeds will be an example for future generations."

As a young man of twenty one, I was responsible for bringing the daily mail to Rabbi Shmuel Salant. This was not ordinary mail. Rather, the letters contained money that was collected throughout the *diaspora,* particularly from eastern European Jews, who supported their brethren living in the old city of *Yerushalayim.*

The delivery of mail was not organized then as it is today. All the colonizing powers, England, France, Germany had their own individual branch post offices because none of them wanted to depend upon Turkey, "the sick man of Europe," that governed Eretz Yisrael.

> [**Ed.** The "sick man of Europe" was the name used for the declining Ottoman Turkish Empire, as it suffered more and more territorial losses during the eighteenth and nineteenth centuries. It's governing policies became more inefficient and inept as time went on.]

Tzarist Russia did not have a branch post office in *Yeru-*

shalayim. All the mail that arrived by boat for Rabbi Shmuel Salant from that country had to be picked up in *Yaffo*. It was transferred to *Yerushalayim* by a reliable person, after special arrangements with the appropriate Turkish government agency were made.[2]

One day, he sent a messenger to tell me that he wished to see me. When I arrived, he explained the reason that he had sent for me, for he was not a man who spoke without purpose.

"I want you to take upon yourself the responsibility of bringing the mail from the *Yerushalayim* train station to me. Many people depend upon the money that I distribute for their most meagre needs. I have authorized your father-in-law, Rabbi Bezalel Lapin, to pick up the letters and the money from the appropriate government agency, and take them to the train depot in *Yaffo*. The train arrives here very early each morning. I want you to pick up the mail at our train station and bring it to me."

I did this job for Rabbi Shmuel Salant for four years, considering it a great privilege to be of service to him. During that time, I learned *menschlachkeit* and became very close to him.

We *davened* each morning with the early *minyon*, then he studied while I went to the train station. He had a set time for learning, always immediately after the *minyon*. He feared that if he would not study then, he would become so involved with the cares of the community later on in the day, that he would not have time.

I remember, even when his sight failed, and he could no longer read, he studied *Mishna* by heart. I had to read the letters to him, and I always started by telling him the return addresses of all his correspondents.

One day he received a letter from a source that was unfamiliar to me. When I read him the return address, his face lit up. "This letter is from my grandson, whose mother was the child of my first wife! Please, read it to me." The letter was written

Our People Return to our Land: Chapter Fifty-Nine

on both sides of extra long paper in a fine, circular scrawl, and I knew it would take a long time to read.

He felt my hesitation, for the hour was getting late, and I had to start my business day. He knew I had to worry about a livelihood for my own family.

"Please," he whispered, "one day you will also have grandchildren. If it should happen that you would not have had any letters from your grandson for many years, you would devour every word that was written. What can I do if my sight is failing and I am dependent upon others to read for me? I beg you, do this great act of kindness, and read me my grandson's letter."

I felt badly that I had caused him such emotional stress. I did not realize that he could feel my haste. I knew that he never imposed his wishes upon anyone, he never asked for favors. How could I refuse him?

I began to read: "Dear grandfather, the exemplary leader of our generation. I am writing to inform you that my eldest son, a pleasant, respectful child, a young scholar who spends many hours every day studying Torah, has been drafted into the Tzar's army. Please, I beg of you, go to the *Kotel* and place a *petek* into the cracks of the holy wall with a prayer inscribed on it that somehow he will be designated exempt from military service, and given a blue card."

[Ed. A *petek* is a note that is tucked in between the stones of the holy wall.]

Rabbi Shmuel shakingly removed a handkerchief from his pocket to wipe his eyes. I could not restrain myself either. I had never seen him cry before. I finished reading the remainder of the letter, folded it neatly, placed it in his hand, and sat quietly for a few moments. He was the first one to break the silence.

"I know it is late and you have to start your business day. But I cannot go to the kotel by myself. Please accompany me, so that I may place a *petek* for my great grandson in it."

Of course, I accompanied him.

Many months passed. One morning, I opened a letter for him from that same address. I read the letter to him. He smiled peacefully. I raced over to the Churva shul. It was filled to capacity with people who had come for the regular morning *minyo*n.

I didn't have time to talk to them; I only wanted to tell them: "You will never believe what happened, you will never believe what happened! His prayer was answered!"

When Emperor Franz Joseph[3] of Austria attended the dedication of the Suez Canal[4], he stopped to visit the holy city of *Yerushalayim*. Before the entrance to Yaffa gate, the embassies of all the governments that had representation in *Eretz Yisrael* set up welcoming stations. The Jews that lived in the Old City decorated their station with antique ark covers and other vessels that were brought from the ancient synagogues in *Yerushalayim*. The consuls of Austria and Turkey waited patiently, hoping the emperor would not by-pass them too quickly.

As the emperor passed, Rabbi Shmuel Salant, leading the Jewish delegation, exclaimed in a loud voice, using a clear and fluent German language: "Permit me , your majesty, to bless you with the same blessing that I blessed your grandfather when I visited him in his palace in Vienna."

The emperor reined in his horse, peered down with trembling and awe at the holy man who had blessed his grandfather. He alighted from his horse, drew near to where Rabbi Shmuel stood, bowed his head, and whispered: "Bless me also, rabbi!"

The approaching visit[5] of Kaiser Wilhelm of Germany to *Yerusahlayim* was announced in enough time to prepare a royal welcome from the Jewish community. At the head of the welcoming committee was Rabbi Shmuel Salant, Rabbi Yaakov Shaul Elishar and the Chacham Bashi (Sephardic chief rabbi).

In order for his majesty's royal carriage to enter comfortably through the Yaffa gate, the entrance was enlarged to accommodate the extra width. The committee also commissioned a gift for the Kaiser: a handwritten parchment scroll engraved in Hebrew and German expressing the blessings of the Jewish community. The Jews thought that the Kaiser would be able to influence Russian Tzar Nicholas II[6] to ease the restrictions he had imposed upon their brethren.

> [**Ed.** The Kaiser met Theodor Herzl, the founder of political Zionism, in a tent camp outside of Yerushalayim, in November, 1898. At first he seemed sympathetic to the Zionist idea. But when he returned to Berlin, he paid no attention to his promise to speak to other rulers to help the Jewish people.]

Rabbi Shmuel Salant passed away on Monday, the 29th day of Menachem Av 5669.[7] He had instructed his grandson Rabbi Tzvi Hirsh ben Rabbi Binyamin Benish: "You know that the children of children are like children. Because my son, your father preceded me in his death, I am obligating you to recite *kaddish* after me."

Tens of thousands of people accompanied his casket to *Har Hazaytim*. When they returned from the cemetery, the heavens filled with heavy black clouds, and torrents of rain poured earthward, an unusual occurrence in *Yerushalayim* at that time of the year. It was as if the heavens were crying over the departure of the "father" of *Yerushalayim*."

A Sacred Trust
— Commentary —
The Determination of a "Yerushalmi"

Fear is the enemy of faith. Affection for the tradition and devotion to its practices will stand us in good stead in peaceful times, but only *emunah sh'leimah*, wholehearted faith, will see us through the times that try our soul.

Most of us are not subject to physical danger in our day-to-day existence. Yet, we are still afraid - afraid of being too closely identified with Judaism. We try to avoid situations in which those hostile to our commitments can show us disdain or disrespect. When we take the path away from integrity, we become strangers to our own heritage. We become estranged from God.

Faith is not a talisman against personal peril or even the enmity of others. But it does allow us to walk the narrowest bridges in our world with a sure step, unafraid.

Having the courage of convictions as Jews means that we are always accompanied by a sense of God's presence.

Rabbi Jack Moline
Agudas Achim Congregation
Alexandria, Virginia

562

Our People Return to our Land: Chapter Sixty

Chapter Sixty
THE DETERMINATION OF A "YERUSHALMI"

Time Line

| 70 c.e. | 600 c.e. | 1000 c.e. | 1400 c.e. | 1600 c.e. | 1800 c.e. | 2000 c.e. |

Location: *Yerushalayim, Eretz Yisrael*

Rabbi Yosef Chaim Sonnenfeld[1] emigrated to *Eretz Yisrael* from Hungary in 1873 and settled in the Old City of *Yerushalayim*. Once settled, he meticulously refrained from remaining outside the walls of the Old City for more than thirty days. Nevertheless, he was instrumental in guiding the expansion of Jewish living quarters outside the walls, to accommodate the increasing migration of Jews, particularly the quarter called *Battei Ungarn* (Hungarian Houses). He led the group of Torah scholars called *Shomrei HaChomot* (the guardians of the walls). He was known for his encouragement of Jewish resettlement in the land, and emphasized the use of Hebrew as the official language of the Jewish people. He strove to establish peace between Arab and Jew during the years when Arab nationalism awakened and consequently opposed Jewish migration from Europe.

During the Nebi Mussa riots of 1920, the Arabs initiated the first of a series of violent attacks upon the Jewish inhabitants of Tel Aviv and Jaffa. The violence reverberated eastward, to *Yerushalayim* under the exhortation of Haj Amin el Husseini, the Mufti of Jerusalem. He had been appointed by the British colonial government as a gesture of even-handedness in their policy to administer fairly between Arabs and Jews.

Our People Return to our Land: Chapter Sixty

The Arabs riot started at the Damascus Gate, and quickly spread to the all-Jewish *Mayah Sheorim* (One Hundred Gates) section, located just outside the walls of the Old City. Only the interference of the *Haganah*, the fledgling Jewish defense forces, interrupted their design to plant fear in the hearts of the people living outside the protection of the walls of the Old City. The air was as tense as a wire stretched taut to its breaking point. For many days afterward, the Jews fearfully moved about their own neighborhoods. They dared not walk alone to the Western Wall, located deep inside the walled Old City.

Only Rabbi Yosef Chaim Sonnenfeld remained unperturbed. He was seen walking toward the Damascus Gate, heading for *Battei Ungarn*, wrapped in his *talit* and *tefillin*, to be the *mohel*, (ritual circumciser), at the *brit* of a newborn infant. His frightened family had pleaded with him not to travel through the Moslem quarter.

"They lie in wait to ambush Jews who dare "trespass" through their quarter. Their keffieh's camouflage their faces. They could remove their *iqual* (thick twisted cord) and strangle you. If one stealthily follows you, darting out from a concealed corner, you will not be able to protect yourself. You should walk around the longer way, through the Jaffa Gate. It will be safer."

He refused to change his direction and murmured: "Rabbi Eleazar said: Those sent to perform a religious duty will not suffer hurt,"[2] and continued walking. The Arabs stared hatefully as he proceeded, but they did not stand up from the stoops upon which they were sitting.

When the *brit* ended, Rabbi Sonnenfeld started to retrace his steps homeward. This time, a friend, Rabbi Moshe Blau offered to accompany him. He refused, saying: "I am not in any danger, for Rabbi Eleazar has taught us that those sent to perform a religious duty will not suffer hurt, neither in their going nor in their returning. However, you, who have not been involved in the performance of this *mitzva*, (religious duty), would be in danger.

The Determination of a Yerushalmi

Rabbi Blau was not satisfied. He persisted. "Why do you insist on going through the Moslem quarter, when it would only take a little longer to walk through Jaffa Gate?"

It took Rabbi Sonnenfeld many minutes to respond. Finally, he said defiantly: "Let me explain something to you. I have chosen to walk through the Moslem quarter because I will not permit any of them to think that they have succeeded in driving us out of our land!"

A Sacred Trust
— Commentary —
A Fragment of Torah

The central elements of this story are three fragments of a *sayfer* Torah, rescued by a young boy, Shmaya, not yet a Bar Mitzvah, from the ruins of a synagogue in Budapest, set afire by Nazi hooligans. Finding the Torah scroll and cradling it in his arms, Shmaya is struck to the ground by the goons who toss the Torah into the flames. Shmaya can only save three torn and tattered fragments from the *sidra* of *Kedoshim*.

What do the fragments symbolize? Certainly the unique values of Judaism reflected in the verses in the fragments —holiness, justice, loving kindness, reverence for parents and rejection of all immorality—that have made the Jew different from all other peoples.

Perhaps they also stand for the Jewish people themselves, torn apart by tyrants far more vicious than any other in their history, yet containing within the 'saving remnant' the seeds of rebirth and redemption.

Even more, the fragments also portray the power of Torah itself to protect and shield the Jew despite all vicissitudes, both physical and spiritual, until that time when all the exiled are gathered from the four corners of the earth to return home, as Shmaya did, to the sacred soil of *Eretz Yisrael*.

Dr. Abraham J. Gittelson
Associate Director,
Central Agency for Jewish
Education, South Florida

Our People Return to our Land: Chapter Sixty-One

The long journey of the three Torah fragments

Chapter Sixty-One
A FRAGMENT OF TORAH

Time Line

| 70 c.e. | 600 c.e. | 1000 c.e. | 1400 c.e. | 1600 c.e. | 1800 c.e. | 2000 c.e. |

Location: Poland to *Eretz Yisrael*

"This is the first *Shabbat* since my nephew, Shmaya, the son of my brother, arrived here in *Eretz Yisrael* on this *kibbutz*, just a few days ago. He saved three fragments of Torah parchment from the hands of the Nazis. These singed parchments are the only remnant of this particular *sayfer* Torah, as it was commissioned by my brother in his son's honor.

Shmaya wants me to place these fragments into our holy ark, because they bear witness to the total annihilation of eastern European Jewry. He asked me to tell you that these fragments inspired him to struggle to survive. He believes that it is only through the strength of Torah that the Jewish people live and rebuild our own land. It is very difficult for him to repeat the story of how he survived. So please allow me to share it with you, just the way he told it to me.

My brother, Gedalya, his wife and Shmaya lived in Budapest, Hungary. One day, early in November, 1944, Shmaya ran hysterically up the stairs of the apartment building where they lived and cried:

"Father, father, the Nazis are pouring gasoline around the *shul*! They are setting explosives. They will blow it up! I ran home all the way to tell you! There are so many people milling around, watching, waiting, whispering. Hurry, we have to

Our People Return to our Land: Chapter Sixty-One

save my *sayfer* Torah from being desecrated and burned!"

"No, we will stay here. It is too dangerous to go out. Those people are barbaric; we know the atrocities they have committed already in the past five years, since they blitzkrieged Poland. We have to keep out of sight, to stay as far away from them as possible. It is our only hope for survival."

"But father, that *sayfer* Torah is my personal *sayfer* Torah. You commissioned a scribe to write it especially for me. I have to save it. I have to save it," pleaded Shmaya.

At that moment, an awesome explosion shook the whole town. Sounds of crackling glass, falling brick, collapsing walls thundered over the howling mob who stood by, cheering wildly.

"I must go! I must go," pleaded Shmaya. "I can run quickly into the *shul*. No one will see me. I have to save my *sayfer* Torah. I will be back in ten minutes."

My brother firmly put his hands on his son's shoulders and said: "I don't want you to go."

Shmaya quivered, crying convulsively in the protection of his father's arms, unable to understand why he could not try to save his *sayfer* Torah. Finally, he shuffled off to his room, lay down on his bed, still crying, still not understanding. He fell into a deep sleep.

My brother must have sat down in his overstuffed easy chair, reflecting recent events. He used to write to me that he spent a lot of time thinking during the past few years. The headlines had been screaming of the Nazi advancement into Hungary. It was obvious that they were determined to deport all of Hungarian Jewry to Auschwitz. His most beautiful memory was the events surrounding Shmaya's birth. This is what he wrote to me on that occasion.

"He is the only one of my children who lived." remembering six other male children who had all died before their *brit*. "When Shmaya was born. I vowed that if he would live I would commission a scribe to write a *sayfer* Torah in his name. At his *brit*, I named him Shmaya, for I prayed that the Almighty would hear my vow.

"I recall the celebration when we carried Shmaya's *sayfer* Torah into the *shul*. Everyone came to march in the procession from my house. We danced and sang, carrying it under a *chuppah*, (a canopy), all the way to the *shul*. The people of my town were overjoyed. They shared my happiness at having fulfilled my vow. They were as joyous as guests who come to a wedding to witness the ceremony uniting bride and groom as they stand together under a *chuppah*. They knew that the *chuppah* under which we carried it symbolized the marriage, the unity between the Holy One, Blessed be He, the Torah, and the Jewish People.[1]

"We dressed the new *sayfer* Torah with a velvet mantle, inscribed with Shmaya's name and the blessing 'length of days,' before placing it in the holy ark."

Recently he wrote that Shmaya was ten years old. Shmaya was permitted to stand on the *bema*, next to the Torah reader, when his *sayfer* Torah was read on Shabbat or on holy days. Each year on his birthday, he had invited all the poor people. Last year, Shmaya told his father that he would like to have his *Bar Mitzva* in *Eretz Yisrael*, in my *shul*. He wanted to take his *sayfer* Torah with him.

He wondered and sobbed, "What will become of the *sayfer* Torah? What will become of my son?"

Shmaya told me that he woke up in the middle of the night, startled. He was haunted by the terrifying thought that his *sayfer* Torah had been desecrated, that it had been burned. He tiptoed around the house and found that his parents were sleeping.

"It's strange," he thought, "when they burned the *shul*, there was such noise. Earsplitting explosions rent the air. Now I hear nothing outside. Something must have muffled the rowdy gangs. Was it possible that maybe calm has been restored to the town?"

"I am going to find my *sayfer* Torah," he decided resolutely. Stealthily, he moved toward the door, unlocked it slowly, silently, stepped into the hall of the large apartment building, pulled the door closed, and ran down the steps. Once outside, he crouched as he ran toward the *shul* through the narrow alleyways, being careful to remain inconspicuous.

Entering the *shul* through the back entrance, he saw that two walls had crumbled from the explosion, the windows were shattered, the benches had been uprooted, holy books were strewn all over the floor, one side of the roof was blown off, but the east wall, the wall where the holy ark stood—the holy ark that housed his *sayfer* Torah—was still intact. Quickly, he opened the ark and removed his *sayfer* Torah, grasping it tightly.

"I knew I could save it, I knew I could save it," he thought.

Suddenly, about fifty "Brownshirts" stormed into the *shul*. They had been parading around the town, laughing raucously at the devastation, throwing rocks into store windows, gathering the booty into a pile, preparing a bonfire, determined to plunder what their elders had left behind. Shmaya told me that they stared harshly at him..

"*Jude*, what are you doing here?" they demanded. "What is that you are carrying?"

"It is mine! Don't touch it! It is holy!" shrieked Shmaya.

"Holy? There is no such thing as holy. Hand it over to me," the leader demanded. "We will burn it with all the other property that we have confiscated from Jewish houses and stores, property that our soldiers left behind."

The leader stepped forward and grabbed the wooden handles of the *sayfer* Torah. Shmaya struggled. He clutched his *sayfer* Torah, kicked the leader, trying to repel him. But suddenly, the Brownshirts surrounded him, struck him on the head, punched him in the ribs, kicking him as he fell unconscious to the floor of the *shul*.

The leader must have taken the *sayfer* Torah, carried it outside, thrown it on the pile of booty, and put a match to the velvet mantle. As was their habit, the Brownshirts must have stomped around the bonfire as it spread, reducing their booty to ashes.

Shmaya stirred towards daylight. He tried to remember why he had been lying on the floor. He pulled himself up, crept towards what was once the doorway of the *shul* and looked in all directions. No one was on the street. It was drenched.

Anguished, he stared at the remainder of the bonfire. From the ashes, he saw a section of parchment and ran to retrieve the remnants of his *sayfer* Torah. Lovingly, he picked it up, caressed it, kissed it, turned it over and over in his hands, crept back into the *shul*, held the parchment up to the dawning light and read: *"Do not contaminate yourselves with any of these, for in all these ways the nations that I cast out before you became contaminated...."*[3]

"That is the end of the Torah reading for *mincha* on *Yom Kippur* afternoon," thought Shmaya excitedly. "It's about halfway through the Torah, right before the laws of "You shall be holy."[3]

"It's just a short time past the holy day season, when we began reading anew from *B'rayshit* (Genesis). Therefore, the majority of the parchment was rolled on one side of the wooden handle, protecting the middle sections from what must have been the licking flames of the huge bonfire. Apparently, that's how it was possible for these fragments of parchment to be saved."

He peered further at the words that danced before him:

Our People Return to our Land: Chapter Sixty-One

> *And the Lord spoke to Moses. Speak to the entire community of the Children of Israel ... be holy, for I, the Lord your God am holy ...*
>
> *Each of you should fear his mother and father and observe my Sabbath ...*
>
> *Do not steal another's possessions; do not deny that another deposited money or objects in your charge for safekeeping ...*
>
> *Do not swear in My Name falsely ... nor curse a deaf person, nor put a stumbling block before the blind ...*
>
> *Do not go as a talebearer among your people nor stand idly by when your fellowman is in danger ...*
>
> *And you shall love your fellowman as you love yourself....*[4]

Shmaya told me that tears welled up in his eyes as he read. He turned the singed parchment over. The second section was not so easy to read:

> *Do not eat the flesh of an animal while there is still blood in its body ... do not make any incision in your flesh ... stand up for an aged man ...*
>
> *If a stranger lives with you in your land, do not offend him, even with words ...*
>
> *Do not act dishonestly ... You shall have just scales, just weights for counterbalancing and measurement...*[5]

He had salvaged only one more section. The tears flowed down his cheeks, blurring his vision, but he persisted to try to decipher the holy words:

> *Sanctify yourselves by abstaining from immorality, for I am Holy. Observe My moral decrees and practice them; I am your God Who consecrates you to serve Me.*
>
> *Do not follow the customs of the nations I am dispersing before you, because they practiced all these....*[6]

Suddenly he sobbed uncontrollably. "Now I know why I am different." He clutched the three sections of the singed parchment to his chest and screamed out: "Blessed are You, our God, Master of the Universe, Who has not made me like one of them!"

Turning, he ran home. When he arrived, the iron gates were bolted. He pounded on them and rattled them. The janitor sleepily shuffled down the path: "Go away," he mumbled. "There is no one here."

Shmaya demanded to know where his parents were. He wanted to go upstairs to his apartment!

The janitor told him that there was a round-up during the night. All the tenants who lived in the building were deported. They bolted all the gates, prohibiting any one from entering the building.

Shmaya decided that he would go to search for his parents. He asked the janitor for a piece of bread. He was so hungry. He hadn't eaten for such a long time.

He took the bread the janitor gave him in one hand. In the other, he clutched the singed parchment sections of his salvaged *sayfer* Torah.

He wandered about for a long time, asking passers-by if they had seen his parents. Most people didn't pay any attention to him. He stopped in front of a big building. Unbeknown to him, this was the headquarters of the Gestapo.

He stuttered to the soldier behind the desk that he was looking for his parents, and asked him to please help find them.

"Looking for your parents, huh," the officer chuckled. "I'll take you to them. Follow me!"

The Nazi led the naive Shmaya down a long dark corridor. By the time his eyes grew accustomed to the darkness, he felt himself being shoved into a dank, crowded cell, a special holding cell for children.

He sat there for days. Only the sections of the singed parchment that he clutched to his chest and the hope that he would one day find his parents encouraged him to struggle to survive.

Our People Return to our Land: Chapter Sixty-One

Then all the children were bound with a rope and herded to the railway plaza. Shmaya was the last child in the line. They were shoved into sealed boxcars, destined for the gas chambers.

They traveled for many days; no food, no water, no sanitary facilities. When they arrived at their destination, they were pulled from the train and forced to march forward. Exhausted, Shmaya stopped to rest for a minute. The rope that attached him to the other children in the line snapped. Yet, he continued to move along with them, waiting for an opportunity to escape.

Noticing a shed in the distance, he dragged himself until he was a few steps away from it, then stealthily dropping out of the line, he crept behind it. He felt a sudden burst of energy. No longer hungry, no longer tired, he slithered silently through the tall grass, hidden by the darkness, not knowing where he was headed.

He dreamed that he was in his house. The *Shabbat* candles were sparkling on the white clothed table. Two golden loaves of *challah* were covered with an embroidered cloth. His father was handing him a few drops of wine from *kiddush*.

He opened his eyes and felt a bitter liquid being poured down his throat. A peasant was standing over him, forcing him to drink. He did not understand a word the peasant said. One by one a group of partisans surrounded him. Some spoke *Yiddish*. Shmaya understood that they would protect him as long as they could.

When the war ended, Shmaya's name was circulated with the lists of names of other survivors, by the agencies that tried to resettle them. They located me, here, in *Eretz Yisrael*, and made arrangements for him to immigrate. I want Shmaya to know that he has come home.

A Sacred Trust
— Commentary —
The Afikoman That Restored Life

"There are six million European Jews for whom the world is divided into two parts: places where they are not allowed to live and places where they can not enter . . .

"There will be a war from which Jews will not escape with their lives.

"Until this war breaks out, we should bring in [to *Eretz Yisrael*] as many Jews as we can."

> *Dr. Chaim Weizmann*
> *First President of the State of Israel*

An excerpt from a speech delivered to the Palestine Royal commission which held its meeting in the Palace Hotel in *Yerushalayim*. Consequently, the Peel commission recommended the partition of Palestine in July, 1937.

Our People Return to our Land: Chapter Sixty-Two

Poland

Vienna
Austria
Budapest
Hungry

Eretz Yisrael

The trail of the *Afikoman*

Chapter Sixty-Two
THE AFIKOMAN THAT RESTORED LIFE

Time Line

| 70 c.e. | 600 c.e. | 1000 c.e. | 1400 c.e. | 1600 c.e. | 1800 c.e. | 2000 c.e. |

Location: Poland to *Eretz Yisrael*

[**Ed.** Holocaust stories that defy imagination because of their barbarity and cruelty have been told over and over. Other stories that describe the underground resistance movement, that depict *Kiddush Hachayim*, the struggle to sanctify life in the ghettos and concentration camps, that delineate miraculous survival remain to be told.]

The family, Rachel and Nachum Krauss and a young girl named Naomi, aged fifteen, sat at their *seder* table with Moshe Levy, an invited guest. They had finished the meal and Nachum distributed pieces of the *afikoman*. The girl became hysterical: "I don't want it, I don't want it," she screeched as Nachum Krauss handed her a the small piece of *matza*.

"What's wrong, *chavivi* (dearest)," he asked. "Why are you afraid of a piece of *matza*?"

She sobbed. "If I take it, they will come and take you away like they took my mother and father. I know it. Please, don't make me touch it!"

Moshe Levy looked at the sobbing girl. Something she said was so familiar to him.

"I believe I know your daughter. Naomi, how long have you been in *Eretz Yisrael*?"

Rachel Krauss responded: "Naomi is not our daughter. She is a survivor and we are raising her."

He turned to the girl and asked: "Where were you born?

What was your father's name?"

She hesitated, for she wasn't sure she could trust him. Then, softly, she whispered: "I was born in Graz, Austria. My father's name was also Moshe Levy!"

Moshe Levy thought it was a dream. He wondered if the girl that sat opposite him could be his own daughter Naomi. He too, had lived in Graz, Austria. He never believed that he would ever see his daughter again.

"Naomi," he said cautiously, "Tell me why you were so upset when Nachum handed you the *afikoman*?"

"I remember a package of pistols and bullets that my *aba* (father) found underneath the table when he was searching for the *afikoman*. It was the last time I saw him. It was many years ago.

"Naomi, he cried joyfully, "I am your *aba*! You are my Naomi!"

"*Aba!* Are you my *aba*?" She ran toward him and threw herself in his arms. He held the trembling girl tightly to his chest, inhaling deeply and rapidly, stroking her curls, tears trickling down his cheeks.

Moshe Levy turned to Rachel and Nachum Krauss. "Since this is the night of telling stories, let me tell you the story of my miraculous deliverance from the clutches of the Nazis."

∽

I was a teacher of Talmud in the *yeshiva* in Graz, located not far from Vienna.

> [**Ed.** The dome-structured *shul* and study hall in Graz were dedicated in 1895. A small Jewish community lived there at that time. After World War I, a tremendous influx of eastern European Jewish refugees migrated and caused tremendous population growth. Many of the refugees became ardent Zionists, organizing both legal and illegal routes to help Jews cross central and southern Europe to sail to *Eretz Yisrael*, successfully thwarting British opposition to Jewish immigration. For almost twenty years, the Jews of Graz tried to lived as normally as possible between intermittent outbreaks of anti-Semitism.]

The Afikoman That Restored Life

On March 13, 1938,[1] the *Anschluss*, Germany's take over of Austria, signalled the beginning of the end of Jewish life. Our cemetery was desecrated, leading members of the community were arrested and tortured. Their property was confiscated. Many people fled.

Somehow, the Nazi invaders took no notice of me, my wife or our daughter. We trembled from the roar of each tank that passed our house, praying the Gestapo would not discover us.

A week before *Pesach*, only four weeks after the *Anschluss*, I wondered how we would obtain *matza* for the holiday. "Moshe Levy," I thought, "What if this is your last *Pesach*? You have never eaten *chametz* on *Pesach* before. Are you going to do it this year?"

Two days before the holiday, I decided to take a chance. I traveled to Vienna by bus, remaining as inconspicuous as possible.

[**Ed.** Vienna had a large Jewish population. 91% of Austria's 181,778 Jews lived in Vienna. They earned their livelihood both in the professional and in the economic sector. They were considered materially successful.]

I alighted from the bus in what had been the Jewish neighborhood. I saw that businesses were destroyed and property confiscated. I was told that Jewish communal leaders had been arrested or deported to a place called Dachau, near Munich, Germany.

Formerly proud Jewish citizens of an emancipated land now cowered in fear in the shadows of their plundered homes. They told me about unspeakable atrocities and brutalities that the Nazis inflicted on the Jewish population.

I sought out a close friend and found him in his apartment, poring over the Talmudic tractate of *Pesachim*.

"I took a chance coming to Vienna to see if I could buy *matzot*, wine and kosher meat for *Pesach*. Could you help me?"

My friend, admiring my courage, stood up from the table

where he was studying and put his arm around me. "Come with me," he said, "I will share with you half of what I was able to procure on the black market."

We were both crying when we parted. We swore to each other that if one of us survived this terrible time, he would recite *Kaddish* for the other.

Two nights later I sat down at our *seder* table with mixed emotions. I was happy that my family was still together, able to eat *matza* and drink wine. But I knew, deep in my heart, that the festival of our freedom was quickly becoming the time of our enslavement.

Just as I began reciting the *hagada*, there was a knock at our door. My lips quivered, my hands froze. When I finally opened the door, a heavy set man, his clothing tattered, his beard speckled with dirt whispered to me in *Yiddish*, "I am a Jew. I fled from Baden Bie Wein. You can't imagine the atrocities the Nazis are perpetrating against our people in Vienna and the surrounding area. I've been running through Graz, searching for a Jewish home. I noticed the *mezuzah* on your doorpost. Please, let me spend this *seder* night with you. Please, let me in."

I invited him in, showed him where he could wash himself, then bade him sit at our *seder* table. Our guest seemed to relax.

"I am so happy that I found you," he said. "Every place I passed as I fled, I saw only wanton destruction." He didn't say much more.

I finished reciting the first part of the *hagada* and we ate our simple meal. To my astonishment, just as I was ready for the *afikoman*, my guest rose, excused himself, thanked us for our kindness and disappeared out the door.

I proceeded with the service. I put my hand under the pillow reaching for the *afikoman* I had hidden at the beginning of the *seder*. I could not find it.

"Where is the *afikoman*?" I playfully asked my daughter,

Naomi. She was giggling gleefully. She urged me to search for it. I looked in all the corners of the small dining room. I opened the cupboard door, and raised the window shades. I could not find it. I bent down to search under the table. I was dumbfounded to find a newspaper wrapped package that I knew had not been there before.

As I unwrapped the paper, I trembled, for the package contained pistols and bullets. I realized that a trap had been set for me. I recalled that the mysterious guest appeared much thinner when he vanished!

I knew I didn't have too much time. I lifted the package, ran upstairs to the attic, and hid the pistols and bullets under the beams of the roof. I tried to calm myself, instinctively waiting for the next knock on the door. In the meantime, I tried to finish the *seder*.

In less than an hour, the door resounded with a thunderous pounding.

"Open Jew! Open the door, in the name of the Gestapo!" voices shouted from outside.

I opened the door. Four men pushed their way inside. Three were dressed in Nazi uniforms. The fourth was dressed in the uniform of an Austrian police detective. I recognized him as the mysterious *seder* guest.

He didn't ask any questions. He grabbed me, my wife and daughter and shoved us against the wall. The three Nazis searched every corner of the house but could not find the evidence.

"You cursed Jew!" he screeched. "Where are the pistols and bullets? I know they are here!"

I refused to speak. He slapped my face and punched me in the stomach until I doubled over in pain. I can still hear Naomi screaming as she witnessed my beating.

The Nazis could not find the pistols and bullets. The police detective grabbed me by the shoulders, pulled me up, and shackled my hands. My wife pleaded, "Please, please, have compassion. We are innocent of any crime. You know the truth. You planted that package under our table. You are a Nazi collaborator!"

He kicked her with his boot and she rolled to the opposite side of the room. He dragged me out of the house, sneering: "I'll get you to talk, don't worry. I have ways of making you talk."

They threw me into a jail cell, placing me in solitary confinement. No food, no water, no light. Days passed. The only thing that kept me from going mad was the lines I etched into the wall, one line each day for the counting of the *omer*.

> [**Ed.** *And you shall count, from the day after Pesach, seven weeks, until you number fifty days.*[2]]

On the fourth day, a man in a Gestapo uniform stood in the doorway of the cell. I recognized that he was my next door neighbor.

"You are accused of smuggling weapons," he whispered.

"It's not true," I said weakly. "I am innocent."

He continued: "Since I was your neighbor, I took it upon myself to watch over you and your family. That's why you were safe after the others were deported.

"The trap that was set for you was meant for me. They wanted to show that I had been protecting smugglers, so they planted the ammunition in order to implicate me. Their plan failed. I can never publicly contradict the story of that Austrian police detective, but I know you are innocent. Right now, I don't know how to help you, but I will try to find a way. Be patient. Give me a few days."

Four more days passed. Then, in the middle of the eighth night, my neighbor reappeared.

"Quick," he whispered, "dress yourself in these clothes and come with me. Hurry! We have little time! Don't ask questions. Don't worry."

I asked. "What happened to my wife and my Naomi?"

He remained silent. I knew I would never see them again. Tearfully, I dressed myself in the clothes he had smuggled into the cell and I followed him to the street. He was very cautious. A car waited at the curb, its motor revved. He helped me into it and extended his hand in farewell.

We traveled a while, then stopped. The driver opened the door and told me to get out. I was standing alone on the shore of the Mur River. I saw a ship anchored in the distance. From the ship, a lantern signalled. I waited.

> [**Ed.** The Mur River runs into the Murz River, then to the Leitha River until it crosses into Hungary.]

I heard the sound of the waves and the rhythm of oars cracking the surface of the water. A dinghy slipped up to the shoreline, the rower frantically urging me to hurry. I jumped in and he rowed back to the safety of a *bericha* ship.

> [**Ed.** Bericha was the "illegal" immigrant organization, part of the Zionist Jewish underground that organized the mass migration of Jews across borders of embattled countries, and engineered their freedom voyage to *Eretz Yisrael*.
>
> The British blockaded the Mediterranean Sea coast of *Eretz Yisrael* during the war years and afterward, firing on, sinking, turning back boats, deporting the survivors of Hitler's concentration camps to British prison camps at a time when Jews needed a place of refuge.]

I'm sure you know, all too well, the work of the *bericha*. I can't believe that I was among the survivors on one of those leaky boats that ran the British blockade.

We docked first in Budapest. Hungary was not overrun by the Nazis until 1944, so it was easier for the underground to operate from there. I stayed and worked with them. We moved Jews from Austria and Poland to Hungary and Yugoslavia and then on to *Eretz Yisrael*.

This is my first *Pesach* in *Eretz Israel*, among my own people. I am eternally grateful to you for inviting me to your *seder*. The Seder I led in Graz was really the *seder* of enslavement. It took me almost eight years to arrive here. Tonight, thank God, I am celebrating my personal *seder* of redemption, together with my beloved daughter, Naomi."

∽

Moshe Levy hugged his daughter again, then he stood her in front of him, arms length, turning her every which way. He still could not believe his eyes. This *seder* night was indeed a night of miraculous deliverance.

There was a silence around the *Pesach* table.

Rachel Krauss cleared her throat. "There is more to this miraculous story. I'm sure you want to know how Naomi came to us.

∽

My husband and I made *aliya* in the early thirties. We settled in Tel Aviv and identified with the *chalutzim*.

[**Ed.** *Chalutzim* were the pioneers who first came to rebuild the land of Israel.]

Just before the war broke out, I decided to return to Poland to visit my aging parents. I travelled with my daughter who was no older than Naomi was then. I tried to convince my parents to return with me to *Eretz Yisrael*, but they refused. They were murdered in a pogrom in their *shtetl* soon after Hitler marched into Poland, for the Poles used the blitzkrieg as an excuse to further persecute our people. My daughter and I escaped with our lives, but she became ill with diphtheria.

I was helpless to do anything, except watch her die. I was alone, frightened and unable to return to *Eretz Yisrael*. Jews were systematically rounded up for "resettlement." My British passport was meaningless to the Germans who were now at war with Britain. I was not permitted to travel, rather I was placed among the deportees. I survived the war years in the Ravensbrueck concentration camp where female resistance fighters from western Europe were incarcerated.

The Afikoman That Restored Life

The first glimpse I had of Naomi was of a frightened girl, huddled into the corner of a transport cattle car. Having lost my own daughter, my heart was filled with compassion for this child who was so alone. I grasped her in my arms and led her with me all the way to the unloading ramp of that hell hole. I pretended that she was my daughter. I cared for her and protected her as best as I could all the years we were incarcerated."

～

Naomi was sitting on the edge of her chair. At first, as Rachel Krauss spoke, she seemed disinterested, for the repressed memories were too painful. But as the story began to involve her, she became more attentive. "*Aba*, let me tell you what happened to me after they took you away."

Her eyes blinked back her tears.

～

"It was worse than a nightmare. At least a nightmare ends when you wake up. This nightmare didn't end for such a long time. I thought it would never end.

Sobbing, she continued: "About two hours passed after you were arrested. *Ima* (mother) was very worried. She must have gone out on the street to look for you. I guess I had fallen asleep, for when I awoke, the house was dark, and I was completely alone. I was scared to be alone. I remember screaming for *Ima*, but no one answered. I ran out of the house looking for her.

"I ran helter skelter, not knowing where I was going. I ran up one block and down another. From the distance, I noticed a familiar shape. I thought it was *Ima*. Under the streetlight, I recognized the dress she had been wearing at the *seder*. I began shouting for her to wait for me.

"Then a shot rang out across the town square and she lay dead under the street light. I remember I was crying. I ran toward where *Ima* lay. I just wanted to touch her.

As I ran across the street of the square, a speeding car hit me. Some passers-by took me to the hospital. The doctor saved my life, but he never could fix these ugly scars on my head and cheeks.

"I was in the hospital two days when someone told the German administrator that I was Jewish. Immediately, he ordered my deportation to a camp for Jewish children. I was thrown into a train with many other children. I didn't know where it was destined. On the way, the train stopped. A barber climbed aboard and all the hair of all the children was shorn from our heads.

"I noticed that the siding of the train had been left open. Since it was night time, I tried to escape under the cover of darkness. Slowly, I wiggled to the open siding and rolled myself under the train. I lay frozen, flattened to the gravel ground under the railroad car. The train resumed its journey without me.

"I wasn't free very long. An Austrian farmer found me wandering in his field and turned me over to the Gestapo. They threw me on to the next transport. I was huddled in the corner when Mrs. Krauss found me."

∽

"There is only one thing you don't know yet," Rachel Krauss interrupted Naomi.

"On April 30, 1945, when Ravensbrueck was liberated, I was able to contact members of the *bericha*. Remember, I had been living here prior to the war, and I had some idea of what to do. I told Naomi to answer every question about her identity with the statement:, "I am the daughter of Rachel Krauss."

"I instructed her to give no more information. It took us many years, even with the aid of *bericha*, to return home. This is the first *Pesach* in eight years that we have celebrated as a family."

∽

Everyone at the Krauss' *seder* table had told their story. Now the room was completely silent.

Suddenly, Moshe Levy opened his *hagada*. Locating the passage, he chanted: "*Ha lachma anya*, whoever is hungry, let him come and eat."[3]

Then, turning to the Krausses, he said: "It is because you truly understand the message of the *hagada* that I was reunited with my Naomi, here in our beloved *Eretz Yisrael*."

A Sacred Trust
— Commentary —
Let Our Work Be For Peace

The *Kotel* (wall) *Ha-Ma-ara-ve* (western) is the one remaining wall from the courtyard of the *bayt hamikdash*, the Holy Temple. The word *ma-a-rav* can be defined in more ways than simply "western." According to the Noam Elimelech, the word *ma-a-rav* means that place where there exists a mixture of holiness, love, fear and praise of God, sweetness, prayer, yearning for peace, righteousness, repentance, acts of kindness without limitations, and the study of Torah.

Rebbe Elimelech of Lizensk, Parshat T'tzaveh

It is no wonder then that Rabbi Avraham Yitzchak HaCohen Kook, the first Ashkenazic chief rabbi before the establishment of the State of Israel, believed that the returning pioneers were fulfilling the dream of *she-vat tze-yon*, rebuilding our ancestral Holy Land. He yearned for the land to be rebuilt with the most exalted of Jewish qualities, the qualities of *"ma-a-rav"* in preparation for the time of redemption.

A student once asked him to explain what all the awe about the Kotel, *Ha-Ma-a-ra-ve*, the western wall was. "After all," the student asked, "the *Kotel* is only a wall of stones."

Rabbi Kook thought for a moment and then responded, "There are two kinds of stones; stones that melt like a human heart, and human hearts that are as hard as stone. The *Kotel* represent those stones that melt our hearts.

Rabbi Avraham Yitzchak HaCohen Kook
Quoted in A. Y. Greenberg, *I-tu-ray HaTorah*.
Tel Aviv. Yavneh Publishers. 1967

Our People Return to our Land: Chapter Sixty-Three

Chapter Sixty-Three
LET OUR WORK BE FOR PEACE

Time Line

| 70 c.e. | 600 c.e. | 1000 c.e. | 1400 c.e. | 1600 c.e. | 1800 c.e. | 2000 c.e. |

Location: Yerushalayim, *Eretz Yisrael*

"I am a fourth generation *Yerushalmi* on my father's side," began Chaim Vigolik, a tall, husky, graying man, who is regional manager of Magen David Adom (MDA). "Rabbi Lipa Meir Vigolik, my great grandfather was born here. My mother's parents were killed in a pogrom in Russia. My mother, two of her brothers and two of her sisters were raised here in an orphanage.

I was born in 1925 in *Mayah Sheorim,* one of the first areas to be developed outside the walls of the Old City. I am the only survivor of six children. Two of my brothers were killed during Israel's War of Independence in 1948.

> [**Ed.** The *Mayah Sheorim* quarter, built in 1874, was one of the new urban developments. Because of increased immigration and a declining death rate, it was necessary to expand *Yerushalayim* beyond the walls of the Old City. The Jews were becoming a majority of the population by the mid 1870s and the new development spread north and northwest. *Yemin Moshe* and *Mishkanot Shaananim* were other newly developed areas.]

I was raised knowing that the British were the enemy. They recruited criminals and drunkards for foreign duty. They cursed and beat Jews who protested their pro-Arab policy. They issued White Papers that effectively restricted Jewish immigration at a time when European Jews desperately needed a sanctuary.

Our People Return to our Land: Chapter Sixty-Three

> [**Ed.** White Papers were issued by the British Mandatory Government between 1922 and 1939. The first one, the Winston Churchill White Paper, assured the Arabs that Palestine would not be converted into a Jewish homeland, but that the existing Jewish community could continue to develop. Jewish immigration could not exceed the economic capacity of the country to absorb new arrivals. The last, the Malcolm MacDonald White Paper stated that the objective of His Majesty's Government is the establishment of an independent Palestinian state in which essential interests of both Arabs and Jews were safeguarded. Immigration could not be allowed to continue indefinitely. The quota would limit 75,000 Jews over a period of five years. After five years, no more Jewish immigration would be permitted.]

November 2nd, was always a day of irritation for the Arabs, and they reacted accordingly. That day marked the anniversary of the Balfour Declaration in 1917. Since our cities were integrated with Arab and Jew living in close proximity, violence easily erupted, especially on that date.

> [**Ed.** The Balfour Declaration was issued on November 2nd, 1917 by foreign secretary Lord Arthur Balfour. He wrote: "His Majesty's government views with favour the establishment in Palestine of a national home for the Jewish people and will use their best endeavors to facilitate the achievement of this object."]

Throughout my schooling, I was inculcated with the words: *"Remember the massacres of 1929."* Haj Amin al-Husseini, the *mufti* of *Jerusalem*, tried to strengthen the supreme Muslim Council and renovated two Muslim mosques, the Dome of the Rock and Al Aqsa. These are located on the eastern side of the Western Wall. When Jews came to pray at the wall the *mufti* alleged that they were taking over the entire area. Clashes followed which culminated in an organized massacre of the Jewish population in four cities Yerushalayim, Hebron, Tiberias, and Tzefat, and in other villages.

> [**Ed.** The *Kotel*, the Western Wall is the remainder of the outside courtyard of the ancient Holy Temple. It is the remnant of what once was Judaism's spiritual center. The *Kotel* is like a bridge which fills the void between heaven and earth. From the *Kotel,* our prayers ascend aloft to heaven. Our rabbis explained that no prayer recited at the *Kotel* goes unheeded. Vayikra Raba 32]

Let Our Work Be For Peace

The British did too little, too late. It took a week for order to be restored. By the time I was fourteen years old, I had already joined the *Palmach*, the crack fighting units, that were stationed in *kibbutzim* all around the country. Our goal was not to confine our activities to the defense of existing Jewish settlements, but to stop Arab attackers before they could attack us.

The fledgling Jewish defense forces were under the leadership of Yitzchak Sadeh, Moshe Sneh, Yigal Allon, Yigal Yadin, and Moshe Dayan. Today their names are in history books, but when I was a teenager, I looked up to them as the defenders of the emerging Jewish state.

In 1945, I enrolled in an officers training course in preparation for service in the *Haganah* The training courses were held in *kibbutzim* such as *Gush Etzyon, Kiryat Anavim, Nevay Yaakov,* and *Bayt Arava.*

[**Ed.** The *Haganah* was a military organization which functioned in *Eretz Yisrael* from 1920-1948 to protect the early settlers. It developed into *TZaHaL, Tzava Haganah L'Yisrael,* the Israel Defense Forces.]

There were three divisions: male university students, female university students, and Jewish students who physically looked like Arabs. The latter were trained in methods of infiltration and espionage. The women performed a special task; they hid arms under their garments and smuggled them into *kibbutzim.* It was our response to the British "search and confiscate arms" policy. As difficult as it was to find sources where arms could be purchased, we replaced much of what they confiscated, in order to be ready to defend ourselves. We stored the ammunition in secret compartments, inside furniture, and behind fake walls.

When I finished officers training school, I became the manager of Magen David Adom in *Yerushalayim.* From its beginning in 1939, MDA was housed in the Hadassah outpatients' clinic, then it moved to the English Mission Hospital. In 1948, we moved to the former Palestine Police headquarters building in the Russian Compound. For the first time, MDA had at its disposal an operating theater, x-ray facilities, a blood bank, an emergency ward, and first aid rooms.

For seven years, I guided the development of the Branch Services Department from our headquarters for the country's new development towns. This department eventually expanded into a regional system spanning the entire country. One of the most important things I did was lay out every street of every city, town, and village on a map, to be able to reach the wounded as quickly as possible during any emergency.

The six months prior to the establishment of the state, from the United Nations vote for partition on November 29, 1947, to the withdrawal of the British military and civilian forces on the morning of May 14, 1948, were filled with bloodshed, retaliation, explosions. Both the Jews and Arabs tried to carve out a larger slice of land from this pitifully small country.

> [Ed. The British Mandate ended at noon on May 14, 1948. Sir Alan Cunningham, the British High commissioner for Palestine terminated the mandate one hour too soon. As his boat sailed away, he glanced at his watch. It was 11 a.m.. He had forgotten the difference between British summer time and Palestine time.[11]

I remember the night when the UN voted for partition. The sound of *shofar* blasts reverberated through the midnight quiet of *Yerushalayim*, proclaiming freedom after two thousand years of exile. Jews rushed out of their apartments in pajamas, robes and slippers, dancing in the streets, swirling in *horas* on every corner. Others marched through the streets, singing *Hatikvah*. We celebrated the promise of an independent Jewish homeland.

Our joy was temporary. The Arabs were thinking of war— of pushing the Jews into the sea. The border between Arab and Jewish *Yerushalayim* was located where the Mamilla project is being built today.

> [Ed. The Mamilla Project, an urban renewal project in the center of *Yerushalayim*, faces the Yaffa Gate entrance to the Old City.]

Small Jewish shops lined the streets. Arab villagers started to loot and burn the shops. *Haganah* soldiers tried to stop the burning and the looting. The British police chased them away.

In February, my brother, who lived in *Nevay Yaakov* and was an officer in the underground, lost his hands and eyes in a mine explosion. From his hospital bed, he asked me to stop fighting. I was now in the underground. He told me that I could accomplish the same objective as a *Haganah* soldier; that I didn't have to expose myself to extreme danger anymore. I didn't listen to him because I believed that the *Haganah* was trying too hard to please the British; that their progress towards taking over after the mandatory government evacuated was too slow.

Near the central bus station in the *Romema* section was an Arab factory that supposedly produced juice. Those of us who were in the underground knew that the factory was actually a terrorist base.

Across the street, there was a home for the aged. Members of our underground mingled with the seniors. The goal was to cross the street and conceal explosives around the perimeter of the building in preparation for blowing it up.

The order was delayed three times because plans to evacuate the home for the aged were incomplete. We did not want to hurt any of our seniors.

Finally the signal was given. We had two minutes to escape before the explosion. There were empty fields between Romema and a new Jewish section called *Bayt HaKerem*. When we entered the safe area, we had to use the password, "the cows are all right."

Following that effort, I was commanded to lead a unit in a diversionary attack against Mount Zion. One of the soldiers in my unit had an Israeli flag in his back pack. He told me that he wanted to put it on top of Mount Zion if we were successful in capturing it.

Grenades and bombs exploded around the graves in the Armenian cemetery and the tomb of King David. I was wounded. I spent six months in the hospital recuperating.

That's where I was on that Friday when David Ben Gurion read the Declaration of Israeli Independence.[2] I listened to the historical proceedings on a battery powered radio.

During the last part of my hospital stay, I lay next to one of my brothers. He died shortly after the declaration of the state, after emergency head surgery. I was released from army service as a lieutenant colonel in June, 1949, and returned to manage MDA.

Until 1985, I served in the reserves. Because I was an officer, I spent forty-five days each year serving my country. The amount of time Israeli soldiers spend in the service of their country adds up to nine years, from basic training until retirement after completion of reserve duty. It is a price we pay for our land to be free.

As the civilian regional director of MDA, I organized first aid stations in every *kibbutz, moshav,* and development town. I set up training programs in first aid procedures, so the settlers would be able to administer emergency treatment. Tragically, we have learned from the experience of five wars, what medical services work and what services need to be improved.

Recently, I instituted a project coordinating volunteers with people in need. I have 109 volunteers; they contact 1,200 people in need every single day. I dream that this type of program will be the main focus of MDA. I dream that MDA will be used only for peace, that I will live to see the time when all of us living in this part of the world will understand what *V'ahavta l'rayacha kamocha* (and you shall love your neighbor as you love yourself) truly means.[3]

I have six grandchildren; three girls that live in Kibbutz *Ayelet HaShachar*, near our northern border, and three boys that live in the *Yerushalayim* area. I dream that I will leave my grandchildren the gift of peace.

A Sacred Trust
— Commentary —
Kfar Etzion

When hopes and dreams are realized, we tend to lose the memories of the yearnings, the visions, the struggles that made them possible. The State of Israel is so real to us that we sometimes forget the story of its birth, of the pioneers who turned barren land into fertile fields and who bravely fought to protect the tiny settlements they founded. The history of Kfar Etzion reminds us how precious is the Land and how high the price paid for it.

The story of Kfar Etzion illustrates the continuity of dreams within families, and how children honored the courage and dedication of their parents. This chronicle of a singular settlement also raises the painful question of the future of the Zionist dream. Will the generations to come be imbued with the spirit and idealism of their ancestors? Will the State of Israel become a country like all others, or will it retain its specialness, its preciousness, its specifically Jewish essence, that so many extraordinary people struggled so hard to secure?

Rivka Haut
co-editor
Daughters of the King:
Women and the Synagogue

Our People Return to Our Land: Chapter Sixty-Four

ERETZ YISRAEL

Yerushalayim •
Kfar Etzion •
Hebron •

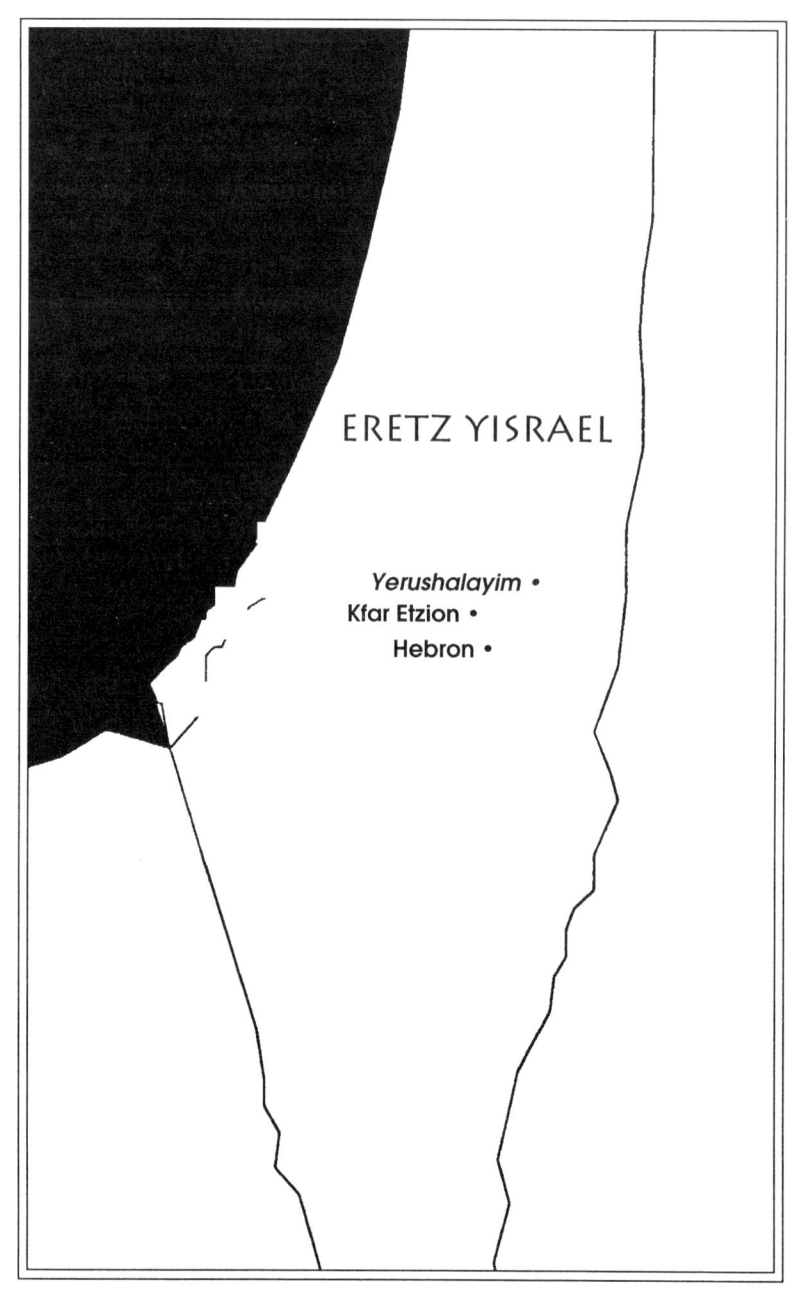

Yerushalayim, **Hebron** and *Kfar Etzion*

Chapter Sixty-Four
KFAR ETZION
The Re-Birth of a Kibbutz

Time Line

70 c.e.   600 c.e.   1000 c.e.   1400 c.e.   1600 c.e.   1800 c.e.   2000 c.e.

Location:
Yerushalayim & *Kfar Etzion* in the Hebron Hills of *Eretz Yisrael*

We looked forward to spending *Sukkot* in *Yerushalayim*. Immediately after gathering our luggage at Ben Gurion Airport, we hired a *shayrut*—a six or seven passenger, shared vehicle, to take us to the Holy City.

We left our luggage in our hotel lobby and walked up King George Street, up the hill as it turned into Nathan Strauss Street. At the top of the hill Malchei Yisrael and Mayah Sheorim Streets merged with it. We were greeted by the happy sounds of people choosing their *etrogim* and *lulavim* which were displayed on long tables. Shoppers measured the *lulavim*, counted the leaves on the willows and myrtles, and smelled the fragrant *etrogim*. As we walked back to the hotel, pleased with our purchase, we noticed that *Yerushalayim* had been transformed into a city of booths, for people were preparing to celebrate *Sukkot*, the "festival of our joy!"

On the first day of *chol hamoed*, the intermediate days of *Sukkot*, we were invited to *Kfar Etzion*, to celebrate, sing and dance with the *kibbutzniks*. People in their thirties and forties were dancing with joyous frenzy. In our liturgy, we recount that *Sukkot* is the "festival of our joy," but I did not understand the intensity of their joy. When I asked, I was told: "We are the generation that has returned."

It made so much sense. Those in their forties were the children who were evacuated during Israel's War of Independence. Some carried their grandchildren on their shoulders. I made a mental note to find someone whose mother was pregnant at the time of the evacuation, and who had returned to rebuild the land for which his/her father died defending. This interview took place in the summer of 1992, in the home of Dorit Una, in *Kfar Etzion*, four years after that *Sukkot*.

⁓

"Do you see that oak tree in the distance, the one in the valley between the two hills," she asked, as she pointed toward it? "For the past forty four years, it has been a symbol of life for those families who survived the Arab massacre during the War for Independence.[1] They vowed to return to rebuild this land.

The opportunity was given to us after the Six Day War in June, 1967. My husband and I were among those families. We are committed to remaining in *Kfar Etzion*.

> [**Ed.** *Kfar Etzion* is located in the Hebron Hills, about 14 miles south of *Yerushalayim*. One of the responsibilities of the settlers, in cooperation with the settlers of three other villages, *Massuot Yitzchak, Ein Zurim*, and *Revadim*, was to guard the entrance to the Holy City from Arab attack.]

We were both involved in *B'nei Akiva*, a religious Zionist youth organization. At meetings, we sat in a circle and sang for hours songs like: *"anu banu artza, livnot u'l'he-ba-not ba:* we have come to the land to build it and to be uplifted by it."

I remember when my mother reminisced how we celebrated all the holidays in Holland, but I never knew the joy of being Jewish until I witnessed the joy of *"simchat bayt ha-sho-e-va"* the first year that I arrived in *Yerushalayim*.

> [**Ed.** *Simchat bayt ha-sho-e-va* commemorates the pouring of water on the altar of the Holy Temple in a ceremony of song, music, dance, torchlight, and *shofar* blasts. It is celebrated during the intermediate days of *Sukkot*. Our sages said: that the person who did not see this joy did not experience joy his whole life. Talmud Bavli, Sukkah 51a (Mishna)]

My father Aharon came here from Zameryiya, Lithuania, in 1933. Being Jewish there was not without its problems. His last name was Lobutzki When he arrived here as a young man imbued with the Zionist dream he changed it to Yavniel, meaning God will build. He immediately set out to work toward fulfillment of his dream, and settled on *Kibbutz Shachal*.

[**Ed.** This kibbutz was named for Shmuel Chayim Landau, who conceived the idea of religious Zionism, which is the ideology that both Torah law and labor could combine in rebuilding the land.]

Later, he moved to *Kibbutz Avraham*, which was located in the fertile valley near *Pardes Channah*. In the early 1940s, the Jewish agency wanted to establish strategic settlements in different parts of the land in order to protect the settlers from Arab marauders. My father was given the choice of remaining or moving to the hilly countryside near *Yerushalayim*.

Meantime, my mother, Leah, who had come from Holland in 1937, settled in *Kibbutz Avraham*, where she met Aharon. She was a *Sephardi*. Her family name was Iteyalandi.

After they were married in 1943, they chose to live in *Kfar Etzion*, one of the settlements in the hilly countryside. A Mr. Holtzman had bought the land with the purpose of establishing a kibbutz. It was named *Kfar Etzion* for him.[2]

The first sight of this land was rock, rock, and more rock. There was very little water, and even less vegetation. When they asked the administrative counselor how they would make a living, he replied: "We will exist by building chicken coops and a rest home; we will gather fertilizer and we will plant fruit trees."

At first, the relationship between the Jewish settlers and their Arab neighbors was relatively amicable. They lived by the maxim, "Honor and suspect!" But when the United Nations voted for partition on November 29, 1947, their attitude changed. My father had an Arab friend who always brought him fresh fruit. The Shabbat morning following the United

Our People Return to Our Land: Chapter Sixty-Four

Nations vote, he appeared with a basket of fruit and said farewell.

"We've been friends for a few years now, but this is the last time I will be able to see you. I want to warn you to stay close to your house. Working in the fields in this area will be very dangerous, so don't wander around."

Almost immediately, attacks began. It was *Chanukah*. The *Haganah* had to defend the settlers that were scattered in isolated *kibbutzim* and *moshavim*. They had to keep supplies flowing and communications lines open, especially to *Yerushalayim*.

The situation became more tense everyday. The British were supposed to maintain law and order. In reality, they were helping the Arabs gain the upper hand. The Jews knew that they would have to fight for survival when the British evacuated at the conclusion of the mandate. The *Haganah* tried to transform settlers into soldiers.

At first, members of *Kfar Etzion* were able to repel the Arab attacks, but the attacks became more and more frequent. The *Haganah* sent a unit of thirty-five soldiers to help the settlers in January, 1948. The men crept forward all night, inching their way through the hills. Toward dawn, they were spotted by a Bedouin shepherd. He warned the Arabs. The young Jews were massacred before the sun rose.

The Arabs slowly gained control of all the hills in the area. A relief convoy was attacked in March. In May, the Arab Legion mounted a major assault on the settlements guarding *Yerushalayim*. The administrative council decided to evacuate the women and children from the area.

My mother and two sisters Geulah and Nili, along with the mothers and children of sixty other families, were taken to a shelter in the new city of *Yerushalayim*, located on Keren Hayesod Street, near the Yeshurun synagogue.

[**Ed.** Geulah means redemption. Nili is an acrostic for the Hebrew: the Everlasting of Israel will not rescind His decree, (I Samuel 15:29), and it symbolizes the young pioneers who arrived in Palestine before World War I who worked for Allied intelligence in the hope of ensuring a future Jewish settlement.]

They remained in the shelter for the next five months, until after the War of Independence. My mother had just learned that she was pregnant before the evacuation. My father was very happy that he would have another child, but he never knew me. When I was born the following January in Hadassah hospital, I was named Dorit Rachel.

[**Ed.** Dorit means freedom. Rachel was the name of my father's mother.]

The war broke out right after the provisional government declared the establishment of the State of Israel. It was Friday, May 14, 1948, the fifth day of the Hebrew month of Iyar, 5708. The state was established with the lighting of the Shabbat candles, but in the Hebron Hills, *Kfar Etzion* was burning. The field radio transmitters crackled with the words: "the queen has fallen, the queen has fallen," for *Kfar Etzion* was the strongest of the four settlements.

The Arabs plundered and burned. The women, who were in shelters in *Yerushalayim*, did not know who was widowed, which children were orphaned, which one of their husbands was in captivity. No one knew of the total massacre for many months.

In August, the government tried to resettle the widows and orphans in various *kibbutzim* on the west coast and in the north, to help them rebuild their lives. My mother took us, together with five more fatherless families, and many displaced persons, and we settled in Kibbutz Yavneh, south of Tel Aviv.

At that time, thousands of Holocaust survivors from displaced persons camps in war torn Europe were arriving in Israel to rebuild their own shattered lives. They were broken in body and in spirit, yet they kissed the ground as they alighted from the decrepit ships that had carried them over the seas to the land of their fathers.

It was not until two years later, in August, 1950, that the Jordanian government permitted Chief Rabbi Shlomo Goren to come to *Kfar Etzion* to remove the bodies of the massacred and arrange for their burial in a mass grave on Mt. Herzl.

"Why did you return here," I interjected.

She responded: "You know, when you wake up in the morning after dreaming during the night, the dream usually vanishes. But, the displaced families from *Kfar Etzion* dreamed a dream, day and night, for nineteen years. The children dreamed of returning while in school, in summer camp, and every year when all the families would gather on Mt. Herzl for a memorial service to their slain fathers. The mothers dreamed when they spoke to their friends, when they sat each Shabbat night, showing their children photos of their fathers from albums that had a large photograph of *Kfar Etzion* on its cover. Our common memory was the vision of that large oak tree. It was the only living object for the nineteen years of the occupation. Meantime, we all grew up and became a close knit family. Some of us were about ready to begin our army service, and some of us were already in the army. We all had hopes for careers, to marry and to have families. And we dreamed of returning to *Kfar Etzion*.

"In the spring of 1967, terrorist raids continued into Israeli territory at an increased rate. Surrounding Arab countries threatened war. Relations between Israel and her Arab neighbors, never peaceful, now deteriorated. Egypt blocked the Straits of Tiran to Israeli shipping, while the other Arab neighbors stationed their forces surrounding Israel's borders. It seemed that another war was imminent, the third in nineteen years. When all of us met for our annual memorial day outing during the last week in May, we discussed the possibility of returning to the *Kfar Etzion* area in the event that Israel would recapture this territory.

"On the fourth day of the Six Day War,[3] when I returned from the nursery school where I had been helping out as a volunteer, I was told that our ancient holy city had been recaptured along with the Holy Wall and the Temple Mount, and that the *Kfar Etzion* area had been freed from Jordanian occupation.

"We had an opportunity to live our dream. When I married, my husband and I decided to settle here. Other couples joined us. They were the grown children of the original settlers.

"The work was back-breaking, but slowly, we built a modern *kibbutz*. We replanted the orchards that had been destroyed, sowed vegetable fields, and rebuilt the chicken coops. We moved rocks, and set down foundations for houses. Our children were born and raised here, and soon they will be ready for their army service."

I looked around the pretty house. It had most of the comforts that Americans are used to: a TV, VCR, telephone, refrigerator, oven, microwave. It was comfortably furnished.

"I'd like to show you around the grounds," Dorit continued, "so that you will be able to better understand our attachment to this land, to the homes we built here. Also, at 1 o'clock, there is a showing of a special video that the members of *Kfar Etzion* made to memorialize those that fell defending this land. Come, let us walk."

Our first stop was the synagogue. I looked up at the stained glass window. It was facing toward *Yerushalayim*. I assumed that the holy ark stood beneath it on the inside.

"What is that shadow on the window?" I asked.

"When we built the synagogue, the administrative council decided to place three rocks on the outside ledge, as a memorial," Dorit whispered in a low voice.

We turned toward the big multi-purpose room. At mealtime, it served as a dining room, but it was also an auditorium. As we entered, my mind was flooded with the memories from four years ago, for it was in this very place that I had first experienced the joy of those who had "returned to rebuild."

We continued walking. The hills were covered with grass. Shrubs bordered the walks. Dandelions turned their sunny, yellow hats to an unclouded blue sky. Neat homes were scattered around. The *kibbutz* nursery school stood in the distance. On a nearby hill, the building for a girl's high school was in the process of construction.

"Some of the children are bussed to the school near the oak tree," she commented. "Forty-four years ago, the leaders of the Haganah planned that this kibbutz would guard *Yerushalayim* from falling into enemy hands. Nothing that they did at that time would have changed what happened, for the entire Jewish population in 1948 was only 600,000, too small a number to defend the land against the armies of seven Arab countries. In time, the Jewish population expanded to four million, the *Haganah* became *TZahal* (Israel's Defense Force), and this land is once again in Jewish hands."

"Do your children feel the same way as you do about this *kibbutz*," I asked?

"Our oldest son is studying in Hebrew University. He has finished his military service. Our middle son is just beginning his service. Our youngest daughter still lives at home. We talk about their future sometime. They are too young to make a commitment, but it is clear to us that the children of this generation think differently than their parents."

We had arrived at the building where the video was going to be shown. Sitting in the theater were ranking uniformed soldiers. Part of their training was viewing this video that was made from the photographs in the same albums the children used to look at on *Shabbat* nights.

It reinforced everything that Dorit told me. As I watched, I realized that I was looking at the faces of real men who had real aspirations, who wanted to live in peace on their land, who wanted to build families and watch them grow, who looked forward to dancing with their grandchildren during *Sukkot*.

As the video ended, the screen upon which it was shown gradually separated to exhibit a stark rectangular hole in the ground. Black marble tiles and a low double chain-linked handrail surrounded it. Grave markers were interspersed, on the places where the defenders fell. The light of a perpetual lantern glowed against the stone wall on which the names of the 240 defenders of *Kfar Etzion* were hewn; a powerful reminder for the children of those who perished in defense of our holy land.

A Sacred Trust
— Commentary —
From Moscow to Yerushalayim

The dream to return to the Holy Land is reiterated in our daily prayers:

"And to *Yerushalayim,* Your city, may You return in compassion, and may You rest within it, as You have spoken. May You rebuild it soon in our days as an eternal structure, and may You speedily establish the throne of David with it. Bless are You, Our God, Builder of *Yerushalayim.*"

The Amida, the silent devotion prayer

It is these words which have kept alive the yearning and the hopes of our people to eventually return to *Eretz Yisrael*, through the inhuman conditions and persecution experienced throughout the Diaspora.

Eleonara, and her parents, raised in assimilated, communist families, represent just one family of the hundreds of thousands who chose to become *refuseniks* after Israel's War of Independence in June, 1967. Despite their infinitesimal knowledge of Judaism, they yearned to make *aliya*, to live in a country where they did not have to worry about the number on their passport. The *refuseniks* manifested their yearning through protest and fasting, The Jewish world responded in kind, and channeled their energy through such organizations as the Student Struggle for Soviet Jewry and harnessed their political clout through the Jackson-Vanik Favored Nation Status Amendment.

Today, it is obvious by the number of *refuseniks* who have resettled in *Eretz Yisrael*, that their insatiable craving to live full and complete Jewish lives in the holy land, is slowly being fulfilled.

—*Authors*

Our People Return to our Land: Chapter Sixty-Five

Novosibirsk, Moscow and Kiev

Chapter Sixty-Five
FROM MOSCOW TO YERUSHALAYIM
THE REFUSNIKS

Time Line

| 70 c.e. | 600 c.e. | 1000 c.e. | 1400 c.e. | 1600 c.e. | 1800 c.e. | 2000 c.e. |

Location: Soviet Russia, London, Washington & Eretz Yisrael

"My family and I were Russian *refuseniks*. I have been living in *Eretz Yisrael* for the past twelve years. My name is Eleonora Shifrin.

I was born in 1948, the same year that Israel was established as a homeland for the Jewish people. I was born into a family that had identified with the communist government since the revolution. My father, Dr. Isaac Poltinnikov joined the communist party after the war,[1] not because he believed in communism, but because everyone joined. It was a way of furthering one's career. Besides, a person who refused to join was considered to be anti-Soviet. My family had no connection whatever with Jewish life.

I grew up surrounded with friends. I was very busy with school. I did what was expected. I joined a young communist group and became a leader. I never thought about the discrepancy between communist theory and the way the state functioned, until I was seventeen years old.

I became ill and had to spend an entire year in bed. For the first time in my life, I had the opportunity to think independently. I came to the conclusion that Marxist theory was wrong. I further decided to fight for what is right.

Mind you, this conclusion had nothing to do with being Jewish, or with Zionism. I had not even heard of the State of Israel. Discussing my feelings with friends later on, we all agreed that our grandparents involvement in communism was embarrassing, and that we had to undo the harm that they had done. But we never thought of leaving our native land.

My father was a colonel in the Russian army. Since the government refused to release specialists after World War II, he became a career officer.

He served as the chief ophthalmologist in the Siberian medical district. After being transferred from base to base, we were finally permitted to settle in Novosibirsk, Siberia. Father's only interest was his profession, his scientific research. Since he had reached the highest position an army doctor could attain, we were considered wealthy. Yet, I remember selling soda bottles to earn extra rubles.

My mother was also a doctor, a heart specialist. She always believed that she didn't know enough, and she yearned to further her education. She wanted to be an expert in the field of electro-cardiology, radiation therapy and neurology. She continued her schooling, but she had difficulty finding jobs because my father was transferred every year to a different base. She didn't care about the money. She only wanted to save lives. She believed that the frequent transfers were because we were Jewish.

Mother suffered her first heart attack at the age of 34. After she recovered, she came to the same conclusions I had reached during the year of my illness, and she joined the struggle for human rights. Her fight was not identified with Zionism either. Her fight was to reunite families, for there were few families that she knew who didn't have one of its members in prison.

She started bringing literature home and I helped her reproduce it, to be distributed to the underground. In those days, there were no photocopy machines. A printing press was out of the question, so we painstakingly made copies by typing each sheet with as many carbon copies as could be legible.

I had wanted to become a doctor, but I changed my mind when I realized that that career would not further my work as an activist. So I enrolled in the university with the goal of graduating as a stage director. Besides drama, this university offered classes in English and history. During the first year, all the Jewish students were expelled. The objective of the government was to train students for the diplomatic corps, and Jews were not allowed in this program.

It was not the first time that I had been made aware of being Jewish, yet nobody I knew could explain to me what being Jewish meant. Either the people I asked were afraid to explain, or they did not know themselves. I searched for answers. To me, it was a case of personal dignity.

On the first day of every school year, when students were asked their nationality, they inevitably responded, "Russian." I was required to respond "Jewish" because of my last name. The students looked at me as if there was something wrong,

Soviet radio stations did not carry much international news. After Israel miraculously won the Six Day War in 1967, people would come over to me and exclaim "you did it!" At first I did not know what they were talking about. Then I understood the reasoning of their Soviet minds: Russian people are taught to respect strength, weak people are to be pitied. When Israel won, Jews were no longer to be pitied.

I knew then that I had to contribute something to the Zionist state, although at that point I did not know what this contribution would be. Little by little, my knowledge of Zionism grew. My mother shifted her energies to the Zionist cause, and we worked together.

In the meantime, my father completed his army service and was waiting to be appointed to the position of chief of ophthalmology at the University in Novosibirsk. The chair had been vacant for seven years. His colleagues elected him as the most qualified, yet the minister of health denied his appointment because paragraph five on his identity card was marked Jew.

He was now unemployed. He could not proceed with his scientific work. All his dreams were tied to being appointed to that chair, with its co-workers, laboratories and experiments.

My mother decided that the time had come for the family to apply for exit visas with Israel as our destination. Father was uncertain. She was so sure of her decision, that she told him that if the exit visas were granted, and he refused to accompany her, she would go without him. He agreed to start the process of procuring letters of invitation from relatives in Israel. This was in 1971.

After I was expelled from the university, I studied on my own. I also had taken ill again, so for this reason, my father, because he had held a high position, was able to obtain a diploma for me. According to the law, anyone who obtained a diploma had to work in the place where they were sent for three years, usually a remote corner of Russia. By chance, I found out about an opening for a drama teacher in the Academy of Music in Novosibirsk. I was sure that as soon as the interviewer saw my passport, he would tell me the job had already been filled. To my surprise, he offered me the job on a part time basis.

I chose to produce George Bernard Shaw's "Pygmalion" for the senior class. We worked very hard on the production. We were scheduled to repeat the performance each night for a week. After the curtain fell on opening night, I asked my students to join me in the dressing room. I told them how much I had been harassed during the entire production of the play.

I explained that parts of the script had been censored. I criticized the cultural bureaucrats for limiting my artistic expression. Then I revealed to them that I felt that my place was in Israel, that my family was in the process of applying for exit visas, that no matter how difficult life would be there for me, how much I had to sacrifice, I had made my choice. I could do nothing for Russia but I could do a lot for Israel. I assured them that I would always love my motherland and I would never forget them.

I knew I had taught them more than drama when none of them went to the KGB to denounce me. They risked a lot by not telling the authorities that I had been conducting anti-Soviet propaganda, even though each one of them were "invited" to do so.

Interestingly enough, had my job been permanent, my colleagues would have been forced to testify about my character. They would have been forced to call me a traitor had they wanted to hold onto their own jobs. I would have been labeled an enemy of the Soviet State, a Zionist imperialist. One of my girlfriends blatantly told me that she could understand if I wanted to emigrate to marry a millionaire, but she could not understand my idealism.

I continued my underground activities for the Zionist cause, but I transferred my base of operation to Kiev, so I could take care of my aging grandfather.

From time to time activists came from Novosibirsk to Kiev to further distribute underground literature. I had been told that if I were caught, to reveal the names only of those refuseniks who had already emigrated. I was not to endanger those who remained behind. The KGB was looking for names of people identified with our cause. Someone accidently revealed my name, and I was taken by the KGB for questioning but was released.

Since I spoke English, I was the person who contacted tourists and journalists to mail the letters from our letter-writing campaign outside of Russia. My activist friends and I wrote letters to the President of the United States, to the United Nations, to world Jewry, to the State of Israel. Our letters emphasized one theme: the struggle of Soviet Jews to emigrate.

After Israel's athletes were massacred in Munich,[2] we wrote a collective letter to the Olympic committee. Then we went to Babi Yar to protest. Apparently, someone had alerted the police of our plans. Most were surrounded as soon as they arrived. A friend had approached me and warned me so I had enough time to escape.

> [**Ed.** Babi Yar is located outside of Kiev. One hundred thousand Jews were massacred there during the Holocaust, after they were forced to dig their own graves. Grass has been planted over the entire area; there is no memorial to their memories.]

I knew that I had to tell the world that the Kiev activists had been arrested. With a group of friends, we drafted a statement that I could read over the phone to whoever answered, at a number I had been given in case I really needed help. I dialed the number, and it turned out to be the Israeli embassy in Paris. Now I know what I did not realize then; the reason the call was allowed through was because the KGB wanted the identity of the people who had signed the statement.

The person who answered did not want to talk. He must have known that the lines were tapped. He kept telling me that what I was doing was very dangerous. I knew it was, but recklessly, I read the statement anyway.

The following day, I was arrested. The KBG tried to intimidate me, but they saw that the more they tried, the stronger I became. They emptied my apartment of half-finished letters, important documents. They asked me trick questions which would have implicated others, had I answered. They warned me to stop my activist activities, and then released me.

The minute I returned to my apartment, I started calling the foreign correspondents who had befriended us activists. It didn't take long for two KGB agents to appear again. They interrogated me for hours, threatened me with imprisonment, then told me that if I would confess, my sentence would be less harsh. They accused me of being part of a Moscow, Kiev, Novosibirsk activist organization. Since they could not prove it, they dropped the case.

My parents joined our cause. My father started distributing Hebrew textbooks and other Jewish educational materials. Fearful that I would be arrested again, my mother searched for someone to marry me.

The law stated that a man who was granted an exit visa could also apply for permission to take his wife with him, and that a married woman could apply separately from her parents. Someone told her that one of the young men that had been arrested at Babi Yar had already obtained his exit visa. She asked him to marry me. She wanted me to be able to leave the country as soon as possible, because she feared that I would never survive imprisonment.

We had to wait one month to get married. The Soviet government wanted young couples to think twice before they wed. The entire month before the wedding, I remained hidden in Kiev. I think the real reason that they finally let me emigrate was that they considered me a trouble maker.

I think they also believed that once I left, my parents would reconsider their application for exit visas. They wanted my parents to remain. My father, who had reached such a high professional level in Soviet society was very well known. They feared that if they granted him an exit visa, then others of his calibre would follow. My father knew what he was doing.

Now, both my parents applied again, on the grounds of reunification of family. I was already in Israel. It was November, 1972. They were refused permission to emigrate because they did not have enough relatives in Israel.

With a group of other activists, my mother went to Moscow to petition the Supreme Soviet. Each was given ten days in prison, but my mother was brought back to Novosibirsk and sentenced to six months.

I had only been in Israel for one month when I heard the news. I knew that my mother would not survive that much time in prison, for she had recently suffered her fourth heart attack and had developed diabetes. I started contacting diplomats and journalists. Most people I spoke to had little first hand knowledge of the real situation inside the Soviet Union. When they asked me how they could help, I found that I had to teach them about Soviet politics before they could grasp the urgency of the *refusenik* movement.

In February, my husband and I were invited by the Student Struggle for Soviet Jewry to the United States, to speak on behalf of the *refuseniks*. They arranged our passports and plane tickets. When we arrived in the United States, we found that the Jackson Amendment was one of the main headlines in the news. Senator Henry M. Jackson was trying to link the emigration of Jews to improved trade relations with the United States.

We travelled around the country, speaking on behalf of all *refuseniks*, but particularly concentrating on my mother's plight. We stressed that the situation was a matter of life and death. We found so many immigrant families who had left loved ones behind who were suffering in similar ways.

When my grandfather passed away at the age of 84 in Switzerland, my mother was denied permission to attend his funeral. He had been permitted the taste of freedom for only a few months.

Mother decided to start a hunger strike, after she was released from prison. My father joined her. I knew that unless someone in the west focused on events in the Soviet Union, their protest would have no impact. I was told that there was no way I could hold a hunger strike in Geneva or in Paris, so I flew to London to begin a simultaneous hunger strike with my parents.

My husband had remained in Washington. He volunteered to join us, so it turned out that we were holding three simultaneous hunger strikes in three different countries; in Russia, in Great Britain, and in the United States.

Senator Jackson needed a popular cause to find further favor for his amendment. Our hunger strike proved to be that popular cause. The newspaper and media headlined the case; we received tremendous coverage. The senator spoke on the senate floor. His aides distributed leaflets throughout Washington.

My husband sat in a black inflatable arm chair across the street from the Soviet Embassy on 16th Street. He had an ulcer which complicated his physical condition during the hunger strike. He grew increasingly unsteady and dizzy, but he insisted on continuing his fast until his in-laws received permission to emigrate.

Before I started my hunger strike in London, I called the immigration office in Novosibirsk. I told them my intention, but promised I would not go ahead with my plan if they let my family go. I told them that they would look very bad in the eyes of the western world. The immigration officer told me that he didn't care if I lived or died, that no matter what I did, they would never let my family emigrate.

The back of the Soviet Embassy in London faces Kensington Park. It would have been an ideal place for my hunger strike, but no one is allowed near that area. I ended up sitting near the front gate.

London is very cold in March and April. I remember that it snowed or rained continuously. The local Jewish community brought warm clothes and blankets, and they also arranged for media and newspaper coverage.

My parents were fasting in the central telephone station in Novosibirsk. On the sixth day, my mother collapsed. The authorities refused her medical treatment unless the entire family stopped its hunger strike.

My husband and I continued our fast for a few more days, ten days in all. We proved to the world that the Soviet Union had not changed its position on human rights. When we stopped, we thought that we were giving the Soviet Union a chance to save face, that they would permit my parents to emigrate. However, we were wrong.

Our People Return to our Land: Chapter Sixty-Five

My family was methodically subjected to ceaseless ordeals and abuse, both mental and physical. My father was accused of experimenting on human beings, his pension was suspended, he was hit by a car, (impossible to prove if it was an accident or purposely set up), his dog was stolen, their phone was disconnected. They were constantly threatened. These were the common measures which the Soviet government used to terrorize Jews who had applied for exit visas. Their purpose was to dissuade others from applying.

Once their phone was disconnected, it was almost impossible to reach them. I had to send a cable to tell them when I would call. They would go to the central telephone station and wait. Either I would be told that they hadn't shown up, or they were told that I didn't call. The KGB schemed to such an extent that my parents felt entirely alone, entirely abandoned.

Eventually, my mother felt that their situation was entirely hopeless. They had no more physical stamina, so they decided that the only way to gain public sympathy was to lock themselves into their apartment. They reasoned that if they cut themselves off from the world, people in the west would know how desperate their situation really was. They stopped corresponding with the three hundred people that had been recipients of their letters.

I received my last letter from them at the beginning of 1975. They told me that they rejected their Soviet citizenship and were applying once more for exit visas. They instructed me to stop writing, to halt all my protest activities on their behalf, because anything I wrote would be used against them. When I read the letter, I was sure it had been written by the KGB. Apparently, they were making an example of my parents. Of course, I did not cease in my efforts to help them.

They had saved some money, so at first, they lowered a basket from their fourth floor window with enough money in it to buy food for a few days. Neighbors shopped for them. When the money ran out, they placed a few personal possessions in the basket each time and asked for food in exchange. Eventually, they were reduced to eating potato peels. My father lost two thirds of his body weight.

I was in constant touch with two United States Congressmen who were pro-*refusenik*. They never stopped their efforts to obtain as many exit visas as possible. Finally, I was informed that my parents had received permission to emigrate. They were both so ill by this time, that the Soviet government decided it did not want to have two martyrs on its hands.

Two weeks after I had been told that they received their exit visas, they still hadn't arrived in Israel. My mother, having been refused the right to emigrate so many times, simply refused to believe that she was free to leave. Nothing my father would say could convince her. She thought it was a trap, that she would be imprisoned if she left the apartment, that she would be killed at the airport.

Finally, my father told my mother that he was leaving. He told her that he would send her photos of him and me together, proving that he had arrived safely in Israel. When the photos arrived, she still would not believe that she was free to leave. She was convinced that even the photos were a trick.

She trusted no one, she felt betrayed by everyone. She was terribly afraid that she was shut off from the rest of the world. She just couldn't go on. She stopped eating even the little food she was able to procure. She was hospitalized, but when she refused to eat, she was taken back to the apartment. The Soviet government insists that people who hold hunger strikes are mentally ill.

Mother died of hunger.

My father had been unable to work for eight years. During that time, he had been so badgered by the KGB that he aged significantly. When he arrived in Israel, it was difficult for him to relearn his unused skills. Normally, he should have been appointed to a department chairmanship in ophthalmology. It took time for him to be able to resume his scientific work. By the time he felt comfortable in it, by the time he was accepted, by the time he was asked to join the staff of a medical institute he had so little time to live

Father died in 1979.

The commissioners of Netanya, the city in Israel where my father lived, decided to honor his memory by naming a new street after him. We have not stopped working for a liberal emigration policy. So many of our brethren still want to emigrate."

Eleonara concluded, "When you write our story, don't forget to include the names of other *refuseniks*. We are in touch with all of them."

[**Ed.** Since that *Sukkot*, 1986, the Soviet government has adopted a system of *glasnost*. What was formerly believed to be impossible is happening: cultural exchanges are taking place between Israel and the Soviet Union, a *yeshiva* has opened in Moscow, and permission to bake *matzot* (March, 1989) for *Pesach* has been granted. But the story of the Russian Jews desiring to immigrate is yet to be told.]

A Sacred Trust
— Commentary —
The Iranian Connection

The state of Israel will be open for Jewish immigration and for the Ingathering of the Exiles . . . it will be based on freedom, justice and peace as envisaged by the prophets of Israel ... We appeal to the Jewish people throughout the Diaspora to rally around the Jews of *Eretz Yisrael* in the tasks of immigration and up building and to stand by them in the great struggle for the realization of the age-old dream, the redemption of Israel.

Eretz Yisrael was the birthplace of the Jewish people. Here their spiritual, religious and political identity was shaped. Here they first attained to statehood, created cultural values of national and universal significance and gave to the world the eternal Book of Books.

After being forcibly expelled from their land, the people kept faith with it throughout their dispersion and never ceased to pray and hope for their return to it and for the restoration in it of their political freedom . . . which would open the gates of the homeland wide to every Jew and confer upon the Jewish people the status of fully privileged members of the community of nations.

David ben Gurion
First Prime Minister of the State of Israel

Excerpted from the Israel Declaration of Independence
May 14, 1948 Iyar 5, 5708

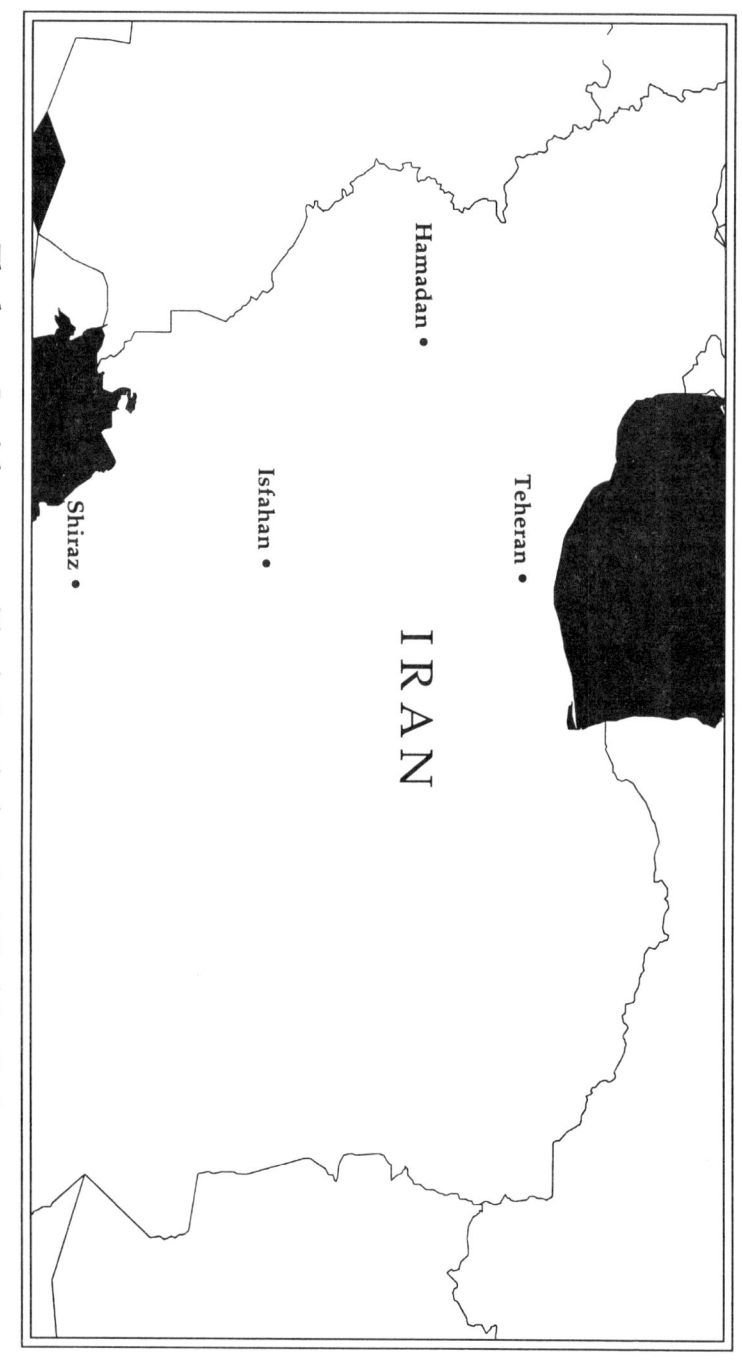

The larger Jewish communities in Iran before the fall of the Shah

Chapter Sixty-Six
THE IRANIAN CONNECTION

Time Line

| 70 c.e. | 600 c.e. | 1000 c.e. | 1400 c.e. | 1600 c.e. | 1800 c.e. | 2000 c.e. |

Location: Iran to *Eretz Yisrael*

"Shall I start from the beginning of Jewish settlement in my country? Do you know that Jews first came to Iran two thousand five hundred years ago, even before the destruction of the first Holy Temple? Do you want me to start from that point? I can give you at least thirty pages of notes!"

"No, why don't you start toward the beginning of the 1900s. I think it would much be more meaningful to know the details of modern Jewish settlement in Iran. I especially want to be able to identify Jews from the middle east who are a great part of today's Jewish population."

He rose for a minute, walked slowly over to a bookshelf and withdrew a large leather-bound book. Opening it to the frontispiece, he pointed to the list of names that were inscribed. "These names reveal seven generations of my ancestors who lived in Iran. It is a family tradition to record the names of the fathers and sons. I remember my grandfather and grandmother, but my father remembered my great-great grandfather and my great-great grandmother," he said.

"In general, the Jews who lived in Iran were either prosperous merchants or professionals; doctors, lawyers, pharmacists, judges. They were the backbone of economic development in Iran. Non-Jews were jealous, even hated us, but the

Shah protected us. Once a Jew was found dead on the streets of Teheran. It was obvious that he had been murdered. I remember vividly when the Shah proclaimed: "Whoever touches another Jew will be executed!"

"The businesses of Jewish merchants flourished, at first through a barter system, until the modern economy developed. Food, fabrics, and shoes were exchanged for medical, legal, and educational services.

"Mostly, the Jews inhabited four cities. Teheran, Isfahan, Hamadan, and Shiraz had sizable Jewish populations. My son-in-law comes from Shiraz. Hamadan (Shushan) was setting for *Megillat* Esther.

"I remember going to a school that must have been similar to the *cheder* in the eastern European *shtetl*. Our teachers were called *mullahs* rather than *rebbes*.

"It was necessary to learn Farsi, as it is the language of business and communication. At age six, we studied Hebrew. At age seven, our teachers transposed the Hebrew language over the similar Farsi sounds. By the time we were eight years old, we were learning French.

"The school system was set up by the *Alliance Israelite Universalle,* but since education was so important to the Jews, it was supported by the local Jewish community. Jewish administered schools, both secular and religious, began in kindergarten and went all the way through university graduation. The worse threat a parent could hold over an 'unwilling to learn child' was: 'Do you want to grow up to be illiterate?' Therefore, wealthy Iranians, Jewish and non-Jewish, sent their children to our excellent schools.

"During our teenage years we attended school in the evening. It was customary for the male children to accompany their fathers to work. They learned his trade or business by working with him. Some pursued a university education, forsaking the family business for a profession.

The Iranian Connection

"We lived in a part of Teheran where mostly observant Jews lived. My father was a respected scribe, and he was known throughout the region. Our home was open to American, English, and Palestinian charity collectors. They came to Iran to collect money from wealthy Iranian Jews to be distributed for the upkeep of their *yeshivot*.

"As was the custom in our society, men married at a young age. I was only twenty years old when I married my wife. We have three children, the two sitting here with us and my eldest son who lives in Israel.

"Did you know that the Iranian Jewish community was the largest Jewish community in all of the Middle East and North Africa? Estimates are that 100,000 Jews lived in Iran before Khomeini.

"After I married, we lived in the same neighborhood as our parents. Teheran was a beautiful city. The Elburz mountain range towers over the city which is 4,000 feet above sea level. Mount Demavent ascends starkly three miles high. We looked forward to the same protected existence as the generations before us.

"Many Iranian Jews knew that the Shah showed genuine goodwill to Jewish Iraqian refugees who were expelled from their country during the early fifties as a reaction to the establishment of the State of Israel. The Shah allowed these Iraqi Jews to live on a campsite outside Teheran. It was used as a base by the Joint Distribution Committee, the Jewish Agency and the Israeli *Mossad* as a way station, an asylum for the Iraqi refugees on their way to Israel.

"As time went on, nationalist Iranians, mostly Shiite fundamentalists, grew more and more resentful of the Shah's western modernization policies. They blamed the Shah and his American ally for morally corrupting their children, for introducing western culture at the expense of Islam, for making Iran dependent upon American technology, for the increased level of inflation, for the Shah's using American made weapons against them. Famine threatened, tenant farmers starved. Food supplies were looted enroute. Peasants protested their fate, going to bed night after night with empty bellies. Meanwhile, two hundred obscenely rich land owners, who lived in palatial dwellings, grew fatter by the minute.

"Rebellion erupted in almost every corner of the land. In September, 1978, the Shah declared martial law to stem the unrest. Dissidents protested in Jaleh Square in South Teheran. The protesters demanded an end to unemployment, an end to inflation, an end to the scheming and intrigue that was known to be part of the royal court. The Shah's soldiers fired into the crowd, killing more than one hundred people. With all this turmoil brewing, the Jews remained relatively secure. We were still protected by the Shah.

"Near the end of 1978, emissaries of the Lubavitcher Rebbe arrived in Teheran. Somehow, they perceived that 2,500 years of Jewish settlement in Iran was rapidly drawing to a close, for the world had begun to feel the tremors and the rumblings of Khomeini's revolution. They feared that the Jews would be the perennial scapegoat. They insisted on taking the children out of the country with them. It was difficult, almost unbearable to heed their warning. But, I sent my youngest son, who was seventeen years old at the time, with them to London, and my daughter to New York. They arranged for my children to live there in Lubavitch schools. Our eldest son insisted on remaining with us.

"So long as the Shah reigned, we were at liberty to emigrate; even to take our property with us. In rapid succession, four of my brothers and four of my sisters, with their families emigrated to America or to Israel. My wife and I and our eldest son remained in Iran, because we were still free to move about. We hoped we could retain our home and our property. I guess we thought the same thoughts that endangered Jews have always thought: a revolution can't happen here, this is a passing phenomenon, we've lived here so long!

"If you think that it is strange that I can recall the exact dates of the revolution, let me assure you that it is not strange to remember dates that signalled the upheaval of one's entire life.

"In January, 1979, my wife and I decided to fly to New York to visit our daughter. January 16, 1979, after months of violent protest against his regime, the Shah flew out of Mehrabad Airport for exile in various countries, including Egypt, Morocco, the Bahamas, and Mexico.

"The Islamic revolution had succeeded in toppling his dynasty, a reign of four decades. His exile lasted eighteen months, until he returned to Egypt at the end of his odyssey. He lived there, daily withering away from the cancer which claimed his life on July 27, 1980.

"Ayatollah Khomeini had arrived in Teheran from Paris on February 1, 1979. Almost immediately a rash of horrifying ordeals commenced. People were arrested without court orders. Telephones were tapped. Citizens were encouraged to spy upon one another and information was revealed to clerics to be used against the accused.

"We heard that businessmen, many Jews among them, were arrested, interrogated, and tortured. Some were held indefinitely in Evin, Lavazon, and Kasser prisons. The most brutal beatings and executions took place in Komiteh Mushtarak Prison in Teheran. Retribution against people loyal to the Shah was swift. Firing squads executed former government officials, military leaders and citizens accused of violating Islamic law. Amir Abbas Hovwida, the Shah's prime minister, Abbas Ali Khalatbari, the Shah's foreign minister, and a Jewish industrialist and head of the Jewish community, Habib Elghanian, who had served as the director of import/export for the Shah were convicted of spying for Israel. All three of them were executed.

"The newspapers and media headlined the Iranian revolution. Wealthy and middle class Iranians tried to escape the new regime, assuming the status of refugees. Among them were Jews, Kurds and Bahia's. They left their country because of political persecution and merciless repression. Jewish organization involved in emigration and resettlement divulged the specifics as it effected the Jewish community. I decided to leave my wife in New York and return to Iran. I thought that it might be possible to sell some of my property.

"As soon as I deplaned, I was arrested and accused of being in Iran to collect money for the State of Israel. I tried to convince my interrogators that I was collecting money for orphanages. Somehow, they believed me. They wrote down my name and warned me not to attempt to leave the country. I hailed a cab and told the driver my address. I remained in Teheran for one month, trying to sell my property, but to no avail. Apparently, word had circulated that it was prohibited for true Moslems to purchase property from Jews. Greatly disappointed, I made my way back to the airport.

"It was very crowded. People pushed and shoved each other, all with the common goal of trying to escape on the limited number of planes that were permitted to fly out of the country. The havoc in the airport made crowd control almost impossible, so the police were not able to check our passports too carefully against the list of detainees. Miraculously, I was able to board a flight, undetected. I returned to New York. When our daughter finished her studies, we decided to settle permanently in Israel.

"My eldest son remained in Iran with his wife and children. He was not permitted to leave until three years ago. He could not sell any of the family property either. Now he lives in Israel with us.

"If you have just a little more time, I want to bring you up to date on the status of Iranian Jews and on the escape routes utilized during the last ten years. There are still 40,000 Jews left in Iran as of this date and many of us keep in constant touch with refugee resettlement organizations, awaiting news of our families.

"There are two escape routes. If a Jew is going to Israel, he usually contacts a Moslem smuggler and pays him in Iranian money. These smugglers are known in the underground. The entire 450 kilometer border zone is a smuggler's paradise. They are brave, dependable, and thus far, honest, meaning that they complete the task for which they were paid, even though their fees are exorbitant. They earn comfortable livings, supporting wives and children by accepting money or property that fleeing Jews turn over to them. They are very experienced motorcyclists, camel drivers, horseback riders, any mode of transportation enabling them to reach the rugged mountainous borders.

"The trip by camel from Teheran to the border takes eighteen hours, but just as often the escapees must travel by foot. Once near the border, the smugglers crawl through the mountain passes, dragging the refugees after them. They lead them through the mountain passes after dark so as not to be detected by the border guards. They head eastward toward Pakistan or northwest toward Turkey The rugged mountain passes are covered with snow, even in early summer, making the trip extremely harrowing. Israeli agents follow their route, once they have crossed the border, contact the refugees and fly them to Israel. The process of resettlement takes about two weeks.

"If the Jewish refugee intends to resettle in the western world, he must contact HIAS, the Hebrew Immigrant Aid Society, once he crosses the border. HIAS workers meet them and guide them to "safe" houses. The refugee must qualify for United Nations refugee status to receive further help. These guidelines state that applicants must have a well-founded fear of being persecuted for reasons of race, religion, nationality, political opinion or membership in a particular social group. Few Iranian refugees qualify, and Turkey refuses to allow them the status of permanent residents. Slowly, the United Nations, the United States consulate or the Canadian consulate procure visas from Turkey or Pakistan to Vienna, where the refugees wait their turn to complete the process of emigration."

"I think I should stop here. I am happy that you will be able to share this information which few people know, and even fewer dare to discuss. My children become very agitated when I repeat this story, and I can tell that even the memories frighten my wife. It is, as if, she relives the harrowing escape of every Jew who followed us out of Iran to replant their roots in *Eretz Yisrael*."

A Sacred Trust
— Commentary —
Why Did You Come to Israel?

"Thus says the Lord: when I shall have gathered the House of Israel from the peoples among whom they are scattered, and shall be sanctified in them in the sight of the nations, then shall they dwell in their land that I have given to My servant Jacob.

And they shall dwell safely there, and shall build houses, and plant vineyards, and they shall dwell in security . . ."

Ezekiel 28:25, 26

636

Our People Return to our Land: Chapter Sixty-Seven

Chapter Sixty-Seven
WHY DID YOU COME TO ISRAEL?

Time Line

| 70 c.e. | 600 c.e. | 1000 c.e. | 1400 c.e. | 1600 c.e. | 1800 c.e. | 2000 c.e. |

Location:
United States, Czechoslovakia, Soviet Union & *Eretz Yisrael*

[Ed. Reporters, journalists, and writers gather information by asking questions. During our trip to Israel in the summer of 1992, one question, prompted by the obvious "ingathering of the exiles" evident at Ben Gurion Airport and on the streets of the cities was foremost in our minds: "Why did you come to Israel?" These are some of the answers.]

Mordechai and Channa

"When I graduated from college, I worked as a manufacturer's representative. I had a special affinity for the business world, and I became successful selling skate boards, the newest rage in America, and windbreaker jackets.

"Driving through Louisiana, listening to an FM station on my way to see a client, the announcer interrupted my reverie.

"Today, June 5, 1967, the State of Israel has been attacked by superior Arab forces and is struggling to survive! We will provide more information as it becomes available," he concluded.

"I pulled over to the side of the road. Sitting in my car, I could not know that the local stations were reporting Egyptian proaganda; that the Israel Air Force had totally destroyed the Egyptian Air Force in three hours, achieving complete air superiority for Israel.

"I began to pray. 'Please God, save my people from destruction. If you do, I swear that someday I will go to Israel and help my people build our land.'

"From that time on, whenever I went on a first date, I always pointed the discussion toward the fulfillment of my oath. I would ask, 'If we marry, will you live in Israel with me?' If she answered negatively, I never asked for a second date.

"Channa and I made *aliya* seven years ago. We settled in Efrat, and I opened a pizza shop in the town square, so my store has become a sort of gathering place for the locals. Since Efrat is a young community, I also organized a basketball and a football team.

"Except for our eldest, our children are *sabras*. We named them after the tribes of Israel. So far, we have six tribes. Our children know that they are helping us build the land."

Rochel and Efraim

"We came from Koshetza, Czechoslovakia just six months ago, and we live in an absorption center where we are learning to speak Hebrew. We have to learn Hebrew before we can find jobs in our professions.

"I am a chemist and Efraim is an electrical engineer. We know that we made the right choice. We are Jews, and this is our land. There are many mixed marriages in Czechoslovakia. Only civil marriages are recognized. We had to be married Jewishly in secret and had to hide our *ketuva*[1]. One could literally feel the anti-Semitism in our native land.

"We had a rabbi[2], but he saw no Jewish future in Czechoslovakia, so he convinced parents of forty children to allow them to make *aliya* with him. Our son was among them. There are very few Jewish children left there. The children now live with many other immigrants in *Kfar Chassidim*, a village outside of

Haifa. As soon as this school year ends, our son will join us here in *Yerushalayim*, just in time for his *Bar Mitzvah*.

"We want him to know that had we wanted to make money, we would have emigrated to America. We came to Israel because we want him always to know that he is a Jew."

Inna Chernitskaya

"I was named Inna when I was born in Moscow in 1924, but in prison camp I was spy number 58-1. My mother was a communist from the time of the Russian revolution in 1917. She was very busy finishing her university education, so my grandmother raised me. It was she who taught me whatever little I know about being Jewish. Anti-semitism was outlawed, yet my passport was stamped with #5, indicating that I was Jewish, and I wanted to understand what that number meant.

"I was an honor student in high school, so I was permitted to enroll in the university. I majored in fine arts and art history. Within two years I was expelled from the university and arrested. They said the reason for my arrest was my American boyfriend who I met through a British correspondent at a party. They said I couldn't be trusted.

"The interrogator called me a dirty cursed Jew. He accused me of wanting to defect to Louvre. He didn't know that the Louvre is a famous museum in Paris; he thought it was a country. He was a Jew who was a loyal communist. When I pleaded my innocence, he sentenced me to ten years. He told me that had he thought I was guilty, the sentence would have been extended to twenty-five years. I was sent to Lubyanka prison.

I had served 43% of my time when Stalin died. I requested release, but I was not given a residence permit for any city until three years later. I was able to find a job as an English typist, then I was promoted to an editor, then senior editor for *APN* (Novosty Press Agency, similar to TASS).

When the newspaper prepared to send journalists to the Montreal Expo in 1978, my boss informed me that even though I was fluent in English, I would not be considered, because I was Jewish.

"I feared loosing my job if I applied for an exit visa. I knew I needed an invitation from a relative to even be considered for emigration. Nevertheless, I applied for my first exit visa in 1977. The application was refused five times until I was allowed to leave.

"I wanted to live in a country where I was not a national minority. I want to live the rest of my life here in Israel, among my people."

Yehoshuah and Emunah

Yehoshuah

"I grew up in Chicago as an American teenager influenced by grandparents who emigrated from eastern Europe. My grandfather was angry at God after marauders killed his entire family in a pogrom in Tzernobyl when he was ten. He wanted no part of organized religion. But my grandmother, an observant woman, always served cold cuts for *Shabbat* lunch, so she wouldn't have to cook.

"My Judaism was matzo balls and a *seder* at someone else's house. I knew something was missing. I searched for answers to being Jewish. Finally, I was able to convince my parents to send me on USY pilgrimage to Israel. The leaders influenced me. They wore *kipot*, (yarmelkes), donned *talit* and *tefilin* and *davened* each day. They talked about Jewish roots as we toured this wonderful land.

"When I returned to America, I decided to wear my *kipa* all the time, but my high school classmates laughed at me. Since I lived near the *yeshiva*, I began studying there. Wonderful rabbis showed me the way. Shlomo Carlebach inspired me.

[**Ed.** Rabbi Shlomo Carlebach[ZˮL] was a scholar, creator of Jewish music, and inspiration to many returning to Jewish life. He died in 1994. Volume Two is dedicated to his memory.]

"Returning to *Eretz Yisrael,* I continued my studies in *Shalavim* and *Mercaz Harav* which are *hesder yeshivot.* This means that I studied and served in the army at the same time. I decided to remain here and make it my permanent home.

"I know that my devotion to this land has affected my children. Even though my mother sent all of us plane tickets to return to America during Operation Desert Storm and the scud attacks, my children refused to leave. I could never take my children out of the Holy Land."

Emunah

"You want to know what I gave up when I left America? I didn't give up anything ... a house, a car, a nice yard ... these are all American values. The standard of living is different in Israel.

"My children collect cards of *tzadikkim* (holy people) rather than baseball cards.

"I was always searching for my Jewish roots. My grandmother's maiden name was Kara, and I knew that our family was descended from great and holy Torah luminaries.[3] I wanted to know who they were.

"I had very little Jewish education until high school. Then my *bauby* took me to a Shlomo Carlebach concert at Queens College when I was about 15 or 16. From then on, I knew that I would have to observe Shabbat.

"I spent a summer in Camp Morasha, and the second half of my twelfth grade year here in *Machon Gold.* I never returned to America. I pray that my children will be the link that will continue transmitting their great grandparents way of life. I want them to know who they really are."

A Sacred Trust
— Commentary —
Don't You Think It's Time?

The relationship between a person and God is, of course, a complicated one, one unique to every person, one tailor-made for every person.

We are, Judaism teaches, each put on this earth for a specific purpose, each of us are to play the part given to us and to us alone. None of us duplicates another's mission, which is why each Jew needs to fulfill his or her mission so that the Jewish People, as a whole, can fulfill theirs.

Thus, no Jew can tell another how to live their life, how to be a "good Jew." That's especially true for those whose mission it was to go through and endure the Holocaust. That some of those who survived became angry at G-d is understandable. But being angry is relating, too, is, indeed, a way of looking for answers, demanding explanations, and so believing there are answers, there was a purpose.

No one knows why G-d brought the Holocaust, but if one believes, one knows it was for a reason.

No one, however, knows that reason.

There are no explanations. But the best explanation I have heard is to think of the life of this world as a beautiful painting of a bright blue sky. To truly bring out the depth of the blue, however, the artist first has to lay down a base of black. If you would walk into the artist's studio in the middle of his work on the painting, you'd see only the black and think the painting was a dark, foreboding one.

But if you waited until it was finished, you'd see the black was absolutely necessary, was the base needed to have the brightness of the blue picture come out.

So with the world, which, when it is finished, will be one of peace and joy—a bright blue sky. But to get there, as only The Artist understands, He first had to bring the period of black, of darkness. If we but wait, if we but trust, when the painting is completed, we will see and we will understand why the black was absolutely necessary to produce the final picture, the bright blue sky.

Each of us must do what we were put on earth to do. For, in the end, if we do that, even in darkness, we will merit to be there when the bright blue picture is revealed.

Joseph Aaron
Editor and Publisher
The Chicago Jewish News

644

Our People Return to our Land: Chapter Sixty-Eight

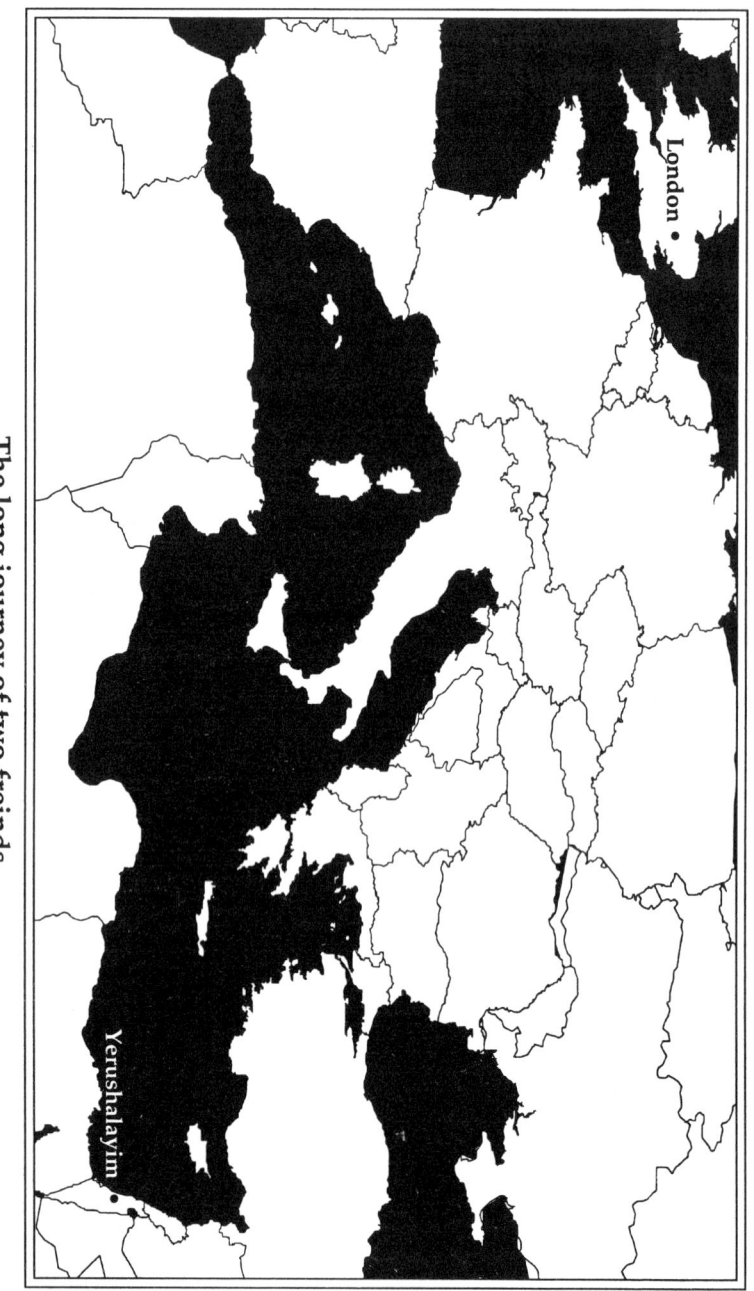

The long journey of two freinds

London

Yerushalayim

Chapter Sixty-Eight
DON'T YOU THINK ITS TIME?

Time Line

| 70 c.e. | 600 c.e. | 1000 c.e. | 1400 c.e. | 1600 c.e. | 1800 c.e. | 2000 c.e. |

Location: London & *Eretz Yisrael*

Shlomo Rosenberg and Maurice Schechter glanced at each other as they completed the long check-in proceedure at El Al's boarding gate in Heathrow International Airport, London.

Shlomo walked behind Maurice through the jetway to the plane. They had been assigned adjacent seats.

The plane departed London for Tel Aviv at 6 a.m. The sun was just rising over the eastern horizon as the jet liner sped down the runway. The darkness slowly dissipated under the face of sparkling morning rays. As the plane lifted, it appeared that it was flying directly into the morning sun. It flew across the English Channel, heading eastward over Germany, while Maurice Schechter sullenly stared at the ground below. He did not encourage conversation between himself and his seat companion.

Shlomo took his *talit* and *tefilin* from the overhead bin and slowly inched his way to the back of the plane where a *minyon* was forming to *daven* the morning service. When he returned to his seat, he tapped Maurice on the shoulder and said gently, "We just finished *davening*. Maybe you didn't feel like joining the *minyon*, but would you like to borrow my *talit* and *tefilin* before I put them away?"

Maurice glowered, "Let me tell you something! I don't need yours or anybody else's *talit* and *tefilin*. I have nothing to do with Him. When they," he slowed his speech and pointed to the earth below, "when they took my youngest son, when they told me to go to the right and shoved my son to the left, from that time until this day, I have no use for Him!"

"You are right," whispered Shlomo. "It was presumptuous of me to interfere with your private thoughts. You don't have to explain anything. But we can still be friends and talk about other matters. After all, we are both going to Israel. But let me ask you just one more question: If you are so angry with God, why are you going to Israel?"

"What do you mean, why am I going to Israel?" Maurice sputtered: "I am angry at God, but not at His people. I love the Jewish people, and I want to spend time with them, especially during this season of the year. Now, on the condition that we don't talk about Him, we can be friendly."

By the time the music over the audio system reverberated with the rhythm of *Haveynu Shalom Aleichem,* and the big jet touched down at Ben Gurion Airport, Shlomo and Maurice had become friends.

Clearing customs, they agreed to share a cab to *Yerushalyaim*.

Shlomo anxiously watched pedestrians as the cab zoomed down King George Street, turned on two wheels at Gershon Agron Street, and sped down David Hamelech Street before stopping in front of the King David Hotel. Breathlessly, he alighted, paid half the fare, and the cab lurched forward without him having an opportunity to ask Maurice where he was staying.

This was Shlomo's fifth annual trip to *Yerushalayim* for *Rosh Hashana, Yom Kippur,* and *Sukkot*. Six years ago, when his wife passed away, he decided to spend these holidays in the Holy City. On his first trip, he found a small *shul* up the street from the hotel, on the side of the YMCA, tucked behind a tall wooden fence, where a middle-aged *chazan davened* with great fervor and sweet voice. He loved that *chazan* and therefore, he returned each year.

Between *Rosh Hashana* and *Yom Kippur*, he walked the streets of *Yerushalayim*, always keeping his eyes open for his new friend Maurice, but somehow, they never met.

During a break in the service after *Yizkor* on *Yom Kippur*, Shlomo walked toward Liberty Park. It was not far from the *shul*, and he thought that he would be able to rest under a shady tree. Usually, the din of children playing resounded throughout the park. On this day, it was nearly empty. Sitting on a bench overhung by a large, broad leafed tree, he recognized Maurice, who was eating a sandwich.

"Listen, I know that you are angry at God and that you want to have nothing to do with Him. The fact that you are eating on *Yom Kippur* is your business ... but, your son, what did he do that you refuse to recite a prayer in his memory?"

Maurice turned sullenly away. "You promised," he reminded Shlomo, and immediately scowled into stony silence.

Shlomo sat on the bench next to him, not responding. Surprisingly, after a few minutes that seemed like an eternity, Maurice blurted out: "You might be right. I thought about it. In fact, I've thought about it for a long time. It is true that I said good-bye to Him in Auschwitz, but I never said good-bye to my son. Maybe it is time to chant a prayer in his memory."

Maurice tearfully turned to Shlomo and whispered: "Somehow, meeting you has inspired me to do something about it. Won't you show me where the *shul* is?"

The two men clutched each other as they walked back. The *chazan* was still standing on the *bema*, for a long line of people waited patiently for their turn to request of him that he recite an individual *El Molay Rachamim* in memory of their loved ones.

The line grew shorter as Maurice and Shlomo inched forward. Finally, Maurice was standing face to face with the *chazan*.

"Please, recite an *El Molay Rachamim* for my son," Maurice stuttered brokenly.

"What was you son's name," queried the *chazan*, gently.

"His name was Pinchas ben Moshe, and he was murdered in Auschwitz"

The *chazan* started to chant *El Molay Rachamim* ... but stopped suddenly.

"Tell me again," he insisted, "what was your son's name?"

"Pinchas ben Moshe."

"*Tateh, tateh,*" cried the *chazan*, "I've been waiting for you!"

A Sacred Trust
— Commentary —
I Have A Dream

Israel seeks the way to peace, not because of fear, or despair, or insecurity, but because of a basic hatred of war. We don't consider it a weakness that, to us, the life of every person is precious and that the death of any young man on the battlefield is a tragedy.

Golda Meir

Excerpted from a speech delivered to the Knesset, July 9, 1971

Our People Return to our Land: Chapter Sixty-Nine

Chapter Sixty-Nine
I HAVE A DREAM

Time Line

| 70 c.e. | 600 c.e. | 1000 c.e. | 1400 c.e. | 1600 c.e. | 1800 c.e. | 2000 c.e. |

Location: *Yerushalayim, Eretz Yisrael*

Today is a very special day. Today I celebrate my fifty-fifth birthday. I will no longer be called for reserve duty. From basic training when I was eighteen years old until today, twenty seven years have passed, nine of them in the service of my country. Nine years? Officers serve forty five days each year in the reserves. I am retiring as a lieutenant colonel.

I decided to walk through *Yerushalayim*. I wanted to see the sights, smell the scents, listen to the sounds of the city as a civilian. It was not easy to walk briskly past the Machane Yehuda marketplace; so many people crowded the narrow sidewalks. I continued along Yaffo Road, turned right at King George Street and followed it as the street named changed to Keren Hayesod. By the time I reached the bottom of Keren Hayesod, I was a bit tired. The lovely shade trees of Liberty Bell Park beckoned me. I crossed Jabotinsky Street, walked down the steps at the entrance, and sat down on a bench. Children played in the park. For a while, I sat and watched Israel's new generation. Then I closed my eyes and I dreamed.

I dreamed. I was a paratrooper in one of the battalions assigned to capture the Old City during the Six Day War.[1]

I was within earshot when Colonel Ahmon responded to a call on the radio from chief of staff General Haim Bar-Lev.

"You must enter the Old City immediately and capture it."

Paratroop Brigade Commander Mordechai Gur confirmed receipt of the order. Then he signalled all the unit commanders to listen on their radios. I heard him say: "Paratroop Brigade 55. We stand on the heights overlooking the Old City. In a little while, we will enter it—the ancient City of *Yerushalayim*—which for a generation (since 1948), we have dreamed of and striven for. Our brigade has been granted the privilege of being the first to enter. Now, move to the gate! We will hold our victory parade on the Temple Mount."

Commander Gur's order turned the momentous assault on the walled city into a race among all the units under his command. They raced toward the Lion's Gate. Tank commander Sergeant Ben Gigi, a Moroccan born tinsmith ordered his gunner, Moshe Haimovsky to open fire, aiming for the upper hinge of the left door. The door canted backwards under the impact, permitting him to see through into the Old City itself.

Behind him was Commander Gur, driven in his half-track by Sergeant Ben Tsur. Gur ordered Ben Tsur to turn sharply to the left. The Temple Mount lay in that direction. The Israeli's leaped out of their tanks and half tracks, and ran up the steps of the Temple Mount, making sure they were no enemy soldiers. Commander Gur was leading. He broadcast to all units: "Cease fire! The Temple Mount is in our hands. Repeat. The Temple Mount is in our hands."

Gunner Haimovsky was peering through the periscope of his tank when he saw the wind unfulring a blue and white flag atop the crescent of the Dome of the Rock.

Another flag was raised on the Western Wall. We paratroopers stood silently, watching. I was overwhelmed. I was conscious that we were the first Jewish soldiers to reach the Western Wall since the Roman destruction of the second Holy Temple almost two thousand years before. I reached to touch

I Have a Dream

the stones. The stones felt wet, as if millions of Jews had cried there before me.

One of the company commanders withdrew his *tefilin* from a velvet pouch and began the morning prayer service. It was the first time a Jew had *davened* at the *Kotel* in nineteen years.

Then chaplain of the army, Rabbi Shlomo Goren appeared on the scene. He was carrying a Torah in one hand and a *shofar* in the other. Two crewmen lifted Rabbi Goren to the top of a tank. He sounded the *shofar*. Then he jumped down from the tank, continuing to blow as he ran all the way to the Temple Mount. Clutching the Torah, Rabbi Goren led forty paratroopers in a *chassidic* dance. The soldiers shouted *Yerushalayim Shelanu, Yerushalayim is ours!*

The dancing ended. Bareheaded soldiers donned their helmets, as they repeated the blessing being recited by Rabbi Goren: *Baruch atah ... shehecheyanu v'keymanu v'hegeyanu lazman hazeh.*

> [**Ed**. Blessed are You ... Who has kept us in life, has preserved us and has enabled us to reach this moment.]

Rabbi Goren continued with *Yizkor* to commemorate the soldiers who had fallen in battle in defense of the Jewish state. He followed this prayer with *Hatikvah*.

I rubbed my eyes, startled. The dream was so real. In my thoughts, I had relived the capture of *Yerushalyaim*. I had been one of those paratroopers who made history.

I focused again on the playing children. Would they have to wear a uniform as I did or would they be able to grow up, unafraid?

Suddenly, I started dreaming again. I was a reservist. We all expected another war, but no one thought that the Egyptians and Syrians would simultaneously attack on *Yom Kippur*, the holiest day of the Jewish calendar year. I was in the synagogue with my family as were many other soldiers who were on leave for the holiday. It was 1973. Less than six years had passed since the last war.

The first few days of the war, seventy thousand Egyptians overran the Sinai. The Syrians attacked the Golan Heights, trying to seize what land Israel had achieved during the Six Day War.

Even though it was easy to mobilize both active soldiers and reservists, because, for the most part, they were in the synagogues, it took almost a week for Israel to drive back the enemy. Because of the surprise attack, four times as many Jewish soldiers were killed as during the Six Day War.

Israel has always been on the defensive. The PLO did not recognize "Israel's right to exist." They never accepted the 1947 United Nations partition plan. Israel does not have to prove its right to exist ... we only want to find a way to live in peace with our neighbors. We have been searching for a way for the past forty five years.

My dream continued. It seemed that all I was thinking about was the wars I fought. It was, as if, I was playing a video tape of my combat experiences.

Israel's usual defensive position changed. At Entebbe, she took the offensive. It was early July, 1976. An Air France plane bound from Tel Aviv to Paris was hijacked, refueled in Libya, and landed in Entebbe, Uganda. The Israeli hostages were separated from the 250 passengers.

Because so many of Israel's citizens are Holocaust survivors, refugees from Hitler's death camps, the separation reminded them of the selections at Auschwitz. They waited dejectedly, reliving their anguish. The world waited for Israel's reply to the hijackers, who demanded the release of forty Arabs held in Israel and thirteen incarcerated in Europe for terrorist acts.

Meantime Defense Minister Shimon Peres and army chief of staff General Mordechai Gur developed a military plan. I was called to active duty. I was one of the paratroopers that flew on that liberation mission.

I Have a Dream

The daring rescue of the Israeli hostages, under the command of General Dan Shomron electrified the world. The released hostages told the waiting press when they landed at Ben Gurion Airport that the first Israeli soldier they saw entering the compound where they were held whispered: "We've come to take you home!" Twice during my military career, I personally witnessed a major historical event.

My mind raced forward, to 1981. It was not until after the bombing of the Osirak reactor in Iraq that Israel revealed its apprehension of a news leak before it actually happened. Israel had to make certain that Iraq would not achieve nuclear capability. France and Italy were helping Iraq build its reactor and were indifferent to Israel's pleas to halt this development. They were customers for Iraqi oil.

After Israel's successful destruction of the Osirak reactor, Prime Minister Menachem Begin said: "Better a condemnation and no reactor, than a reactor and no condemnation." He knew that the world would not "publically" understand Israel's preemptive strike for self-protection. It was not until the scuds fell on Israel eleven years later that he was proven right.

Very little time elapsed between Israel's lightning strike against Iraq and its embroilment in its longest, most controversial war. The Lebanese War, originally called "Operation Peace in the Galilee," was fought with the hope of destroying the PLO forces in Lebanon that were shelling and subjecting Israel's northern borders to terrorists incursions. The controversy rages until this day: was the war offensive or defensive? Was it necessary for six hundred Israeli soldiers to lose their lives? The whole time that war was being fought, I wondered if it would ever end?

And then came the scud attacks with Operation Desert Storm. Israelis sat like lame ducks through the winter months of 1991, while one person was killed, twelve died indirectly, two hundred were injured, one thousand six hundred forty four families were evacuated from Tel Aviv and Ramat Gan and four thousand ninety five buildings were damaged. We wondered if we would have to use the gas masks that were distributed by the civil defense authorities in the event that poisonous chemicals were attached to the scud missiles. The kits with the gas masks also contained syringes for injecting atropine (an antidote for nerve gas) and powder and gauze for use in case our skin was exposed to mustard gas.

I had to select a room on an upper floor of our building, prepare it as a sealed room, with taped windows and plastic sheeting in the event that it would be needed. Can you imagine my grandchildren's hysteria? The TV station broadcasted continuously, to familiarize people how to use the equipment. Our nerves were taut as we waited the alert siren sounding throughout the country eighteen times between January 18th and February 25th.

Tears trickled down my eyes as I stared at the children and wondered about their future, for my dreams that day in the park were filled with pain. Would the migration of Russian Jews continue? And the Ethiopians that have already been absorbed as Israeli citizens, how will they fare? How many Americans will make *aliya?*

What will this country be like in the twenty first century? Will Israel ever achieve the respect of the nations of the world? Will they ever stop condemning her?

Three thousand years ago the prophet Isaiah described the glorious time when peace would reign supreme, when the word for war will have been eliminated from every dictionary. He prophesied:

> *And it shall come to pass in the end of days,*
> *That the Lord's House shall be established*
> *At the top of the mountains,*
> *And shall be exalted above the hills.*
> *And all nations shall hurry to it.*

And many people shall go and say,
Come, let us go up to the mountain of the Lord,
To the House of the God of Jacob,
And He will teach us His ways,
And we will walk in His path.
For out of Zion shall go forth the law ,
And the word of the Lord from Yerushalayim.
And He shall judge between the nations,
And shall decide for many people;
And they shall beat their swords into plowshares,
And their spears into pruning-hooks.
Nation shall not lift up sword against nation,
Neither shall they learn war any more.[2]

I pray that I will live long enough to be part of that peace. I pray for my children, for your children and for all the world's children.

Sources, Further Readings and Footnotes for Volumes Two and Three

PART FOUR
— The Silver Age —
— of Polish Jewry —

Chapter Thirty-Two:
—Kaddish
Sources:
Yaakov Yisrael HaKohen Beyfus, Kuntros Zeh Yenachameynu: Yalkut Lekach Tov, Kefar Chasidim Israel, Tashber HaRav, 1990.
M. Kasher, Y Belchrovitz, Anshay Ma-aleh, Yerushalayim, Defus Maarav, 5734, 1974.
Rabbi Shlomo Zalman Sonnenfeld: Guardians of Jerusalem, Brooklyn, Mesorah Publications, 1969.
Footnote:
[1] Rabbi Asher ben Rabbi Yitzchak HaKohen died 1582.

Chapter Thirty-Three:
—The Repentant Tailor
Source:
M.S. Kasher, Baalay Teshuva, Yeru-shalayim, Maarav Publishing Co., 1974.

Chapter Thirty-Four:
—Equal Citizenship
Sources:
M. S. Kasher and Y. Belkrovitz, Anshay Mofayt, Yerushalyim, M.S.D. Publishing, 1976.
Menachem Mendel, Sepuray HaChag: Rosh Hashana, Yerushalayim, Defus Hanachal, 1983.
Y. Weintraub, HaMaharsha: Rąbbi Shmuel Eliezer Edels, Yerushalayim, Sifrei Kodesh: Maayan Chayim, 1991.
Footnotes:
[1] Volhynia, located in north west Ukraine, was once part of Lithuania. It was annexed to the Polish crown in 1569.
[2] The Jewish people fled to Poland from the Franco-Germanic lands, seeking relief from persecution. The stories in Part 2 describe the lives of the Jewish people led in those lands. Blood libels, disputations, kidnappings, expulsions, and massacres were common occurrences.
[3] The parnas acted as the civil leader of the Jewish community. Today, his role would be equivalent to the president of the local Jewish federation.
[4] **Biography:** Maharsha (1555-1631) is an acronym for Moraynu (our teacher) Harav (our rabbi) Shmuel Eliezer ben Yehuda Edels, and he is remembered for his commentary on the Talmud. His commentary was composed as a result of studying with students. He understood that if earlier explanations on the Talmud were vague to his students, and he could clarify them, then his commentary would become a valuable study aid for future generations.
[5] The *kahal* was the local autonomous Jewish governing council, similar to today's city council.
[6] The charter of citizenship extended to the Jewish people by King Boleslav in 1264 and reaffirmed by King Casimir in 1344 regulated relations between Christians, Jews and the government. The charter protected the Jews from molestation, safeguarding their person and property and provided unrestricted travel throughout the country; it laid the foundation for the purchase of land and the expansion of autonomous Jewish communities; it encouraged the development of a mercantile class; and it prohibited the allegations of blood libels that were one of the reasons that forced Jews to flee to Poland/Lithuania from the Franco/Germanic lands.
[7] The Sejm was the Polish Parliament.

Chapter Thirty-Five:
—The Rabbi's Daughter
Sources:
Aviezer Bernstein, Moray Dayah, Tel Aviv, Zioni Publishing House, 1963.
Rabbi Zechariah Fendel, Challenge at Sinai, New York. Hashkafah Library Series, Rabbi Jacob Joseph School Press, 1978.
Marcus Lehman, Faith and Courage, London, Honigson Publishing Co. Ltd., 1965.
Kuntros M'vo Hash'orim, Yerushalayim, Defus Hayd, 1983.

G. Mah Tov, Ma-a-say-hem Shel Tzadikim, Vayikra, Yerushalayim, Hamesorah, 1986.

Footnotes

[1] **Biography:** Rabbi Shabse Hakohen, the Shach, (1622-1663) was one of the most illustrious Polish rabbinical leaders. He was known as a child prodigy, and he was privileged to study with the leading rabbis of the time.

His major work, *Siftay Kohen*, is a commentary on the Code of Jewish Law dealing with the laws of kashrut, mourning, family purity, vows, and charity. It was completed when he was but twenty-four years old. The name Shach is derived from the acronym of this work. In the introduction to his book, he wrote:

"In truth and sincerity I toiled greatly and I expended much effort. I occupied myself with nothing else, nor did I indulge in sleep or drowsiness for many years until I succeeded in fulfilling my intention. I clarified and weighed every thought carefully, I searched every aspect of every question, not once or twice, but rather one hundred and one times, together with beloved and worthy colleagues...."

Once, when he was a defendant in a legal case, he astounded the rabbinical judge by exclaiming that the verdict, based upon his work, could not go against him, since a person can't be convicted by his own words.

His commentary, included in the standard edition of the Code of Jewish Law today, is a monument to his memory. Fleeing persecution most of his short life, he died at the age of forty one.

[2] Rabbi Moses Isserles was known as the Rama (1530-1572).

[3] 1648-1649.

[4] 1618-1648.

[5] Talmud Bavli, Shevuot 39a

Chapter Thirty-Six:
—The Forgotten Story
Sources:
S.M. Dubnow, History of the Jews in Russia and Poland, Philadelphia, The Jewish Publication Society, 1916.
Y.Y. Klapholtz, Tales of the Baal Shem Tov, New York, Feldheim Publishers, 1970.
Annette Labovitz, Secrets of the Past, Bridges to the Future, Miami, CAJE, 1983.
Dr. H. Rabinowicz, A Guide to Chassidism, London, Thomas Yoseloff, 1960.

Footnotes:

[1] **Biography:** Rebbe Yisrael ben Eliezer, Baal Shem Tov (Besht-1700-1760), known as the Master of the Good Name, succeeded in infusing life and vitality into the Jewish people, who were suffering from the misery of diaspora living. He taught them to serve God with great joy, despite personal feelings of hopelessness and helplessness; he imbued them with a love for Eretz Yisrael and a yearning for the days of the Messiah; he nurtured a deeper understanding of learning and observance; he emphasized prayer as a focal point of Jewish life; he stressed an all pervasive, abiding love of every Jew. These were his legacies, the tenets of the emerging chassidic movement, a movement which still pulsates with life around the world, more than two hundred years after his death.

Chapter Thirty-Seven:
—The Righteous Proselyte
Sources:
M. Dick, Gayray HaTzedek, Vilna, 1862.
Annette Labovitz, Secrets of the Past, Bridges to the Future, Miami, Central Agency for Jewish Education, 1983.
Meir Meisels, Judaism: Thought and Legend, Yerushalayim, Philipp Feldheim, Publishers, Ltd.
Menachem Mendel, Otzar Hachag: Shevuout, Yerushalayim, 1984.

Footnotes:

[1] **Biography:** Rabbi Elyahu ben Shlomo Zalman, the Gaon of Vilna (1720-1797) was born into a family of great Torah scholars. At a very young age, he was recognized as an *illui* (genius). He followed in the illustrious footsteps of his forbearers. He was totally devoted to Torah study, having the ability to block out distraction that might disturb his thought processes. In addition to his *halachic* commentaries, his writings stress *middot tovot*, character traits that imitate God. To him, ethical sensitivities were a prerequisite for Torah scholarship. When asked how he became the Vilna 'Gaon' (acknowledged religious leader), he played the name of the city where he lived, Vilna, against the Yiddish word 'vilnor' (if you will it): "Vilnor, un du vest oychet veren a Gaon" (if you will it, you can also become a religious leader).

[2] 1749

[3] *Devarim*, Deuteronomy 6:4

Chapter Thirty-Eight:
—The House of Rothchild
Source:
Mordechai Ben Yechezkel, Sayfer Hamaseyot, Volume I, Tel Aviv, Devir Pub. Co.,

Sources, Furthur Reading, Footnotes and Three Volume Index

Reprinted 1973.
Footnotes:
1. **Biography:** Mayer Anshel (1743-1812) was the founder of the legendary House of Rothschild. With his wife Gitel Shnaper, who he married on August 29, 1779, he raised five sons. They expanded the family fortune to include branches in most major European cities including London, Paris, Naples, and Frankfurt. The Rothschilds were advisers to kings and princes; they lent large sums of money; supplied armies; purchased securities and government bonds; speculated and increased their investments; and built Austria's first railroad. The family supported agricultural settlements and institutions in Eretz Yisrael and in the Jewish communities of their native countries. The Nazis tried to expropriate their wealth, but they transferred it to holding companies in neutral countries. After World War II, they continued their phenomenal careers in investment banking.

Chapter Thirty-Nine:
—An Unusual Torah Scholar
Sources:
S. Kasher, Baalay Teshuva, Yerushalayim, Maarav Publishing House, 1974.
Niflaot Tazdikim, Ha-admor Harofay, Yerushalayim.
Footnotes:
1. Rabbi Dovid Lelever (1746-1814)
2. Rabbi Yaakov Yitzchak HaLayve Horowitz (1745-1815)

Chapter Forty:
—Just One Kopeck
Sources:
S.M. Dubnow, History of the Jews in Russia and Poland, Volume I, Philadelphia, Jewish Publication Society, 1916.
Yitzchak Raphael, Sayfer HaChassidut, Tel Aviv, Zioni Publishing House, 1953.
Dr. H. Rabinowicz, A Guide to Chassidism, London, Thomas Yoseloff, 1960.
Footnotes:
1. **Biography:** Rebbe Menachem Mendel ben Moshe of Vitebsk (1730-1788) grew up under the influence of the emerging chassidic movement, and was one of its prominent leaders, influencing both simple and scholarly Jews in Lithuania and White Russia. He tried to mend the rift between the *chassidic* and *mitnagdic* movements. When he found himself unsuccessful, he decided, in the spring of 1777, to make *aliya*, to live the remainder of his life in Eretz Yisrael. He left with three hundred *chassidim* and they settled in the Galilee region, near Tiberias and Safed. Their settlement in Eretz Yisrael paved the way for other *chassidim* to follow.
2. **Biography:** Rebbe Shneor Zalman ben Baruch of Liadi (1745-1813), the Alter Rebbe, created *Chabad Chassidut*, an acronym for wisdom, understanding and knowledge. He was blessed with an insatiable thirst for the study of Torah. He lived modestly and abhorred materialism. He considered Rebbe Menachem Mendel of Vitebsk his teacher and colleague. *Chabad Chassidut* spread through the far corners of Lithuania/White Russia under his leadership from Liadi, located on the estate of Prince Lubomirski.
3. **Biography:** Rebbe Layve Yitzchak of Berditchev (1740-1809), descendant of an unbroken chain of twenty-six generations of leading Torah scholars, was one of the most charismatic *chassidic* rebbes. When the Baal Shem Tov heard of his birth, he commented: "A great and holy soul has been born into this world: he shall be an eloquent advocate for the Jewish people." Rebbe Layve Yitzchak spent his entire life fulfilling that prophecy. People said that he never found fault with any Jew. He loved God and Judaism, but his love for the Jewish people exceeded his love for both God and Judaism.
He is also remembered for the famous soliloquy that showed his truly personal relationship with God:
"Good morning to You, Lord of the Universe!
I, Layve Yitzchak, son of Sarah of Berditchev, have come to You to complain on behalf of Your people Israel.
What have You against Your people Israel?
No matter what happens, it is:
Say to the children of Israel.
No matter what happens, it is:
Speak to the children of Israel.
My children Israel ...
Father dear! How many other people are there in the world?
Babylonians, Persians, and Edomites ... the Germans—
What do they say?
Our king is a king!
The English— What do they say?
Our sovereign is a sovereign!
And I, Layve Yitzchak, son of Sarah of Berditchev say:

Sources, Further Reading, Footnotes and Three Volume Index

Hallowed and magnified be Your Name, O God, Our Father, Our King! "

Chapter Forty-One:
—The Pintele Yid
Source:
Mordechai Ben Yechezkel, *Sayfer Hama-seyot*, Volume I, Tel Aviv, Devir Publishing Co, Reprinted, 1973.
Footnotes:
1. The Sejm was the name of the Polish Parliament.
2. The sixth of the ten commandments is "You shall not murder." Sh'mot, Exodus 20:13
3. Vayikra, Leviticus 17:14
4. **Biography:** Rebbe Avraham Yehoshua Heschel (1765-1835), the Apter Rav, was descended from a long line of religious leaders. People believed that he was blessed with divine inspiration, even when he was young. He was so personally disturbed by this, that he prayed to the Almighty to remove from him the responsibility of this gift. He served as *rebbe* in three *shtetlach*: Kolbesof, Apt and Yaas, but he was called the Apter Rav because he felt his rabbinate there was the most important part of his career. He spent the last years of his life in Medziboz, the cradle of the *chassidic* movement. Shortly before his death, he told his followers to inscribe his tombstone with two simple words, "*O-hayv Yisrael*, The Lover of Israel."
5. Rabbi Shaul Levinshtam 1755-1790.

Chapter Forty-Two:
Remember Who You Are
Sources: S. M. Dubnow, *History of the Jews in Russia and Poland*, The Jewish Publication Society, Philadelphia, 1916.
G. Mah Tov, *Ma-a-say-hem shel Tzaddikim*, Volume II, Yerushalayim, Hamesorah, 1986.
Footnotes
1. **Biography:** Rabbi Yitzchak Isaac "Chaver" Wildmann (1789-1853) served the communities of Rozinoi, Volkovsysk, Tikocyn, Siauliai, and Suwalk, located in the center of northern Poland/Lithuania, in the area between Vilna and Bialystock. He was called *Chaver*—a title first used in *geonic* times, (Babylonia, ninth to eleventh centuries)—to symbolize a person who devoted himself to both the study of Torah and the needs of the Jewish community. It was used for centuries to honor distinguished scholars and communal leaders.
2. See *Rachel and Akiva* and *These I Remember in Volume I.*
3. The quote is from *U'Netaneh Tokef, I Will Die A Jew, Volume I.*

Chapter Forty-Three:
—The Holy Shekel
Source: Yosef Hillel Kenig, *Se-pur-im Nif-la-im*, Yerushalayim, Givat Shaul, 5727 (1967).
Footnotes
1. October 28, 1868.
2. **Biography:** Rabbi Avraham Shmuel Binyamin Sofer (Shreiber-1815-1871) was one of the leading decisors of Jewish law. As head of the famous *yeshiva* in Pressburg founded by his father, Rabbi Moshe Sofer, the Chasam Sofer, (1762-1839) he insisted that the interpretation of every halachic problem be based upon Talmudic precedent, for he believed that Jewish tradition had withstood the pain of exile because of Talmudic learning. He could trace his family lineage back to Rashi (Rabbi Shlomo ben Yitzchak, 1040-1105, foremost Biblical commentator) and from there to Rabbi Judah the Prince (second century codifier of the Mishna) and King David. When the Hungarian government agreed to his appointment as chief rabbi, the Jews rejoiced.
3. Avot 3:15
4. Avot 1:6

Chapter Forty-Four:
—Quick Thinking
Source: Menachem Becker, *Parparot LaTorah: Shmot*, Yerushalayim, Omen Publishers, 1983.
Footnotes
1. **Biography:** Emperor Francis (Franz) Joseph of Hapsburg (1830-1916) ruled Austria from 1848 until his death during World War I. Because of his liberal attitude toward his Jewish subjects, he won their loyalty and support. He cancelled restrictions on Jewish occupations and ownership of real estate, assented to their emancipation, and made them full citizens of the state. When he died, Austrian Zionists eulogized him as the "donor of civil rights, equality before the law, and the benevolent protector of the Jews." The Jews referred to him as "*HaKaiser, yarum hodo*: the emperor, may his majesty be exalted!" Synagogues were always full of worshippers on his birthday as a sign of the love of the Jewish people for him. Anti-Semites, who tried to sway him, called him "Juden Kaiser." He called

Sources, Furthur Reading, Footnotes and Three Volume Index

them "a scandal and a disgrace in the eyes of the world." (Judaica)

2. **Biography:** Rabbi Shimon Sofer (1820-1883) was the son of Rabbi Moshe Sofer, the Chasam Sofer, (1762-1839) the founder of a dynasty of rabbinic families whose leadership spanned the eighteenth, nineteenth, and part of the twentieth centuries in Austria/Hungary. His brother Rabbi Avraham Shmuel Binyamin (1815-1871) was known as the Kesav Sofer for his responsa and expositions on the Torah, and Rabbi Shimon was called Michtav Sofer for his writings on Jewish law and homiletics.

Chatper Forty-Five:
— A Woman Ahead of Her Time
Sources:
Rabbi Leo Jung, Jewish Leaders, New York, Bloch Publishing Company, 1953.
Rabbi Elyahu KiTov, Sayfer Hatodaah (The Book of Our Heritage), Yerushalayim, Alef Publishers.
Devora Rubin, editor, Daughters of Destiny: Women Who Revolutionized Jewish Life and Torah Education, Brooklyn, New York, Mesorah Publications, 1988.

Footnotes:
1. Sara Schneirer, 1883-1935.
2. **Biography:** Rabbi Shimshon Raphael Hirsch (1808-1888) introduced the philosophy of *"Torah im derech eretz:* the study of Torah with the ways of the world," a philosophy which encouraged participation in the modern world as long as this participation did not repudiate the eternal values of Torah. He is considered to be the father of the day school movement.
3. *Bayt Yaakov* means the House of Jacob. The schools were thus named from the biblical passage: "Thus should you say to *Bayt Yaakov,"* (Sh'mot, Exodus 19:3) based upon the interpretation of Rashi, one of greatest of our biblical commentators, that *Bayt Yaakov* means "the women."
4. Phone interview with the authors, November, 1994.

Chapter Forty-Six:
— Don't Let the Lights Go Out
Source:
Yechiel Grantstein, Shemesh Ba-a-nan, Yerushalayim, Mosad Harav Kook, 1975.

VOLUME III
PART FIVE
— The Jewish —
— American Experience —

Chapter Forty-Seven:
— The First Jews in New Amsterdam
Sources:
Azriel Eisenberg and Hannah Grad Goodman. *Eyewitnesses to American Jewish History.* Part One. New York. Union of American Hebrew Congregations. 1976.
Arthur Hertzberg. *The Jews in America. Four Centuries of an Uneasy Encounter.* New York. Simon and Schuster. 1989.
Allon Schoener. *The American Jewish Album, 1654 to the Present.* New York. Rizzoli International Publications, Inc. 1983

Chapter Forty-eight:
— A Light of a Small Candle Shines at Valley Forge
Sources:
"The Light of a Small Candle Shines at Valley Forge," from *Time for My Soul,* Annette and Eugene Labovitz, Jason Aronson Publishing, 1987.
Howard Fast, *Haym Salomon: Son of Liberty.* New York. Julian Messner. 1941. Reprinted, 1963.

Chapter Forty-Nine:
— Rebecca and Judah
Sources:
Jacob Rader Marcus, This I Believe: Documents of American Jewish Life, Northvale, New Jersey, Jason Aronson, Inc., 1990.
Allon Schoener, The American Jewish Album: 1654 To The Present, New York, Rizzoli International Publications, 1983.
Richard Tillinghast, The Spires of Charleston, The New York Times, May 23, 1993.
Rachel Heimovics, New Orleans, (The Jewish Traveler) New York. Hadassah Magazine, January, 1987.
Bernice Scharlach, San Francisco, (The Jewish Traveler) New York, Hadassah Magazine, January, 1993.
Helen Silver, Charleston, (The Jewish Traveler) New York, Hadassah Magazine, April, 1987.

Footnotes
1. "Who is rich? He who is happy with his portion." *Pirkei Avot,* Ethics of the Fathers 4:1.
2. Tehillim, Psalms, 31:6.
3. The Mikveh Israel synagogue functioned without a rabbi for the first four years. Isaac Leeser was elected to its pulpit in 1829.
4. Judah Touro (1775-1854)

Chapter Fifty: Concerning the Jews
Source: Samuel Langhorne Clemens (Mark Twain 1835-1910), Concerning the Jews,

Sources, Further Reading, Footnotes and Three Volume Index

Charles Neider, Editor, The Complete Essays of Mark Twain, Garden City, N.Y., Doubleday & Co. Inc., 1963.

Chapter Fifty-One:
—The New Colossus
Sources:

Emma Lazarus. *The New Colossus*.

Rabbi David Geffen. *"Give Me Your Tired, Your Poor..."* Los Angeles. *The Jewish Calendar Digest & Magazine*. Isaac Nathan Publishing Co., Inc., Passover, 1994.

Deborah Pessin, *Giants on the Earth: Stories of Great Jewish Men and Women from the Time of the Discovery of America to the Present*, Behrman House Publishers, New York, 1964.

Allon Schoener, *The American Jewish Album: 1654 to the Present*, Rizzoli International Publications, New York, 1983.

Chapter Fifty-Two:
—*Parochet* Comes to the *Glodeneh Medinah*
Sources:

Ronald Sanders, Shores of Refuge: A Hundred Years of Jewish Emigration, New York, Henry Holt and Company, 1988.

Allon Schoener, The American Jewish Album: 1654 to the Present, N.Y., Rizzoli International Publications, 1983.

Footnotes:
[1] The *shul* was built in 1888. Rabbi Elyahu Chaim Meisel (1873-1912) served as the rabbi.
[2] The Russo-Japanese War (1904-1905), was fought because of an imperialistic conflict that grew out of the rival designs of Russia and Japan on Manchuria and Korea.

Chapter Fifty-Three:
—Snippets from A Bintel Brief
Sources:

Isaac Metzker, editor. *A Bintel Brief: Sixty Years of Letters from the Lower East Side to the Jewish Daily Forward*, Doubleday and Company, Inc., New York, 1971.

Irving Howe and Kenneth Libo, editors. *How we Lived: A Documentary History of Immigrant Jews in America*, 1880- 1930. New York. The New American Library. 1979.

Chapter Fifty-Four:
—Tuition
Source:

This story was told to the authors by one of the children. Although the story is true, the names have been changed to protect this family's privacy.

Footnotes:
[1] Rabbi Joseph Telushkin, *Jewish Literacy*, New York, William Morrow & Co., 1991.

Chapter Fifty-Five:
—One Survivors Story
Footnotes:
[1] *Tehillim*, Psalms 27:1. Commentary of Rabbi Shimshon Raphael Hirsh.
[2] *Genocide* (VHS) A documentary on the Holocaust produced by the Weisenthal Center, Los Angeles, California.
[3] George E. Berkley. *Vienna and Its Jews: The Tragedy of Success*, Maryland, Madison Books, 1988.
[4] The activity of the American Jewish Joint Distribution Committee reached its peak after the war. Between 1945 and 1952, the sum of $342 million was spent on the feeding, clothing, and rehabilitation of 250,000 displaced persons in camps and the remnants of Jewish communities in Europe. (Judaica Encyclopedia)
[5] 400,000 displaced persons who had been uprooted by World War II entered the United States between 1948 and 1950. (World Book Encyclopedia)
[6] Quoted in William B. Helmreich's *Against All Odds: Holocaust Survivors and The Successful Lives They Made in America*. New York. Simon & Schuster. 1992.

PART SIX
— Our People —
— Return to Our Land—
Introduction
Footnotes:
[1] *Tehillim*, Psalms 137:4,5.
[2] The *Amida*, the Silent Devotion prayer.
[3] Grace After Meals.

Chapter Fifty-Seven:
—Be Careful How You Speak
Source:

This story was told at the House of Love and Prayer in San Francisco by Rabbi Shlomo Carlebach[Z"L] during the 1970s.

Footnotes:
[1] For a biography of the Baal Shem Tov, see footnotes to *The Forgotten Story*, Chapter 36.
[2] *B'rayshit*, Genesis 21:33.
[3] *B'rayshit*, Genesis 28:12.
[4] *B'rayshit*, Genesis 37:12, 14.
[5] *Yirmeyahu*, Jeremiah 32:9.
[6] Natives and tourists alike recognize the gravesites of these rabbis. The graves of Rabbi Akiva and Rabbi Mayer overlook the Sea of Galillee. The grave of the Rambam is in the city.

vii
Sources, Furthur Reading, Footnotes and Three Volume Index

[7] Bogdan Chmielnicki, leader of hordes of Ukrainian peasants, ravaged the Polish countryside, burned towns and villages and massacred both Poles and Jews in an attempt to revolt against Polish political, economic and religious exploitation. The Chmielnicki massacres are known in Jewish history as *Gezayrot Tach v'Tat*, the pogroms of 1648-1649.

Chapter Fifty-Eight:
—When Will The *Messiach* Come?
Source:
Yitzchak Raphael, *Sefer Hachasedut*, Tel Aviv, A. Zioni Publishing House, 1955.
Footnotes:
[1] For a biography of Rebbe Menachem Mendel of Vitebsk, see footnotes to Chapter 40.
[2] There are thirteen *Principles of Faith* written by Maimonides, which delineate the beliefs of a Jew. They can be found in his introduction to *Perek Chaylek*, which is the eleventh chapter of the Babylonian Talmud, *Tractate Sanhedrin*, and in his introduction to the tenth chapter of his commentary to the *Mishna Sanhedrin*. Based upon his principle, the *Anee Maamin*, (I believe) was formulated. The twelfth principles states: *I believe with complete faith in the coming of the Messiach, and even though he delays, nevertheless I anticipate every day that he will come.*

Chapter Fifty-Nine: Once He Cried
Source:
Yaakov Rimon and Yosef Zundel Wasserman, Shmuel B'Doro, (Biography of Rabbi Shmuel Salant, Rabbi in *Yerushalayim*, 1855-1909), Tel Aviv, Maslul Publishing House, 1961. (This book was loaned to the authors by Rona Schwartz, the granddaughter of Rabbi Shmuel Salant.)
Footnotes:
[1] Rabbi Shmuel Salant (1816-1909).
[2] A traveling post office for the Turkish mail service aboard the first railway connecting *Yaffo* with *Yerushalayim* started in 1897. Mail was sorted during the journey. Other countries were not permitted to use this service. *The Jerusalem Post*, International Edition. October 17, 1992.
[3] Emperor Franz Joseph (1830-1916).
[4] Suez Canal was dedicated in 1869.
[5] Kaiser Wilhelm visited Yerushalayim in October, 1898.
[6] Russian Tzar Nicholas II (1848-1918)
[7] July/August, 1909.

Chapter Sixty:
—The Determination of Yerushalmi

Source:
Menachem Baker, Parparaot LaTorah, Vayikra, *Yerushalayim*, Omen Publishers, 1983.
Footnotes:
[1] Rabbi Yosef Chaim Sonnenfeld (1849-1932).
[2] *Talmud Bavli, Pesachim* 8b.

Chapter Sixty-One:
—A Fragment of Torah
Source:
Menachem Mendel, Otzar HaChag, *Yerushalayim*, 1980.
Footnotes
[1] "The Holy One, Blessed be He, the Torah, and the Jewish people are One." Zohar, Emor 93b.
[2] *Vayikra*, Leviticus 18:24.
[3] *Vayikra*, Leviticus 19:2.
[4] *Vayikra*, Leviticus 19: 2, 3, 14, 16, 18.
[5] *Vayikra*, Leviticus 19:26, 28, 32, 33, 36.
[6] *Vayikra*, Leviticus 20:7, 8, 23.

Chapter Sixty-Two:
—The Afikoman That Restored Life
Source:
Otzar HaChag, *Pesach, Menachem Mendel, Yerushalayim*, 1984.
Footnotes:
[1] The tenth day of the Hebrew month of *Adar Shayne*
[2] *Vayikra*, Leviticus 23:16 -17.
[3] HaLachma, *Hagada of Pesach.*

Chapter Sixty-Three:
—Let Our Work Be For Peace
Source:
This story is based upon an interview during the summer of 1992 between the authors and the regional manager of Magen David Adom, the Israeli equivalent of the Red Cross.

Footnotes:
[1] Larry Collins and Dominique LaPierre, *O Jerusalem*, New York. Pocket Books (Simon and Shuster), 1972.
[2] Iyar 5, 5708 (May 14, 1948) is Israel Independence Day.
[3] *Vayikra*, Leviticus 19:18

Chapter Sixty-Four:
—Kfar Etzion
Source:
This story is from a personal interview with Dorit Una in *Kfar Etzion*, summer, 1992.
Footnotes:
[1] Israel's War of Independence began the night after independence was declared on May 15, 1948. A cease-fire went into effect on July 17, 1948.
[2] In Hebrew, Holtzman translates to *Etzion*.

Sources, Further Reading, Footnotes and Three Volume Index

3. Six Day War, June 5-10, 1967.

Chapter Sixty-Five:
—From Moscow to *Yerushalayim*
Source:
The authors met Eleonora Shifrin while visiting *Eretz Yisrael* during *Sukkot*, 1986.
Footnotes:
1. World War II.
2. September, 1972.

Chapter Sixty-Six:
—The Iranian Connection
Source: The authors interviewed this family when they visited their relatives in Miami Beach in August, 1988. They did not want their names used in the story.

Chapter Sixty-Seven:
—Why Did You Come to Israel?
Source:
These vignettes are based upon personal interviews with the authors.

Footnotes:
1. The *ketuva* is the marriage contract that the groom gives to his bride during the wedding ceremony which is both a religious and a legal rite.
2. We met Rabbi Daniel Meyer on a trip to Prague during the summer of 1982. He had just returned from Moscow, where he was trained as a rabbi. He was not permitted to study outside of the Iron Curtain countries. He recently made *aliya*.
3. Rabbi Joseph Kara (b. 1060 -1070?) was a French Biblical commentator. He also explained much of the religious poetry that was written in medieval Europe. Consequently, he was known as the "commentator." Rabbi Avigdor ben Isaac Kara (d. 1439) was a German kabbalist and poet. He was appointed a *dayyan* (judge) for the Jews who lived in Prague.

Chapter Sixty-Eight:
—Don't You Think It's Time
Source:
Rabbi Shlomo Carlebach [Z"L] told us this story.

Chapter Sixty-Nine:
—I Have A Dream
Sources:
Abba Eban, Personal Witness: Israel Through My Eyes, New York, G.P. Putnam Sons, 1992.
Abraham Rabinovich, The Battle for Jerusalem, Excerpted in The Jerusalem Post International Edition, June 6, 1992.
Yitzchak Shamir, Osirak: A Truth Begin Understood, Excerpted in The Jerusalem Post International Edition, June 19, 1993.
Rabbi Joseph Telushkin, Jewish Literacy, New York, William Morrow and Company, Inc., 1991.
Footnotes
1. June 5-10, 1967.
2. *Yeshayahu*, Isaiah 2: 2-4.

Also available

A TOUCH OF HEAVEN:

Spiritual and Kabbalistic Stories for Jewish Living

complied and edited by Rabbi Eugene and Annette Labovitz

Stories of *Simchah*—Joy • *Ahavas Harayah*—Loving Fellow Man • *Gemilus Chasadim*—Acts of Kindness • *Hachnasas Orchim*—Hospitality • *Emunah*—Faith • *Tefillah*—Prayer

Second Printing • Revised with new stories added to original

— $20 —

Send to:

The Isaac Nathan Publishing Co., Inc. 22711 Cass Avenue, Woodland Hills, CA 91364, (818) 225-9631

Send check for $20 for each copy. We Pay Shipping.
California Residents add 1.60 for state tax.

Three Volume Index

Volume I, Pages 9-288 • Volume II, pages 313-450 Volume III, pages 451-657

Subject Index

A
absorption center, 638
aleph-bayt (alphabet), 22 - 23
aliya (to Eretz Yisrael), 145, 147, 246 - 7, 252, 254, 517, 556, 586, 638, 656
allya (to the Torah), 528, 543 - 545, 555
Anschluss, 581
anti-Semites, 431 - 432, 457 - 459, 580, 638, 639
apostate, 146, 148, 190, 366, 367, 406, 407, 409
arendar, 397
arrogance, 55 - 56
Auschwitz, 570, 647 - 648, 654
auto-da-fe, 263, 368, 376

B
baal tefilah (prayer leader), 391
baal teshuva, see repentance
Babi Yar, 618
Balfour Declaration, 594
bayt din (court), 54 - 57, 286
bayt midrash (study hall), 379, 386, 545,547
bayt mikdash (holy temple), 423
Bayt Yaakov Schools, 440 - 441
Ben Gurion Airport, 646,655
Bericha (illegal immigration organization), 585,588
Birkat HaChodesh (blessing of the new month), 57
Black Plague, 154, 165, 166, 220
blood libels, 145, 153 - 160, 195, 199, 201, 202, 209
brit millah (circumcision), 45 - 48, 120-121, 212,219, 231,564, 570, 571
British, 585, 593, 594, 596, 597, 604
burial outside of Yerushlayim, 17
burning books, 146, 148, 164, 190

C
caliph, 61
Cantonist Laws (military conscription), 417 - 418
cardinal (church), 105
chair of Elyahu, 121
challah, 332, 334
chalutzim (pioneers), 586
chametz (leaven), 69

Chanukah, 167, 195, 437, 445 - 450, 463 - 466
charter of privileges, 329, 344
chassidic movement, 361-368,391 - 413
chassidim, 551
cheder, 407, 499, 628
chicken soup (as a remedy), 72
childbirth, 219, 252, 255, 389, 392
childlessness, 87 - 88
Chmielnicki pogroms, 546
chosen people, 528
chuppah (wedding canopy), 61, 62, 153, 147, 155, 165, 437, 491, 571
collaborators, 582 - 584
communism, 613- 624,639 -640
compassion, 53, 57
concentration camps, 520,586, 588
conquest of the Holy Land 131 - 132
conversion (to Christianity) 104, 113 - 114, 164, 193, 194, 202-208, 241 - 242, 261
conversion (to Judaism), 211, 231, 373 - 375, 413
conversos, 253, 261, 262, 267 - 273, 277 - 278
covenant, 432 - 447
Crusades, 105, 127, 131 - 132, 135 - 142, 147, 153, 195
cup of *Elyahu*, 155

D
Damascus Gate, 564
death/mourning, 222 - 223, 336
Declaration of Independence (Israel), 598
decree of expulsion, 107, 340, 342 - 344, 354, 356, 409
defense of Jewish people, 137
deicide, 141
destruction of first Holy Temple, 18, 46, 195, 627
destruction of second Holy Temple, 15 - 18, 146, 195, 652
devil, 165
diaspora, 545 - 547, 556
discrimination, 614 - 616
disputations, 146, 241 - 247
Dome of the Rock, 652
dowry, 380, 385,437
dreams, interpretation, 62, 63,

115, 153, 160, 231, 284, 287-288

E
economy (Babylonia), 71
economy (Constantinople), 87, 252, 272
economy (eastern Europe), 173, 175,339,340,379,381,403 - 405, 492, 494, 516, 518
economy (England), 135 - 136
economy (Iran), 627 - 628
economy (medieval *Eretz Yisrael*), 230, 257, 273
economy (medieval Europe), 119, 145, 153, 164, 216, 218
economy (medieval Spain), 236
economy (USA after World War II) 526 - 528
education (for women), 29 - 31, 216, 435 - 441
Ellis Island, 496
emancipation, 389, 423, 436
enlightenment, 389
Entebbe, 654
Eretz Yisrael, 423,441,473,518, 569, 586, 589, 641
ethical will, 220 - 221, 440, 470, 475, 476
Evian conference, 517 - 5 18
evil, 30, 35, 71, 237
execution—innocent Jews 365, 367, 376
exilarch, 61 - 66
exit visas, 616, 619, 622, 640

F
fasting (atonement), 331, 393
Final Solution, 445
forced conversion , 397, 398
forgiveness, 186, 376, 386
four captive rabbis, 77 - 80, 235

G
gaon, 77
gas chambers, 576
Gestapo, 519 - 522, 575, 581, 583, 584
ghetto, 157, 183, 184, 185, 215, 423, 445, 521, 522, 524
Goldene Medina, 494-495, 497
Golem, 199 - 200, 208
gossiping, 183, 375, 380, 386, 420, 574

H
hachnassat kallah, (providing

x
Sources, Further Reading, Footnotes and Three Volume Index

a dowry for a poor bride), 77, 216
Hadassah hospital, 595, 605
Haganah, 564, 595, 597, 604, 608
halachic (legal) decisions, 121, 163, 190, 551
Hatikvah, 653
hatred of the Jewish people 88 - 89, 98, 105, 137, 145, 148, 160, 163, 165, 166, 169, 186, 194
havdalah, 31 - 32, 334
Heavenly voice, 120
heresy, 376
HIAS, 497, 633
Holocaust, 445 - 450, 515 - 524, 569- 576, 579-589, 605, 645-648,
Hoshana Raba, 277, 280
hospitality, 72, 155, 221, 364, 394
hunger strike, 620 - 623

I
identity papers, 419
immersing utensils, 69
infidels, 136, 153
innocent Jews (execution of) 123, 139, 142, 145
Inquisition, 251, 262-263, 270, 271, 457
Iranian Jewry, 627 - 634
Islam, 65, 629, 631

J
Jaffa Gate, 560, 560, 565, 596
Jewish Agency, 629
Jewish Daily Forward, 505
Jewish section (of a town) 372
Joint Distribution Committee (JDC) 525, 629
justice, 54

K
kabbalah, 179, 199, 283 - 288, 376
kaddish, 223, 319-324, 376, 522, 560, 582
kahal (autonomous governing council in Poland), 319, 327, 328, 343, 403, 407, 417
kashrut (kosher), 30, 31, 177, 351, 390, 420, 435, 508, 518, 529, 574, 581
ketuva, 638
kibbutz, 569, 595, 598, 601-609
kiddush, 155, 156, 284, 334, 363, 576
kidnapping, 31, 103 - 104, 107, 270, 350, 351, 417 - 420
kindness, 21, 22, 53, 155, 163, 164, 165, 189, 210, 216, 273, 343, 350, 354, 436, 500, 556, 557, 558
kipa, 640

Kol Nidrel, 261 - 263, 279
Kotel (western wall), 544, 555, 558, 594, 607, 652, 653

L
lamed vav tzaddik, 336
landsman, 495, 526
love your fellowman, 574, 598
Lubavitch, 630

M
Maccabbees, 1 5
Magen David Adom, 593 - 598
martyrdom, 114 - 115, 135 - 142, 153, 335 - 41, 376, 420
matchmaking, 57, 88, 123 - 126, 147, 210-212, 217, 287, 379, 380
matriarchs, 255, 257
matzot, 155, 156, 475, 582, 624
Mayah Sheorim, 564, 593, 601
medicine, 72, 91 - 92, 122, 174, 175, 270
Megillat Esther, 628
mutual co-existence, 229

N
Nazism, 441-445, 523, 525, 569, 575, 580, 582, 583
Nebi Mussa riots, 563
neilah, 492, 500
netilat yadayim (washing hands before meals), 95, 156, 175 - 179
New World, 457 - 459

O
Operation Desert Storm, 641,655
Operation Peace-Galilee, 655
ordination of rabbis, 41
Osirak reactor (Iraq), 655

P
Pale of Settlement, 362, 389, 418, 545
Palmach, 595
parnas, 340, 344, 353 - 355, 493, 495
parochet (cover of the holy ark), 491, 493, 495, 500 - 501
partisans, 576
partition of Poland, 431
patriarchs, 255,367
peace, 598, 656 - 657
persecution (medieval Europe) 135 - 202, 229, 244, most of Volume 2
persecution (under Rome), 15 -18, 21-25, 29-32, 45-48, 35-41
Pesach, 69, 71, 140, 155-159, 165, 195, 200-201, 254, 367, 380, 384, 408, 436, 469, 475, 579-589, 624
Pharisees, 15,16
philosophy, 71

pintele yid (spark of holiness), 403
piyyut (religious poetry), 103, 114, 146
PLO, 654 ,655
pogrom, 412, 593, 640
poisoning wells, 165,168
polygamy, 100
Pope (Jewish), 103 - 109
poretz, 319 - 321, 327 - 330, 334, 383, 384, 397, 398, 400
prayer, 333, 375,392, 394
Purim, 195

R
rabbinic authority, 71
ransom, 77, 78, 149
ransoming captives, 77 - 80, 145-150, 319-324, 353, 397 - 400
redemption, 39, 61, 64, 243, 244, 545, 547, 548, 551 - 552, 586
refuseniks, 613 - 624
relatively secure, 113
religious tolerance, 339, 344
repentance, 56, 330 - 331, 334, 344, 367-368, 389, 394, 403 - 413
responsa, 149, 153
Revelation, 376
reward, 93
righteous gentiles, 521
ritual murder charages, 367, 408 - 410, 412
Roman siege of *Yerushalayim*, 15
roots (Jewish), 393, 394
Rosh Hashana, 57, 103, 109, 115, 267, 279, 342, 344, 420, 436, 475, 491, 506, 518, 521, 646, 647

S
Sabra, 638
Saducees, 15
Sanhedrin, 18, 285
scribe, 277
searching for *chametz*, 380, 581
seder, 155 - 159, 262
Sejm, 345, 406 - 410
Sh'ma, 37, 38, 263, 376, 407, 420, 441
Shabbat, 24, 39, 135, 153, 158, 160, 165, 177, 179, 183, 201, 217, 23 1, 283 - 284, 328 - 334, 356, 357, 362-364, 367, 372 375, 390, 432, 436, 437, 440, 448, 458, 470 - 472, 474, 475, 498 - 500, 512, 516, 521, 528, 534, 569, 574, 576, 586, 603, 605, 606, 608, 640,641
Shabbat Hagadol (preceding Pesach) 140
shammash, 446, 465

Sources, Furthur Reading, Footnotes and Three Volume Index

shammish, 333 - 336, 379, 411, 413, 446, 450, 492 - 494, 518
shekel, 423 - 428
Shevuot, 165, 184, 376, 436, 469, 534, 535
shochet (ritual slaughterer), 516
shofar, 269, 270, 393, 516, 552, 596, 653
shtetl, 321, 361, 362, 364, 367, 379, 382, 390 - 391, 394, 403, 405, 411, 418, 436, 439, 492, 504, 515, 518, 520
shul (synagogue) 135 - 137, 139, 158, 183, 288, 330, 331, 336, 362, 363, 371, 375, 392, 394, 437, 445 - 450, 491, 492, 499, 500, 555, 569, 570, 571, 646, 647
Sicarii, 15
Simchat Torah, 165, 448
Six Day War, 606, 615, 637, 651, 654
Soviet Jewry, 613-624
stealing, 94, 96
Student Struggle-Soviet Jewry, 620
Sukkot, 40, 342, 418, 436, 469, 493, 521, 601, 608, 646
survival (of Jewish people), 77, 137, 195
synagogues (in the United States) 471 - 472

T
talit, 141, 279, 321, 448, 564, 640, 645 - 646
Talmud, 9, 51 - 57, 189, 191, 436
taxes, 80, 90, 142, 135, 145, 146, 148, 215
tefilin, 165, 179, 321, 432, 535, 564, 640, 645, 646, 653
Tehillim (Psalms), 256, 280, 282
Temple Mount, 254, 652
Ten commandments, 470
ten martyrs, 35 - 41
thanksgiving, 280
throne of Solomon, 93
Tisha B'Av, 278
Torah learning, 18, 22 - 24, 37, 64, 79, 177, 211, 212, 218, 231, 273,
Torah reading and study, 135, 183, 332 - 336, 362, 373, 374, 393, 394,
Torah scrolls, 447, 449, 569 - 575, 653
transmission of Torah, 51
tzedakah (charity), 39, 77, 178, 179, 222, 379, 398 - 400
tzena u'rena (Yiddish Torah translation), 435
U
u'n'taneh tokef (prayer), 420
USY, 640

V
Valley Forge, 463 - 466
vows, 24 - 25
W
wandering Jew, 189
War for Independence (Israel) 593, 602, 652
White Papers, 517, 593 - 594
witchcraft, 91, 142
Women, education of, 435 - 441
Women, honor of, 24, 29, 218 - 219, 273
Y
yeshiva, 24, 71, 74, 77, 79, 121, 127, 145, 148, 153, 154, 212, 230, 272, 390, 410, 435, 440, 506, 512, 516, 517, 556, 580, 629,
Yiddish, 423, 496, 497, 505, 520, 526, 576, 582
yizkor, 647, 653
Yom Kippur, 38, 262, 278 - 279, 342, 390, 392 - 394, 420, 436, 491 492, 500, 506 - 507, 521, 573, 646, 647, 653
Yom Kippur War, 654
Z
Zealots, 15
Zionism, 614, 617
Zohar, 283

✡

Order Today

A SACRED TRUST

Stories of Jewish Heritage and History

Volume I

by *Rabbi Eugene and Annette Labovitz*

• The Talmudic and Post-Talmudic Age •

• Medieval Europe: The Middle Ages and the Renaissance •

• The Sephardic Age •

— **$18** —

Send to:

The Isaac Nathan Publishing Co., Inc. 22711 Cass Avenue, Woodland Hills, CA 91364, (818) 225-9631

Send check for $18 for each copy. We Pay Shipping.
California Residents add 1.44 for state tax.

—Books published by the Isaac Nathan Publishing Co.—

- **A Sacred Trust: Stories of Jewish Heritage and History, by Rabbi Eugene and Annette Labovitz.** Two thousand years of Jewish history, from the fall of the Second Temple to the founding of the new State of Israel. Told in story form. 3-volumes.

  Vol. One: The Talmudic and Post Talmudic Age, Medieval Europe: The Middle Ages and the Renaissance, and The Sephardic Age. ISBN 0-914615-12-2. $18.

  Vol. Two & Three Combined: The Silver Age of Polish Jewry • The American Jewish Experience • Our People Return to Our Land (Eretz Yisrael). ISBN 0-914615-02-5. $24

  Three Volume (2-book) Set (from Publisher) $36.

- **A Touch of Heaven: Spiritual and Kabbalistic Stories for Jewish Living. by Rabbi Eugene and Annette Labovitz.** Stories of basic Jewish concepts of Jewish living, compiled by these master storytellers. ISBN 0-914615-04-1. $20.

- **How to Explain Judaism to Your Non-Jewish Neighbor: A Primer to Better Understanding of the World's Oldest Monotheistic Religion, by Rabbi Ed Zerin.** ISBN 0-914615-20-3. $12.95.

- **The Art of Engagement: How to Build a Strong Foundation of Communication for Marriage, by David & Sheila Epstein.** For soon-to-be and just-married couples. ISBN 0-914615-16-5. $12.95.

- **Circumcision: Its Place in Judaism, Past & Present, by Samuel A. Kunin, M.D.** A basic explanation of the ritual as well as controversies concerning this ancient Jewish rite. ISBN 0-914615-07-6. $12.95.

- **What This Modern Jew Believes, by Rabbi Isaiah Zeldin.** The story and beliefs of the builder of a 3,000 family congregation and new 750 student Jewish community high school. ISBN 0-914615-01-7. $15.

- **Threads of the Covenant: Growing Up Jewish in Small Town America, by Harley Sachs.** Ten charming stories of the only Jewish boy, from his Bar Mitzvah until his wedding and the ten Jewish families struggling to retain their Jewish heritage. (A Real Delight!) ISBN 0-914615-03-3. $18.

- **Withered Roots, The Remnants of Eastern European Jewry, by Stuart Tower.** Poetic prose from the travels of a sensitive writer to Eastern Europe searching for the remaining Jews. ISBN 0-914615-11-4. $18.

To order, send check with requested titles and your full return address to: **Isaac Nathan Publishing Co. 22711 Cass Avenue, Woodland Hills, CA 91364** We pay the postage on all orders within the United States. (California, please add 8% state tax.)